Kauai As It Was In the 1940s and '50s

Kauai As It Was In the 1940s and '50s

Recollections and photographs of the days when Grampa Mike was a Teenage, Coast Haole Bachelor living on Kauai during the two years prior to World War II and four years following the war

Mike Ashman

A Publication of the Kauai Historical Society
Lihue, Kauai, Hawaii

ISBN 0-8248-1766-4 (cl)
ISBN 0-8248-2904-2 (pa)

This book is printed on acid-free paper and meets the
guidelines for permanence and durability of the council
on Library Resources.

Designed by Santos Barbasa Jr.

Printed by The Maple-Vail Book Manufacturing Group

Contents

1

Discovering Your Family Roots Are Buried in a Carton of Junk

Dear Lynne, Keoki, Megan, Kaely, Miki, Michael, David, Kenji, Andrew, Billy, Kevin and all your curious offspring who one day may wonder why you are the way you are. You know, in part it's because I was the way I was. And I've just happened to pass some of me along to you.

For more than half a century, Grandma and I have carried with us from town to town, city to city, and country to country a cardboard carton containing an assortment of old photographs and letters. Now the box has been laid open, revealing a vivid collection of moments of the past that almost were tossed aside as outdated, useless junk.

What follows here is an assortment of recollections, some pictures of your Grandpa and others taken in the 1940s and early '50s along with bits of items from *The Garden Island* weekly newspaper and portions of letters I wrote to my parents in 1940 and '41. The letters had been saved and given back to me at about the time Grandma and I were married in 1944.

It was in my eighteenth year that I landed at Nawiliwili, Kauai, following four-and-a-half days on Matson Line's SS *Matsonia* from San Francisco to Honolulu and an overnight voyage to Kauai on the interisland steamer *Waialeale*. When I arrived it felt as if I had just emerged in the Land of Oz—facing an uncertain future—not yet an adult but beyond being a youth.

Passing through San Francisco's Golden Gate on board the ocean liner SS *Matsonia,* Grampa is heading westward for a new life on an unfamiliar teeny-tiny dot in the South Pacific Ocean somewhere way out there in that direction. He's wearing his favorite all-wool, heavy tweed suit that he's planning to wear to Sunday school and church in Hawaii. (Mistake number one.)

Up to that time, for nearly two years, I'd been working full-time as an all-night disk jockey in San Francisco and attending junior college during the day. Still, this was going to be a journey into the unknown because it was my first attempt at living away from home.

It wasn't long before I learned that my position in the hierarchy of Kauai was that of a coast *haole*—meaning a *malihini* that had just arrived from the mainland. The immediate future was anticipated to provide some good work experience. It turned out to be a magnificent adventure.

Last year I began writing short captions for the old photographs rescued from the carton. But, I soon discovered there were so many precious memories associated with them. The short captions became longer and longer until they evolved into brief stories.

To help in your search for understanding from where you came, here are some pictures and recollections of the wonderful, exciting life your Grandpa lived in the far-away Territory of Hawaii on the Island of Kauai during the two years preceding World War Two and his return following the war.

Aloha, Grandpa Mike
October 10, 2001 (my 80th birthday)

2

Docking at Nawiliwili and Leaving the Nest

Spring of this year of 2000 was the sixtieth anniversary of my arrival at Nawiliwili aboard the interisland steamer *Waialeale* as a teenage, coast-*haole* bachelor seeking fame and fortune in The New World.

All I knew about Kauai was that it was a teeny-tiny dot on a large ocean map somewhere way out there from the West Coast of the United States. For me, a wide-eyed kid who grew up in a working class San Francisco neighborhood, I knew as soon as we entered Nawiliwili Harbor that I had found my Shangri-La.

This South Sea Island seaport seemed to have been copied from an MGM movie. With binoculars borrowed from the *Waialeale*'s friendly skipper, Captain O.O. McIntyre, I became fascinated by the deep green crown of sugar cane growing atop the bluff overlooking the harbor entrance. Spreading out below the cliff was a broad, crescent sand beach fronting a spectacular garden that was prettier than any place in San Francisco's Golden Gate Park.

There in the center of this tropical greenhouse-without-walls was the magnificent white plantation-style mansion of retired Territorial Senator Charlie Rice. How frightening, some months later, was my first invitation from the Senator to attend a Sunday afternoon *luau* at HIS palatial estate on Kalapaki Beach. (I had never seen a politician up close before. Wait—I take that back. As a real little kid, I once peeked through a fence and saw San

Since Grampa was a little over six feet tall, this surfboard must have been about thirteen feet in length. Shaped from a three-inch-thick solid piece of redwood, the board felt like it weighed a million pounds when you had to drag it across a stretch of sand.

Francisco's famous mayor and California's future governor "Sunny Jim" Rolph looking out the window of his house. You may touch me.)

The public didn't use Kalapaki Beach much in those days, probably because it looked as if it was Charlie Rice's exclusive property. But sometimes, during the lazy summer months when Kauai's off-island students were home for vacation, we'd go moonlight skinny-dipping late in the evening.

The boys bodysurfed waves on one side of the big black rock while the girls bathed on the other side, way down at the far end of the beach. That sounds very Victorian and so naive today. But those were the rules and we never ever thought to question them. Yeah, right! Well, maybe "thought" isn't the right word. Let's say the girls never knew for sure whether we peeked or not. (Incidentally, the name "Kalapaki," I was taught later, came from an ancient and beautiful Hawaiian legend that told of an *alii* who lived in that cove and whose chickens always laid eggs with two yolks. Some legend.)

At one edge of Charlie Rice's property was a narrow stream emptying into the cove. Alongside was the small cottage of the Aiu (Ah You) family. They always were very kind in lending their thirteen-foot-long, solid redwood surfboard to ride waves of occasional high swells coming in from the south. The board was so heavy it took two people to haul it across the sand to the water's edge. Nobody wanted to be the last to use it because the others would have disappeared. That meant you'd have to hunt around for someone to help drag this giant plank back up to its proper place in the Aiu's neat little garden.

The morning of my arrival, as Captain McIntyre maneuvered the ancient *Waialeale* around the ten-year-old breakwater, I could see the mouth of a much wider stream, actually a river, at the other end of the harbor. This area was aptly named Niumalu, "in the shade of coconut palms." Among the ironwood trees, *wiliwili* and palms, two cottages could be seen. One belonged to the Coney family; the other to the Lovells.

The Coneys had fishing rights for the adjoining

Huleia River. Permission had to be asked (those were the rules) when a few of us young fellows wanted to spend a night paddling a small canoe up the river, casually laying out crab nets along the way. After several hours we slowly drifted back, hauling up those baskets to see if the stinky codfish bait tied to the nets had attracted any Samoan crabs. I never did learn how to swallow raw crabmeat as the others did. But I did enjoy our conversation, dumb jokes, and lies we told about all the fantasy girlfriends of our past.

The Coneys' neighbors were the talented musical members of the Lovell family. Their frequent *kanikapila* music sessions eventually turned their home into Lovell's Tavern, a favorite nightspot during the forties and fifties. And not far from the Lovells could be seen the Wilcox family's beach house, Papalinahoa, set within a grove of tropical trees and shrubs.

Back on the interisland steamer, I wondered was that the old *Waialeale* creaking and shuddering as it eased closer to the pier or was it my knees shaking from realizing the moment of truth was at hand? Down below me was my new boss, Charlie Fern, the only person standing on the dock who looked like he was a businessman. He must recognize me. I'm the only *haole* among the dozen passengers.

Why is he looking at me for such a long time with no expression on his face? Did he now suspect I was only eighteen years old when my job application suggested my age was twenty? (I really didn't say I was twenty years old. What I wrote was, "Any twenty year old would jump at the chance of working at a brand new radio station in Hawaii." If he assumed I was writing about me, he guessed wrong.)

His stone-faced look made me begin to worry. I began asking myself questions about the wisdom of seeking a job in Hawaii. Why didn't I stay home with my happy family of seven older brothers and sisters? Why did I give up a budding career that already had nearly two years of being the only all-night disk jockey in Northern California? I couldn't believe I left in order to take a job at Kauai's first radio station, KTOH—not even built yet! Why did I have to look over the classified ads in the back of that broadcasting magazine last year and apply for this job? Wish I could delete everything that has happened since then.

Was he thinking he had wasted a pile of money buying me a ticket on the *Matsonia* and two nights at the Alexander Young Hotel in Honolulu, plus this passage to Kauai? As these thoughts zipped through my mind, I halfway expected Charlie Fern to turn around, run into the sugar storage shed and hang himself.

I wanted to smile and wave to him but couldn't lift my arm. My lips were frozen stiff. Hour after hour, it seemed, he just kept staring at me—like he couldn't believe it. Eventually there was a small grin and a friendly wave of his hand. The worst was over. From now on everything was going to be up to me.

While Charlie Fern moved toward the boarding gangway being lowered, I returned to surveying my new home. A few small cottages were down the road leading away from the pier.

One belonged to the Malina family whose daughter, Sarah, married Melvin Kailikea who had come from Oahu to work on the new breakwater. Over time, Sarah and Melvin established their Luau Garden nightclub and Menehune Garden conservatory on the property.

One other house I could see down the road from the pier belonged to former Territorial Senator, part Hawaiian, Chris Holt. A spectacular flower garden lay between his cottage and the road. It had to be impressive because his tiny wife was seen every evening holding a kerosene lantern, kneeling among her blossoms, and deftly picking every single bug that dared crawl on her plants.

One son, "Slim" Holt, became a rental car pioneer in Hawaii. Another, the Waimea High School football star Benny, later married the celebrated "Kauai Annie" who, during the late '40s, reinvigorated Kauai's *hula halau* by creating a troupe that appeared at all the most important events on the island. A Chris Holt daughter, Kealoha, was distinguished as one of the Territory's foremost teenage hula dancers. In 1939, at the age of nineteen she was brought to Hollywood to be featured in the MGM hit movie *Honolulu* starring Robert Young and Eleanor Powell along with comedians George Burns and Gracie Allen.

At the time of my arrival in 1940, around the corner from these homes lay the village of Nawiliwili with a narrow side road leading left, up *mauka,* to the high school. The road and school still are there.

At the bottom of that road was the cottage of Manji and Emma Ouye and their daughters Betty and Marian. It was with them on my first New Year's Day on Kauai that I was initiated into the enjoyable Japanese custom of "eating up" with house-to-house feasting. They served a delicately-flavored *miso* soup, sweet rice balls with a red-colored filling that tasted something like chocolate, cone *sushi* and *sushi nori,* a giant platter of *ahi sashimi,* plates of *teriyaki* chicken and beef, all kinds of special tea cakes, jiggly squares of colored gelatin, and the most delicious macaroni salad anyone has ever eaten.

As masters of local-style food preparation, they began serving *saimin* and other light foods at tables on their front lanai in 1946, calling their little café "Hale Aina," House of Food. A few years later, the family established the highly successful Club Jetty out on the nearby breakwater, bringing another enterprise to help make Nawiliwili the nightlife capital of east Kauai.

That morning of my first arrival on the *Waialeale* was extremely hot and humid. It was *kona* weather. The air was completely still. Down below me was a big, ferocious dog chasing a poor little kitten across the dock. It was so hot they both were just walking. Except for activity on the dock, there was no movement of any kind in the village. I supposed everyone was lying somewhere in the shade.

The road from the pier passed through the little community of Nawiliwili and then ascended to Lihue somewhere out of sight over a hill. Only a few buildings were scattered along both sides of the route through Nawiliwili. A narrow, two-lane divided bridge in the middle of town crossed a stream running from the mountains into the Kalapaki cove.

My Word, How You've Grown!
I Can Hardly Recognize You.

It's noontime on the main road in Lihue on a spring workday in the years 1940 and 2000. Back in 1939, with 5,761 registered vehicles, Kauai recorded 72 accidents with property damage, 38

accidents with 54 injuries, and only one traffic death. Compare that with 1999's 57,000 vehicles, 471 major accidents costing $3000 or more, 1,019 minor crashes and eight traffic fatalities. Now, in the year of 2000 there is one registered vehicle for every man, woman and child living on the island.

Although Kauai's population has only doubled during the sixty years between 1940 and 2000, the former tiny "Montgomery Hotel" County Jail has ballooned into this major correctional facility covering more than nine acres.

Former Senator Charlie Rice's imposing Kalapaki Beach home and its access

road from Nawiliwili town were totally destroyed by the deadly April 1946 tidal wave. The photo below shows the unfrequented strip of sand as it appeared for the remainder of the 1940s.

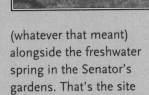

After the tidal wave, not many beachgoers chose to walk from Nawiliwili Road to the abandoned homestead. Gramma was photographed in what was, in those days, called a "cheesecake pose"

(whatever that meant) alongside the freshwater spring in the Senator's gardens. That's the site

of today's acre-size swimming pool of the 356-room Marriott Resort and Beach Club with its additional 232 vacation ownership villas.

On one side of the bridge was the small two-story Kuboyama Hotel with its ten rooms for traveling salesmen who wanted lodging near the pier. Not far away was the warehouse of the former Waimea Stables whose operator, Clem Gomes, was in the midst of changing from smelly horse-drawn wagons to spiffy small trucks. Nearby was a tiny gas station with two pumps—the kind where the amount of gasoline in the glass storage tank at the top of the pump was measured by eyeball. If the attendant was tall, you'd get more gas. If he was short, his eye measurement gave you less.

On the other side of the road were several small businesses. One of them, Don Drug, really should have been located in Lihue so people wouldn't have to walk or catch a ride down to Nawiliwili for drugstore shopping. We were told Lihue Plantation didn't want competition for its big plantation store and wouldn't lease land in Lihue to the pharmacist. (No competition was another rule.)

Close to Don Drug were a pool hall, a barbershop and Jack Wada's small appliance sales and repair shop. Jack Wada was the local radio technician who assisted the engineers in setting up the transmitter for KTOH. Above his shop was a room for rent: bed, dresser, chair, light bulb hanging from the ceiling and a few coathooks on the door. Here I lived during my first month on the island. Can't remember a bathroom but there must have been one in the building or nearby. The rent was five dollars a month, the same as it would have been at the ten-room Kuboyama Hotel across the stream.

After the first month, Sheriff Willie Rice offered a room at his garden-terraced Lihue Hotel, also for five dollars a month. And that's where I contentedly settled down in my new home. Three meals a day, all you can eat, totaled one dollar. This landmark Lihue Hotel was across the street from the present Ben Franklin/Ace Hardware store. Later the hotel expanded into the Kauai Inn. The site now is Kalapaki Villas.

On the hotel side of what is now called Rice Street up in Lihue was Charlie Rice's large pasture between Lihue Hotel and Kalena Street. From there on up to the County Building was a stretch of mostly unimproved land with a scattering of businesses such as the Royal Theater, a few one-story enterprises including the Kauai Filipino News, a *Mama-san* & *Papa-san* store with a gas pump, and the two superstores: H.S. Kawakami and S.H. Kress separated by a narrow road that people called Kress Street.

The only buildings over on the Kapaa side of that road from Nawiliwili were about a dozen large, white plantation homes running all the way from the present Ace Hardware on up to the County Building. You'll find some of these houses have been transplanted to the road above the Lutheran Church on Lihue's German Hill.

A big attraction in Nawiliwili at the time of my arrival was the roller-skating rink. This imitation roller-drome with its heat-seeking corrugated iron roof was usually, but not always, open for three hours each evening and for matinees on weekends. Sometimes roller-skating dances would be held with live music by the Ambassador Orchestra. You had to come real early if you wanted to rent a pair of skates and get in the whirling circle. Otherwise you had to pay your quarter and stand around until somebody got dizzy and quit. If you organized a group large enough to make it profitable, the rink would operate at other times and anyone else who showed up could join in the delight of doing circles.

That's all there was to the town of Nawiliwili sixty years ago. Most private homes were hidden among trees on both sides of the road and up Nawiliwili Valley. There may have been other buildings around the waterfront but, if there were, they've been covered in my memory by the sands of time.

Not long ago I sat on the lanai of one of the dazzling homes hanging down from the steep Kalapaki bluff where sugarcane once grew. Today that headland has been transformed into a magnificent golf course surrounding a series of peaceful lagoons.

Sitting up there, I was cogitating like an old codger's supposed to do. (You know, there's rules.) It was as if I had become a soaring albatross with a birds-eye, kaleidoscopic view blending dim visions of days and nights past. Nawiliwili played a very significant part in my young life.

Looking across at the tremendous changes that have taken place, I recalled how six decades ago I was standing on the deck of the old SS *Waialeale* waiting to meet my new boss, Charlie Fern. That day I was like an innocent baby chick cracking the shell that would allow me to enter the realm of grownups. I thought of all that has happened since then. It didn't take any convincing at all to make me realize how lucky I've been to be me.

3

Boneyard Beach and The Night Marchers

One recollection that's been haunting me for the past sixty years is the memory of playing stupid games with real, honest-to-goodness human skeletons! I can't believe I ever did that. My knees go wobbly today when I only think about holding a dead man's bones in my hands.

It wasn't like that a half century ago on Kauai when the isolated sand dunes at a beach beyond Poipu were littered with bones of what must have been hundreds and hundreds and hundreds of people.

Some local folks claimed those were fallen warriors' remains from a failed invasion by forces of a Maui *alii* in the 1300s. Others believed they came from thousands of bodies washed ashore following an attempted invasion by Kamehameha the Great in 1795. At that time, it is said, a hurricane-like storm swamped the canoes of thousands of warriors as they approached this side of the island. Kamehameha retreated to Oahu with few survivors. Bodies of many others, they say, must have been washed ashore.

We who walked along that out-of-the-way shoreline during the middle of the past century sometimes wondered if these sands might have been an ancient burial ground. However, as far as we could tell, there were no remains of children. Today the area is the setting of expensive homes and fine condos neighboring the prestigious Hyatt Regency Hotel Resort.

How did anyone happen to begin this ghoulish game of creating do-it-yourself skeletons?

Well, there really wasn't much to do on Kauai in the early 1940s. Young folks were bored, just as they are today. Options for free time included hanging out in the stillness of the library in Lihue, walking down to the roller-skating rink in Nawiliwili, or hiking up at Kokee or along closer mountain trails. You could go to a Filipino, Japanese or Hollywood movie, take part in a sports activity, or disturb the peace by walking around playing an ukulele.

In addition to Boy Scouts and the YMCA, various churches planned activities for young people in the Lihue area. The Young Buddhist Association of the Hongwanji Mission in Kapaia found ways to involve kids in healthy pastimes. The nearby Korean Christian Church in Kapaia and the neighboring Immaculate Conception Catholic Church along with the Japanese Christian Church at the end of Kress Street in Lihue tried to find something to entertain youngsters in leisure-time activities. The German Lutheran Church up on German Hill wasn't very active because services were held only once a month with Pastor Dr. Arthur Horrmann coming over from Honolulu to lead the worship service. The two Congregational Churches, English and Hawaiian, near Pualoke tried their best to keep teenagers busy and out of trouble. But sometimes you wanted to do things on your own.

Being out of doors was the big attraction for people of all ages. In every town on the island young people's leagues featured junior baseball, barefoot football, soccer and basketball for those youth that were into team play. Golf and tennis were for the old folks. In good weather, shore casting, spearfishing, crabbing or frog hunting was the way to go.

As far as I know there weren't many surfboards on the island when the 1940s began. The only one I ever came across was that solid redwood plank, three inches thick with a tapered forward end, that belonged to the Aiu family. When southerly swells entered Nawiliwili Bay, that board was like magic—creating rapture where monotony normally was a young fellow's way of life.

And then, for real fun, there was the ultimate thrill of bodysurfing! No place on earth was better for this sport than the exciting break in front of Dr. Brennecke's house at Poipu.

I hung out in a gang of five fellows from Lihue and Nawiliwili—not the kind of trouble-making gang you hear about today—but just a group of what were then called "pals." Two were Hawaiian, one Japanese, one *hapa*-Filipino and I, a coast *haole*. All of us were the ages of recent high school graduates.

When the normal tradewinds disappeared and clammy *kona* weather set in, we felt it would be a great day for bodysurfing. The two Hawaiian kids gathered ripe bananas, guavas, oranges, sometimes alligator pears, mangoes, figs and lychees from their backyards. Bread, rolls and other leftover Lihue Hotel food was scrounged by our Japanese buddy who worked in the hotel kitchen. Our *hapa*-Filipino friend scooped up tasty *bunelos*, *lumpia* or *pancit* from his home. And I contributed transportation in the bright yellow Chevrolet Coupe provided as part of my employment with KTOH. Two of us sat in front and the three others squashed themselves into the snug rumble seat.

It seems there never was anyone else surfing by Dr. Brennecke's. I'm sure there were others at times because this beach was renowned as Kauai's finest. But because there were very few cars on the island in those days, not many surfers would want to walk all the way from Koloa, the nearest town. Poipu was a community of about two dozen scattered homes separated from Koloa Landing by a long stretch of coconut palms and *kiawe* bushes along a narrow road bordering the shoreline.

Once at the beach, we'd ride waves until sunset if the surf was good. We had plenty of food and could always find lots of drinking coconuts. Mrs. Brennecke was very kind each time we asked if we could drink from her garden hose. Who could want anything more? It was a young man's paradise.

How to Have Fun
Without Spending Money

While hiking through the muck of Alakai Swamp atop Mt. Waialeale, the wettest spot on earth, sometimes the bog would be ankle deep and even up to your knees. If you were like Grampa and weren't careful you could fall into a deep hole and get yourself drowned.

When you were looking for something that was fun to do, you always could—

Go bamboo-pole fishing on the Port Allen dock. Or, spearfishing on the Lydgate reef. Wear out your *palaka* shorts on the Waipahee slippery slide.

Find some church that's having a *luau*. Walk around town disturbing the peace. Grampa's with pals Lana Fountain and Barney van Wagner.

You'd think terrifying ghosts would be hanging around Grampa like flies. Just imagine—he actually took people's leg bones and spelled out his real name.

The ultimate thrills were the super-long rides when bodysurfing in front of Dr. Brennecke's house at Poipu.

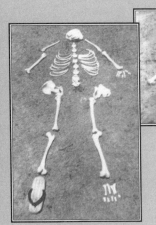

If the waves were junk, we'd walk over the hill to a wide expanse of sand covering the slopes all the way to Mahaulepu. It was here countless human bones could be seen lying among occasional tufts of weeds. Many more bones were lightly covered with sand.

If you didn't give it any thought, this was a great place for young people to play. We sometimes saw small neighborhood kids building bone houses and teepees. They constructed bone forts. They tied bones together and dragged them over the sand dunes as choo-choo trains.

Because we five teenagers were at a competitive age we invented a contest to see who'd be the fastest in putting a complete skeleton together. It wasn't easy to distinguish an arm bone from a leg bone or tell the difference between a toe bone and a finger bone. Still, we managed to create something reasonably accurate.

One thing we didn't do was to touch a skull. That would have been too spooky and probably would cause the *Obake-man* to hide under our beds at night until we fell asleep. And then strike!

Our skinless masterpieces were left right on the sand where man had created them. Years later I wondered whether detectives ever were called to investigate the decapitated remains of a murder victim. I decided no respectable cop would take a second look at this weird, decomposed body with leg bones sticking out of his armpits.

About ten years later, after I had acquired a wife and three children, our young family lived in a house across the road from Dr. Brennecke. There still were no hotels, resorts or condos at Poipu. Just a few more houses had been added during the prior decade.

Between our home and that of our neighbor, George Aguiar, was an empty lot. We were told no one would build there because through that piece of land ran an unseen trail over which Night Marchers walked from mysterious Boneyard Beach, across the west side of the island, all the way to the eerie cliffs at Polihale, the spirits' parting place from earth.

I don't believe in ghosts. I'm positive Night

Marchers never walked between the Aguiar house and ours. That's why I told my family those strange sounds they sometimes heard at night either were night body-surfers walking down the road to the beach, or a neighbor who couldn't sleep and decided to pound some *taro,* or a family nearby that was practicing the *hula,* or the wind was causing coconuts to fall to the ground, or whatever else I could think of.

The real reason I was certain there weren't any Night Marchers is because I knew that I once had played macabre games at nearby Boneyard Beach. I had even left my true name spelled out in leg bones. (That was real dumb!) And if Night Marchers actually were on their way to Polihale they wouldn't just pass my house, they'd be sneaking in under the back door.

I still can't believe I really played that gruesome game. But, it's true. I clearly remember not just disturbing but actually fooling around with bones of dead people. Although I'd prefer denying it, there are photographs on the desk beside me documenting what was done. Sadly, what we five teenagers and others did on that historic battleground is part of the history of Kauai and can never be erased.

Today I sincerely regret the disrespect we showed. The only explanation that can be offered is that we were thoughtless young people looking for something different to do. Perhaps this terrible behavior can be blamed on the influence of no television.

4

Radio Station KTOH Becomes Kauai's First Broadcast Station

"That sounds like a stupid idea," was the sentiment of many folks on Kauai when the Garden Island Publishing Company in 1938 announced plans to construct a broadcast radio station. Some people laughed—"Who's going to listen; nobody has a radio." Others observed, "We already have two stations in Honolulu. Why do we need more?" The last two statements were quite correct: that there weren't many radios on the island and the Territory of Hawaii did have a total of three stations, two in nearby Honolulu. The first comment, however—that it was a stupid idea—was dead wrong.

In 1938 not many people on Kauai owned a radio set. The Honolulu stations, KGU and KGMB, did offer a wide variety of programs from before sunrise to late in the evening. Reception from Honolulu wasn't always dependable during the day but at night the Oahu signals came in loud and clear. Nighttime reception from KHBC, the Territory's only other radio station, broadcasting from Hilo, also was acceptable.

Owners of radios on Kauai primarily were people with a healthy disposable income: businessmen and government employees' families who lived in single-family homes. But the bulk of the population living in plantation camps and rural farming areas owned very few radio sets. If they wanted to listen, they'd have to find a neighbor who could afford such a luxury.

In the face of widespread skepticism over estab-

It's Just Like
Having A Magic Carpet

The Grove Farm Plantation tunnel creating a shortcut for cane-haul trucks between Puhi fields and the Koloa Mill is finished. Crews drilling from both sides of the mountain are just half an

inch apart in elevation when they meet at the middle of the bore. The public is not allowed to view the construction. But KTOH is there for them as plantation manager William Alexander describes the feat to Charlie Fern. The wire recorder is being powered by the car battery and the quiet celebration is broadcast with great fanfare on the evening news.

A tiny homemade, one-tube amplifier made it possible to connect a studio microphone to the telephone line to the station.

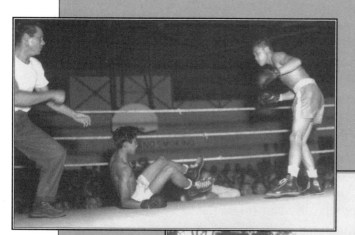

Folks listening to KTOH are taken to—
- Saturday night boxing at Isenberg Gym in Lihue
- Sunday afternoon barefoot football in Waimea
- Von Hamm Young Company's auto showroom in Lihue for the introduction of next year's models
- Sharon Sue's fashion show at the Kauai Inn

The new highway between Hanapepe and Waimea is inaugurated by County Chairman William Ellis. Listeners to the evening news will hear speeches by Territorial Highway Engineer Robert Belt, the

County Chairman and Councilman Yutaka Hamamoto as well as hearing the sound of scissors snipping the ceremonial ribbon.

After listening to broadcasts from many parts of the island, Kapaa High School Principal Gladys Brandt remarks, "KTOH is just like having a magic carpet that takes you wherever something is happening."

lishing a local station, there were some residents who championed it as a great idea. For them it would bring entertainment and the latest news right inside a person's home rather than having to wait for the weekly *Garden Island* newspaper or walk to the nearest plantation town to see an out-of-date newsreel along with a cartoon and movie.

A few sharp businessmen agreed with the publishing company's board of directors. A radio station on this island would provide much wider coverage for marketing their goods. That, simply, was the compelling reason the costly decision had been made. Charlie Fern, publisher of *The Garden Island,* convinced his board of directors that owning the island's radio station would give the company control of virtually all advertising.

So in 1939 near Lihue town, a small site was cleared in a cane field on the road to Ahukini Harbor. Today, the Jack Harter's Helicopters office is on the spot where the 150 feet tall antenna stood. A total of ninety antenna ground wires, 180 feet long, were buried a foot underground, stretching out like spokes in a wheel. People marveled at the close-up sight of a communications tower reaching as high as a fifteen-story building.

Merchants began adding more radio sets to their inventories and featuring them in newspaper advertising. Many styles of table and console models became available but only two kinds of portable radios existed. One was impractical; the other expensive.

The tiny transistors, capacitors, diodes and chips used today hadn't been invented yet. All radio receivers needed a number of glass vacuum tubes, about the size of light bulbs, along with very heavy, bulky, iron transformers, plus an assortment of metal variable condensers and other devices.

One of those two types of portables was a full-size radio that needed to be connected to a huge, weighty car battery. You really wouldn't want to take that one along on a picnic. It was more suitable for people who didn't have electricity in their homes.

The other portable was the size of a small suitcase.

It weighed at least twenty-five pounds. I know because my friends in San Francisco gave me one as a bon voyage gift. It wasn't turned on very often because the battery, about the size of a loaf of bread, cost too much. Even with a special discount from Jack Wada's appliance shop in Nawiliwili, it still took one week's pay to replace the battery.

Well, there really was a third portable—the crystal set. It was more like a toy to be used when a radio transmitter is nearby. With the aid of earphones, the listener scraped a wire across a small quartz chip about the size of a candy Lifesaver. If he had lots of patience and was lucky, the thin wire would get stuck in a crack of the chip and "surprise!"—something could be heard. The sound couldn't be made clearer or louder, but voices and music seemed to be coming from right inside of that peewee chip.

Installation of the KTOH transmitter began on April 16, 1940. Power was limited to 250 watts during the day and 100 watts after sunset. For a location like Hawaii and for certain frequencies, the Federal Communications Commission restricted nighttime power. This was to make sure signals from stations around the U.S. didn't interfere with each other. Our having maximum power of 250 watts was pretty good in those days. Broadcast stations now radiate in the thousands and tens of thousands of watts.

On April 20, four days after the crew began installing equipment, a two-week test program of music and station call letters went on the air from 1:00 to 6:00 A.M. Because the broadcasting was at night, reception was good. Over the next few weeks letters came from all around the Pacific as well as from a few limited pockets in North America.

The very first report came on the first night. Kauai's former Senator Charlie Rice had set his alarm clock for 1:30 A.M. He telephoned KTOH saying that when he twisted the radio dials, lo and behold he could hear beautiful Hawaiian music.

When the month of May 1940 arrived, the small staff was engrossed in developing three inaugural pro-

The Sunday Parade of Hits

It was Sunday madness every week as groups of musicians from all around the island gathered outside the main studio waiting to entertain KTOH listeners. There were the Smoky Mountaineers, Skyriders and other cowboy bands from Kalaheo and Hanamaulu. Anahola's

Kaui family with its dozen brothers, sisters and cousins, the Kaluahine sisters with "Rusty" Akuna, as well other Hawaiian groups singing island favorites. Music was played by Filipino, Japanese, Puerto Rican orchestras, high school combos and other groups performing one after the other all day long.

Even the Kauai Police Department's Hawaiian troupe, that entertained at many civic functions, appeared from time to time.

Each group was allotted twenty-nine minutes. That allowed only a one-minute rush to change places in front of the single, hanging, studio microphone. The confusion couldn't be heard on the air. People at home just laid back and marveled at what was coming out of the box called radio.

grams, English, Japanese and Ilocano, as well as drawing up the future regular English daily schedule.

Station manager Dean Stewart, a *kamaaina,* came to Kauai from a radio station career in Honolulu. Mainlander Bob Glen was responsible for engineering the project along with Kauai's ingenious technician Jack Wada. Bill Parsons, a former isle resident, and I were announcer/engineers coming from stations in San Francisco.

(FCC requirements called for a Federal First Class Radio/Telephone licensed engineer to be operating the transmitter at all times. Small stations sought announcers with engineer's licenses to avoid having to employ both an announcer and an engineer. Bill Parsons and I had the indispensable credential as well as on-air experience.)

To these four station members was added a one-person office staff, Lorraine Fountain, daughter of school-teacher Eva and police sergeant Eddie Fountain.

All the selling of commercials, engineering, announcing, programming, script and commercial development, coverage of remote events, and the administrative work was carried out by this busy team of five early settlers in the land of broadcast radio.

Two part-time employees were the janitor, Barney van Wagner, teenage son of *The Garden Island's* linotype operator, and Pedro Sampayana, gardener, who also tended the flowers and vegetables at Charlie Fern's home.

Working on the creation of the Japanese-language program were two Garden Islanders, Chitoko Isonaga and Shoichi Hamura. During the day they sold advertising, translated it into Japanese, and then for an hour each evening, except Saturday, they brought music from the homeland along with news and events of local interest for Japanese-language listeners.

Preparing for the twice-daily Filipino program were Abe Albayalde and Leonora Currameng, editor and assistant editor of the island's weekly printed *Kauai Filipino News.* Their two half-hour shows, in Ilocano, were broadcast at *pau hana,* 4:00 P.M., and again in the early evening at 7:30 P.M.

Both foreign language programs showcased local ethnic entertainers.

The big day, May 10, 1940, finally arrives. World-wide attention is focused on Europe where the Nazis on that day invade France, Belgium and Holland and on England where Winston Churchill is named to replace Prime Minister Neville Chamberlain.

Here on Kauai (probably because they haven't yet heard the world news) residents have gathered around radios concentrating on picking up the first sound of their very own radio station. It's Bob Glen's voice saying, "This is radio station KTOH, **K**auai **T**erritory **of** **H**awaii, broadcasting on an assigned carrier frequency of 1500 kilocycles by authority of the Federal Communications Commission."

Then, for three hours, a parade of island musicians and singers entertain in the main studio that opens onto an outdoor covered auditorium. Only some seventy-five special guests had been invited but there are many more first-nighters than the 100 folding chairs could seat. This important event is a formal occasion: with men speakers wearing white dinner jackets and most ladies dressed in *holoku*.

Annie and Benny Holt's Kekaha Hawaiians along with the Kekaha Parents Club bring greetings from Kauai's west side. There are Hawaiian songs by Nora Chang and Margaret Kilauano's Leinaala Glee Club as well as the Lei Ilima Club led by Nick Koani and Keawe Aipoalani.

Musical greetings from around the island continue with Billy Waialeale's Aloha Hawaiians from the Koloa side. Joe Rapozo's Lihue Hawaiian Serenaders, Sam Peahu's Transco Hawaiian Serenaders, Henry Sheldon's Kapaa Chorus, and the Latter Day Saints Choir directed by Louise Sheldon represent the east side. From the North Shore come Jacob Maka's Hanalei Singers. And Eddie Kanoho's CCC Rangers travel all the way down from Kokee to make the grand opening an island-wide celebration.

During the moments that the musical groups are exchanging places in the main studio, KTOH staff mem-

Would You Like to be
Clean For A Day?

Can you imagine a group of housewives eagerly gathering at a store to compete in tossing pennies into a small *koa* wood bowl? How unsophisticated that would be today. Back in the 1940s, during the Lihue Store Radio Party, they didn't seem to mind standing up in front of everybody to blow balloons to see whose would be the first to pop. Or, throwing darts at pictures of animals on the huge target. Prizes usually were merchandise certificates or small electrical appliances from Lihue Store. How many folks today would inch up close to the radio to hear a play-by-play account of a balloon popping and darts whizzing through the air? Maybe even an instant replay?

On the Mainland, one of daytime radio's most popular programs always

began with the question, "Would You Like to be Queen For A Day?" Then, women told sad stories about their lives and the audience voted by applause for the most miserable contestant who'd receive gifts to alleviate her problem.

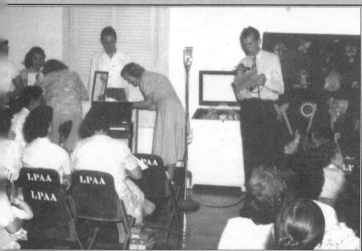

Well, here on Kauai, Lihue Store sponsored a series of weekly radio parties which asked, "Would You Like to be Clean For A Day?" Housewives were interviewed about the wonderful things that had happened in their lives and the winner would receive an assort-

ment of soap, sponges, brushes, brooms, buckets, wash rags, etc. as her prize.

Once Grampa bestowed himself as part of the grand prize, agreeing to work three hours in cleaning the winner's house. Later that week, when he arrived in his work clothes, the homemaker wouldn't let him touch anything. Instead she had invited her neighbors to sit around in her living room to eat cake, drink coffee, talk story and giggle.

bers are introduced. Then come politicians, plantation managers, private businessmen, County and Territorial officials, and other dignitaries who join in welcoming the new era in communications and entertainment.

Beloved *kamaaina,* Dora Isenberg, pays tribute to those who have brought "a vital service and family entertainment to the residents of the island." Kauai's chief librarian Thelma Hadley whose father, K.C. Hopper, had once saved *The Garden Island* newspaper from bankruptcy, is honored. A.H. "Hib" Case, Grove Farm's chief financial officer and corporate secretary of the publishing company, describes the many steps, beginning in 1936, that led to the creation of this fourth radio station in all of the Territory of Hawaii

Regular daily broadcasts then began at six o'clock the next morning. During the next two evenings grand inaugural festivities introduced KTOH Radio to Japanese and Filipino audiences.

From Monday through Saturday the KTOH evening world news was received late each afternoon via a United Press mainland short-wave radio transmission. The rapid stream of dots and dashes in Morse code was deciphered by radio operators Herman Loebel and Frank Westlake at the wireless station atop Mount Kalepa above Hanamaulu.

On very stormy afternoons no one wanted to attempt the drive up the narrow muddy road to the wireless station. So, world news was skipped. We explained to listeners why, and they all seemed to be sympathetic. J.C. Plews, Garden Island Motors manager, an avid short-wave listener, often called in to KTOH with news of significant world events, sometimes hours before United Press and the Honolulu radio stations carried the story.

Within a week after going on the air, the station gave its first on-site coverage of a crisis. A cloudburst hanging motionless over the east side of the island all day and into the evening brought the heaviest rainfall ever recorded on Kauai. Lihue *Mauka* Camp Nine recorded a total of 25.43 inches of rain pouring down from hovering, dark clouds. In the one-hour period from 11:00 A.M. to noon, Lihue was inundated with three inches of rain from a gigantic cloudburst. Rivers in the Lihue and Kapaa areas reached heights never before seen.

KTOH covered the disaster using the telephone at M.S. Carvalho Store in Kapaia. The terminal of the telephone line at the station was patched in to the control panel. The two reporters struggled through the torrential downpour getting stories to relate to radio listeners.

Breathlessly they described rushing water over Wailua Falls Road near Kapaia rising from three inches to three feet in a matter of minutes. In other places houses were lifted and floated away from foundations. An automobile and boat had a collision. At Kapaia a car, from which three men had jumped at the last minute, was swept to the edge of a precipice where it teetered and fell. The flash flood bulldozed its way through a road above Kapaia leaving a gorge 150 feet across and 75 feet deep.

The destruction was a catastrophe for many Kauaians. For radio listeners in other parts of the island the broadcast was a live news event with excitement that a newspaper story couldn't duplicate.

In future years the drama of flash floods in Waimea, Hanapepe and the North Shore also were brought directly into homes through KTOH's use of a homemade, tiny, leather-bound amplifier. The box was designed so that a studio microphone could be connected to send a normal sounding voice over a phone line to KTOH rather than just talking through a poor-quality telephone instrument.

This little amplifier case, about the size of a half loaf of bread, contained one vacuum tube plus several tiny resistors and capacitors. A cord connected the box to an electrical outlet. The twin ends of a telephone line were fastened to the box. There also was a connection for earphones and one for a microphone. That was it—doing the work of today's deluxe amplifiers. Now, for Kauaians, instead of squeaky telephone voices on the radio, there was a microphone creating studio-like sound.

On twice-weekly Boat Days, as the old interisland steamer *Waialeale* prepared to depart from the dock at Nawiliwili for Honolulu, the Hawaiian-music sendoff was broadcast to night-owls who'd stay up real late to hear the 9:30–10:00 P.M. show. The station went off the air at 10:00.

The tiny magic box brought listeners to interesting events all around the island. We'd broadcast political rallies, Board of Supervisors' meetings, store grand openings, and the twice-weekly evening departures of the interisland steamer from Nawiliwili. Here on the pier at Nawiliwili, as musicians sang Hawaiian music in the background, travelers were interviewed about why they were making a trip to Honolulu.

There also was live coverage of all kinds of sports played at plantation and high school gymnasiums and athletic fields: football, boxing, wrestling, basketball, and baseball.

Horse racing on July 4 always brought huge crowds to the Wailua Racetrack. Now the exciting races were being enjoyed by those not able to attend in person. At our first Independence Day racing coverage one horse in the Kauai Derby, the main event, didn't take off with the rest of the nags. When it was over, the jockey explained to KTOH fans that his horse was asleep when the starting signal was given.

At Hanapepe Baseball Park one Sunday, Charlie Fern and I arrived early—his job to make ready the team lineups and mine to set up equipment and drum up color stories to fill the time between innings. We spent the entire afternoon describing this important game play by play. Only nobody heard it. The connection to the telephone line had come loose and we hadn't noticed it.

The phone circuit to the station in those days enabled one-way traffic only. Before going on the air with a remote program, the phone line was connected to our little amplifier and we could hear whatever KTOH was broadcasting. Then we'd wait for the cue: "We now take you to the Hanapepe ballpark where Charlie Fern and Mike Ashman are waiting to bring you . . . etc." The engineer at the studio would close a switch and then it was our turn—we were on the air.

On this afternoon, however, one of my connections had jiggled loose shortly after we started and frustrated sports fans were treated to several hours of phonograph records while waiting for the play-by-play report to resume. The studio announcer had no idea what went wrong and didn't know what to say except, "Stand by."

All during the year there were dance band remotes at plantation and high school gyms on Saturday nights. People were interviewed at the many community carnivals and E.K. Fernandez Circuses.

On June 28, 1940, the first prominent international entertainer on Kauai since 1924 gave a one-night concert at the Roxy Theater in Kapaa. She was the celebrated Metropolitan Opera star Marian Anderson. This wasn't just a rinky-dink affair. This was the most spectacular musical event in sixteen years. Tickets for the program, sponsored by the East and West Kauai Lion's Clubs, went for $4.40—a monumental price at a theater where movies were enjoyed for 45¢.

The KTOH Steinway grand piano was carefully trucked to Kapaa and tuned up for the recital. Lovely usherettes were outfitted in Asian and Polynesian ethnic

Hey, Mom! I'm Gonna Be on KTOH!

Because afternoon audience numbers are low, KTOH begins taking a fabulous new invention, the wire recorder, to the island's three high schools. With programs such as these, teenagers race home to turn on the radio.

It's the teacher who has to answer questions.

The band practices in a closet-size room.

Girls talk about sewing gowns for their senior prom and the boys describe items being made for their homes. The wire recorder, seen nearby on the shop floor, is picking up the interviews for broadcast later in the day.

Younger folks also are used to pressure parents to turn on KTOH. Together with store sponsorship, a kids version of the Lihue Store Radio Party is presented on Saturday mornings.

Ratings increase dramatically. Mothers can't avoid hearing the commercials. Surveys show that once a radio has been tuned to KTOH, it's left on indefinitely.

costumes. As excited concertgoers arrived, many dressed in white dinner jackets and formal gowns, they were interviewed on the sidewalk Tinseltown style. Coverage was as majestic as at any Academy Awards presentation. It was 100% pure imitation Hollywood.

That evening concert was such an important event that the SS *Waialeale* departure was moved from ten o'clock to eleven o'clock to make sure the opera celebrity wouldn't be left stranded on the Nawiliwili dock.

On one Saturday night in mid-June of 1940, Grove Farm Athletic Association presented its annual carnival in Puhi. A one-hour broadcast was scheduled for 9:00 P.M. Live talent was lined up from around the island to appear on the stage of the community hall.

I'd been invited to a chicken *hekka* dinner given by a Japanese family living in the camp near the Community Center. Before the meal, the remote equipment was set up at the community hall and then I joined a good-sized group at the nearby home. Hot *sake* was offered and I accepted my first-ever taste of an alcoholic beverage. It burned my throat going down but the flavor was sweet and the initial sharpness turned mellow. I liked it.

Folks had told me that if you drink too much *sake* you might go blind. How much is "too much" I wondered. Watching the others, I figured they knew all there was to know about drinking *sake* and would know when to quit before losing their vision. So, I matched them cup for cup. At 8:30 when I left to test the broadcast equipment I remember floating across the ballpark and into the spacious clubhouse.

By a quarter to nine the hall was full and I began warming up the audience. After fifteen minutes of tipsy nonsense we were about to go on the air. I stood poised in front of the microphone waiting for the cue from the station to begin the show.

Without warning, I suddenly went blind. Total darkness everywhere. I imagined people were aghast, horrified by the shock on my face, as I stood there speechless. I was certain they could tell it was no joke.

They were looking at a frightened sinner who had just been struck by the hand of God.

It was crystal clear to me that at age eighteen any chance of my living a normal life had just been destroyed by my lust for that demon *sake*. I thought about the pledge I'd signed on my twelfth birthday promising never to let alcohol pass between my lips.

As I stood there hopeless in the coal-black darkness, holding on to the microphone stand for support, people began mumbling, then raising their voices. I could hear many crying, "Let's get out of here!" I had created bedlam and panic in a crowded hall with closed doors.

It seemed an eternity before a tiny reddish glow appeared. Maybe this blindness was going to be temporary. There was the sound of doors being pushed open when a second gentle radiance became visible. I could hear anxious voices and shuffling of feet. Then a third glimmer. Slowly my vision began returning. Eventually I could see dim shapes of people and then upraised hands. They were holding lighted matches. It wasn't my eyesight. It was the electricity that had failed.

Once again a remote broadcast was nothing but dead air. Bewildered listeners were treated to phonograph records and the voice of the engineer at the station suggesting, "Stand by."

Regularly throughout the year, that little leather amplifier box brought Sunday church services to island shut-ins, to folks who had no transportation to a church, and to those who wanted to worship but were too lazy to dress up.

Each week this unique remote equipment box and a single microphone were taken to Lihue English Church (later called Lihue Union Church). The church telephone was disconnected and the phone line attached to the little amplifier. Then after the service was over the phone was reconnected.

Well, it was rejoined most of the time.

Once in a while the reconnection wasn't fastened securely and the pastor, for several days, would wonder why nobody had called. Elsie Wilcox solved the problem

Imitation Chef Conducts Cooking School

Making believe he knows how to cook, Grampa conducts the General Electric Radio School of Cooking. It's more like exchanging recipes, household hints and dumb jokes than teaching how to make a pineapple upside-down cake.

Itsue Kawaguchi Kaui (left) performs the tasks in producing the program and Winona Keahi plays the piano for the theme song and sing-along.

Housewives share all they know about culinary arts.

Gifts from General Electric are presented to participants.

Each week a glee club is formed from volunteers in the audience. Sometimes Joe Rapozo, head of the store's home furnishings department, joins pianist Winona Keahi by accompanying the singers on his guitar or ukulele.

by offering to pay the monthly charge for a permanent broadcast line costing about five dollars a month—more than KTOH could afford.

In those days, putting out five dollars each month would take a big chunk out of the station's bottom line. Income was not great because the cost of advertising on the new station was very inexpensive. A one-minute commercial could be purchased for as little as twenty-five cents, depending on time of day and the number of ads bought. Mainland advertisers were charged almost ten times as much. They knew the value of radio advertising while local businessmen still had to be convinced.

To prove to potential advertisers that there really were lots of residents listening to KTOH, several times each year teams of high school students were hired to conduct listener surveys in towns and plantation camps. They'd go house to house with tabulation sheets asking questions such as:

Is your radio turned on?

If so, which program are you listening to? (We never asked "which station" since many listeners didn't remember station call letters.)

What time did you turn on your radio today?

Which programs do you remember hearing?

How long do you think you'll leave the radio on today?

Do you listen to the early morning wakeup program? Regularly? Sometimes? No?

Do you listen to the six o'clock evening news? Regularly? Sometimes? No?

Do you listen to the Japanese program? Regularly? Sometimes? No?

Do you listen to the Filipino program? Regularly? Sometimes? No?

Do you have a favorite program?

How big is your family? How many work? How many in school?

The results were used to set advertising rates and sell radio time to local businesses. Sometimes the comparison with Honolulu's stations was so exceptional that we picked up national advertisers who had been selling through the two Oahu radio outlets.

The surveys showed very high listenership in the south-side communities from Eleele through Koloa and the east-side towns from Lihue to Kealia. It was low on the west side and also around Anahola where the KTOH signal was weak. And almost no one could hear the station on the Hanalei north shore except those who had strung an antenna wire between the house and a nearby tree.

Peak audiences came during the wakeup morning hours and for the six o'clock evening news as well as the two foreign language programs. The Japanese and Filipino shows stood at the top of the ranking. Weakest was the period from right after lunch to around four o'clock when kids were arriving home from school and dinner was being prepared.

To bolster this mid-afternoon time slot a request program was inaugurated with dedications being added later. The ratings soared as both housewives and students listened to hear their names being spoken over the radio.

For the early afternoon period, we created a talk show at an age in radio broadcasting when such entertainment was virtually non-existent. At one o'clock every weekday "The KTOH Party Line" went on the air. With Kauai's thin telephone book in one hand and an opened paperclip in the other, I began the program with a few thoughts on the question for the week. The next step was to turn to any old page in the phone book and randomly pinpoint a name.

The person answering the phone was told what was going on. Once in a while the homemaker abruptly would hang up—sometimes because she didn't want to be interviewed and at other times we didn't speak the same language.

Most of the time the conversations were good fun with some of the most beautiful pidgin English you'd ever hear. The discussions would begin with talk about the listener, her family, and whatever else happened to come up in the friendly chat. Then came the question of the week.

We asked for an opinion—never on the subject of politics or religion. Usually it was something like, "What should we do about the millions of pesky *bufos* hopping around in everybody's yard and all over the roadways?" Or, "If a magic genie popped out of a bottle and granted you one wish, what would it be? Or, "What is the recipe for your family's favorite dish?" Or, some equally significant topic.

It would have been wonderful if we'd had some way to save those candid dialogues. They'd be perfect examples today of the various patterns of pidgin: Chinese, Portuguese, Filipino and Japanese. But, tape recorders hadn't been invented yet.

Everything on the air had to be done live except for music on phonograph records and material received on transcriptions. The backbone of America's radio stations at that time was the electrical transcription industry. Several mainland recording companies produced large, 16-inch-diameter permanent disks that could play up to seventeen minutes on each side.

Commercials for national advertisers and programs such as soap operas, dramas, comedies, kid shows, public service programs, etc. filled most of the air time all around the country through the use of transcriptions.

These giant platters also brought us mainland entertainment such as big name bands, singers and other musical groups. From five to six songs would be recorded on each side, each tune lasting from two to three minutes. Classical music tracks sometimes were longer.

The one big drawback to the early transcriptions was that these song tracks were not connected to each other. So, every piece had to be played individually.

This meant if you were working alone, as we so often did at KTOH, you couldn't be away from the turntable for more than about two minutes or so. It was real torture when you had to go to the bathroom. The longest musical performance we had was a concert orchestra playing Modeste Moussorsky's "A Night on

Bald Mountain" that ran for twelve minutes and sixteen seconds. When a regular program was interrupted to run this piece, it meant you know what.

If "A Night on Bald Mountain" was followed by the fifteen minute transcription from the Red Cross describing "Safety Tips for Home and Recreation," then the poor announcer/engineer was having trouble. It was like sending out a SOS. Those of us with radio licenses including Jack Wada and Katashi Nose (Kauai's other radiomen with Federal licenses) would rush to the station to offer relief. When more than one of us showed up, we'd *jan ken po* to see who'd finish the shift so the suffering soul could go home.

There actually was one other means to make recordings but it wasn't used very much. This was an aluminum disk with a shiny black coat of acetate. Using the regular turntable and a special diamond-tipped needle, we could cut an audio groove on the surface of the disk. The result was okay for a few uses but, because the acetate was soft, it quickly deteriorated. Besides, it was expensive.

That was the extent of recorded programs prior to World War Two.

But, the technology of war brought some significant advances. I left KTOH and spent most of the war years overseas. When peace came there were no plans to return to Kauai. I wanted to be an entertainer—in the spotlight on Broadway and before the cameras in Hollywood.

I thought I was about to make it big in December of 1947. While studying piano, opera coaching and orchestration at the San Francisco Conservatory of Music, I had a two-week vaudeville engagement on the stage of San Francisco's RKO Golden Gate Theater. One afternoon, following a matinee, I opened the stage door to the street and there standing on the sidewalk, smiling, was Charlie Fern. We went for a cup of coffee. He made an offer. I made a phone call home to my very pregnant wife and six weeks later, shortly after our second child was born; I was on Kauai as KTOH station manager. In a matter of minutes, the course of my life

had been altered 180 degrees. There never has been a moment of regret.

The new technology now provided the ability to record sounds on spinning reels instead of flat disks. The first to appear was a wire recorder. Here a very thin steel wire from a spool on one side was drawn across a magnetic recording/playback head to a spool on the other side. The sound was quite tinny but it allowed us to cover remote happenings without being limited to going live by telephone line.

Now for the first time we could bring noteworthy events to listeners at the most convenient time. Newsmakers' voices were heard on the evening newscast. Teentime reporters at the island's three high schools were recorded at the school every week with their chitchat broadcast during the after school request program.

The wire recorder, about the size and weight of a case of beer, had one other shortcoming apart from the high-pitched sound. The very thin wire often would

The new KTOH wire recorder took listeners all over the place—even right into people's kitchens. Who can remember today what might have been interesting then about somebody's ordinary kitchen? But devoted daytime listeners (probably just being nosy) followed this new invention each day on its unpredictable journey to the unknown and the unusual. You'd never know which of your neighbors was going to be featured on the program "KTOH Explores—Inside Kauai."

snap in two when being rewound. This meant tying the two ends into a knot and losing a few seconds of audio. This knot produced a strange gulping sound as it slid over the playback head. Sometimes it was embarrassing as a VIP was speaking and it sounded as if he had belched in mid-sentence. Without saying, "Pardon me."

Each time the spool of wire was used, a little bit of all the former recordings remained. There was no total erasure. After a while it was necessary to replace the high-cost spool because the residual noise made it sound as if the talker were speaking in a noisy barroom.

So, we were glad when Ampex and a few other manufacturers produced a mechanism that used quarter-inch acetate and Mylar tapes. The first one at KTOH was as big as a Pullman suitcase and weighed a ton. It had to be huge because it was filled with vacuum tubes, heavy iron transformers and bulky speakers made with

The invention of the tape recorder brought a big addition to KTOH programming—so big it had to be wheeled around on a table. Here Itsue Kawaguchi Kaui (the station's total office force) sets up a taped commercial during her daily morning broadcast devoted to women's interests.

weighty metal magnets. Today, thanks to miniaturization, the same application comes in a gadget that fits in a shirt pocket.

After the Ampex tape recorder arrived, KTOH had high-fidelity recorded audio. The sound was as real as broadcasting a live show.

That KTOH tape recorder cost me countless sleepless nights and chopped a few years off my life span. Today I'm older and grayer than I should be because of one incident on one election eve.

Candidates for office often came down to the station to record campaign speeches to be played for audiences at different times of the day. For this, the tape recorder was an excellent device.

For the evening before one election, Clem Gomes, who was in the Territorial Senate, had arranged to record a five-minute address to be played right after the 6 o'clock evening news. It was his most important campaign speech. He chose the top radio listenership moment to solicit support of undecided voters.

He didn't show up at the appointed time of 2:30 P.M. Or 3:30. Or even 4:30 while there was a second

Wailua's old county fairground and racetrack became a US Marine Corps Barracks during World War Two. It also became the final resting-place for the ocean freighter SS *Andrea Luckenbach* that ran aground in March of 1951. The KTOH tape recorder made regular visits to the site to interview the men in charge of trying to salvage the vessel. Among them was future Honolulu Mayor Frank Fasi who was interested in recovering the steel hull and superstructure.

When the Boss is Away the Cast Will Play

For members of KTOH's original staff, it wasn't always just work, work, work at the station. Here Lorraine Fountain (who is the entire office force) and Grampa explain to Bill Parsons

(announcer/engineer) how to turn the crank on the ice cream maker, while Lorraine's brother, Lana (who brought the ice cream gadget), hollers, "Turn it faster or it won't freeze!" Bob Glen (chief engineer) is in the control room spinning phonograph records on the air.

When the ice cream is ready, Bill

goes inside with his giant bowl full to take over on-air duties while the rest of us relax, eating delicious mango-

coconut ice cream. From left is Abe Albayalde (Filipino program), Bob Glen sitting alongside Lana, Grampa, Dean Stewart (station manager) and Lorraine. It's a real friendly, festive, fattening experience—seven people and a gallon of high-fat ice cream.

Grampa was really just a kid pretending to be a grownup. You didn't see any plantation supervisor or store manager or bank employee wearing baggy pants like these. Sixty years later young folks of the 21st century again have adopted this fashion—except Grampa's fly is not down around his knees.

Grampa's faking it again as he reads the evening news like he was Walter Cronkite.

Whenever equipment breaks down, so phonograph records no longer can be played, there are three choices: sit in front of an open microphone and tell stories or play the piano or stop broadcasting until repairs are completed. There was some of each.

The subject of the bet has long been forgotten but there's no question over whether Lorraine or Grampa was the loser.

person available to make the recording. When he hurried in a little before 5:30, I was the only one around.

There was just a quarter of an hour before I had to go on the air with a 30-minute live broadcast to be followed immediately by his recorded speech. The taping was completed with about two minutes to spare. The tape recorder was wheeled from the studio into the control room with my intention to rewind it back to the beginning while I was speaking live on the air.

This early machine didn't have a trustworthy instant stop. You usually let it rewind completely, when it would make a loud "flap, flap, flap" sound (that I did not want listeners to hear). Or, you used your fingers to slow the reel down and stop it. Also, in this way you did not have to re-thread the tape.

I chose the fingers.

It was the wrong thing to do. As I was speaking I tried to slow the reel down, the tape snapped and pieces flew all over the control console. While announcing what movies were playing at the island's theaters that evening, I blindly Scotch-taped pieces together and set the recording back to the start.

Right after the news ended, the tape recording of Republican Senator Clem Gomes was introduced and the very important election-eve speech began. After about a minute, the sound of his voice became garbled, unintelligible, incomprehensible. That was the broken portion of the tape running backwards. In my scrambling to assemble the pieces, I'd taped wrong ends together. The jumbled fragments didn't last long but without question they made Democrats laugh and Republicans cry.

Senator Gomes called me immediately. I tried to explain but he was too upset to comprehend what I was trying to say. He also called Charlie Fern and accused him of plotting the whole thing. The next day he lost the election after twenty-four years of elected public service.

I was unable to broadcast the news the next evening. The lead story reported, "Long time public servant Senator Clem Gomes has died of a heart attack."

The guilt I carried was a tremendous burden. It was noticeable in my work. Dr. Sam Wallis, Lihue Plantation physician and regular KTOH listener, asked me to stop by the clinic to have a talk with him. He assured me that humans don't die from sudden shock or fright or anger unless the heart already was in a condition about to fail. It might have happened at that moment anyway or the next day or someday soon.

I don't know if that's correct. But that's what I needed to hear and is the consolation I still carry with me a half century later.

As the decades passed, Kauai's pioneer station KTOH's ownership and call letters have gone through several changes including the call letters KIVM and KIPO. Today it's radio station KQNG, popularly known as KONG-AM 570 in Lihue. A new FM station reviving the KTOH call letters is expected to go on the air in the year 2001.

5

Torrential Rain and Flash Floods Bring KTOH Its First Major Live News Coverage

It was just three days after KTOH went on the air that the small four-member broadcast crew plunged into its first significant live news story. A torrential rainstorm drubbed the east side of the island leaving from twenty to twenty-five inches of rain in the area around Lihue and Kapaa. It was so heavy that during the one-hour morning period from eleven to noon more than three inches of rain pounded Lihue.

This was an awesome moment preparing for our first remote broadcast. This was going to be a really big story. In all my eighteen years I'd never felt so excited. Charlie Fern was at the newspaper office keeping in touch with weather bureau and County officials and assigning reporters to cover the storm. Dean Stewart, station manager, was at the studios coordinating radio coverage with *The Garden Island* newspaper. Bill Parsons was on the air keeping listeners up to date on flash flood warnings. Bob Glenn, our engineer, and I set out to give first-hand reports.

With much difficulty we drove out of KTOH's unpaved parking area. Our car was skidding from side to side in deep mud, raising waves of water. It looked like 1,001 Dalmatians had passed by—thinking the new radio tower was a fire hydrant.

We didn't know which side of Lihue to put on the air first. There were sizeable streams on both sides: Kapaia and Nawiliwili. We chose Nawiliwili because both the Huleia River and Nawiliwili Stream, with rising waters, could inundate homes along the banks and low-lands of the two normally gentle rivers.

The following is a letter written to my family on May 13, 1940.

"Dear Ma and Pa . . . Tragedy hit the island of Kauai today. The worst was around the village of Lihue. It was so terrible that estimates of the amount of damage cannot be made for quite some time.

"The heaviest rainstorm in the history of Kauai battered against the tiny wooden huts and business houses in an eight-mile wide streak demolishing every house, barn, fence, tree, and automobile that was the least bit unsteady in its foundation or out in the open where no solid piece could hold it.

"Between the hours of five this morning and eleven, twelve inches of steady rain fell. Then between eleven o'clock and noon a little more than three inches of rain was hurled from the sky.

"When I woke up this morning at a quarter to five to go to work, the sky had a beautiful gray haze that is peculiar to Hawaii in the early morning. Since it seemed to be a normal day here I dressed in the usual fashion: a shirt, slacks, and shoes and stockings.

"As I left the foyer of the hotel I could see way over in the distance a huge mass of threatening black clouds. To me they seemed to be far above the mountains somewhere out in the Pacific. Incidentally, this morning as I went to the car, I saw for the first time the peak of Mount Waialeale, the wettest spot on earth. Usually it's covered with fog or white fluffs of clouds.

"But the dark clouds were not as far distant as I had supposed. No sooner had I started the car than a drop of rain splattered against the windshield. A second later it was a bucket of rain, then torrents of water came down like an upside-down geyser. By the time I had driven onto the road in front of the hotel, the rain was so heavy that it formed a thick film on the windshield. I could see just a short way ahead of the car.

"A small truck of plantation workers passed by. I followed right behind but I couldn't see it ahead of me. The police department of Lihue placed visibility at one hundred and fifty feet. The rainstorm was no more than ten minutes old but the highway was at least four inches under water.

"Not knowing much about Hawaii, I thought this must be one of those tropical showers that come and pass away quickly.

"Six o'clock came. The station went on the air and all seemed fine to me until Mr. Fern, the station owner, rushed in with a warning. Rain was falling heavily and was expected to continue for several hours. Motorists were to be advised to drive carefully.

"Seven-thirty came. The kids were in school and everyone was working . . . hoping that the rain would let up. But it didn't.

"At nine-thirty we received word to ask residents at Nawiliwili to prepare to abandon their homes if the rain didn't lessen. Nawiliwili is the village at the harbor, about a mile and a half from here. Through the center of that town a tiny stream, about eight feet wide, passes from the mountains to the harbor. All along its sides are houses. . . .

"At a quarter to ten, the police department gave us word that evacuation was to start immediately. Very few radios are in that section of the island so word of threatening disaster was slow in reaching the unfortunate people there.

"When the telephone operator had notified as many of those who were fortunate to have telephones, the people began to leave with the little they could carry. The men had all gone to work and the children were in school, so the women carried furniture, bedding, and clothing, all they could lift to their backs into the highlands.

"Bob Glen and I took the remote equipment down to Nawiliwili to broadcast what was going on at this point. We were ready to go on the air when the lights went out. The power had failed. There was no electricity in this part of the island.

"We went to the bridge over the tiny creek running into the harbor (in front of Kuboyama Hotel). Behind us was the railroad trestle crossing the same

When It Rains It Pours

How much did it pour? Sometimes plenty! Lihue Mauka Camp in May 1940 was soaked by 25.43 inches of rain from a heavy rainstorm that began at sunrise and continued into the evening. Up at Kokee in August 1950 an unbelievable 50 inches drenched Mt. Waialeale in 40 hours. In Lihue town in May 1940, more than three inches were measured during the hour between 11:00 A.M. and noon. And there were more rainstorms year after year.

Until serious flood control measures were undertaken in the 1950s, flooding was routine in riverside communities such as Waimea, Hanapepe, Anahola, Kalihiwai, Hanalei and Wainiha. Sometimes unexpected flash

floods turned normally peaceful streams into watery wastes in areas around Nawiliwili and Hanamaulu and the inconspicuous channels bisecting Kapaa town.

In these photos, the Bishop Bank branch in Waimea stands in several feet of rising river water. It wasn't unusual for Garden Island residents to find themselves marooned as if they were on their own little island. On one unhappy weekend, the tents, Ferris wheel and other attractions of the E.K. Fernandez Carnival stood deserted. The glowing anticipation of attending an infrequent big-tent spectacle was doused by a tremendous rainstorm that hovered over Kokee and sent a surging river sweeping through the center of town. A home was set adrift by a rising Nawiliwili Stream but was saved by a tree. And, as always, the Red Cross was there with blankets, cots, something to eat, and a place of shelter.

Meanwhile, as folks battled a devastating flood on one side of Kauai, sunbathers in other parts of the island often were basking in the sunshine of a partly cloudy day.

stream of water once only eight feet wide but now nearer to fifteen. Underneath us were passing fences, trees, live poultry, and parts of wrecked homes.

"About three hundred yards upstream a house began slowly to move on its dirt foundation. The stream began to rise more and more. Slowly but steadily the house moved. Then as if a rope holding (it) snapped, it swirled to the middle of the stream twisting and turning until it reached the center. Then straightening out it headed for the only outlet of the stream, underneath the bridge.

"The police rushed to the bridge, grabbing small children watching the house. Picking up speed, the house was sent down the stream, smashing into the bridge. Large splinters of wood flew in all directions. The bridge was not very high because usually the water is very shallow. The sides of the house, now braced at the bottom by the bed of the river and at the top by the bridge, formed a dam.

"The stream, now more like a river, rose to the level of the highway and flooded over. Houses were lifted from the ground to the top of the water.

"We rushed for our car parked on the side of the hill. Along the way we passed families . . . watching the rushing water carry away everything that meant home.

"I'd like to describe the expression (on) the faces of these poor people. I had never seen an expression like this before. I couldn't imagine it either. One could see the lumps in their throats from the look in their misty eyes.

"We had gone only a short way when suddenly there was a ripping sound. . . . The wooden dam (formed by the house caught at the bridge) had broken. The water, pouring through the bridge, undermined the train trestle, causing it to crash to the water with a grinding sound. The last means of crossing from the harbor side of the island to the rest of the island had been washed away. Not until the river receded could anyone on the other side get to a safe shelter. A Nawiliwili Transportation Co. warehouse wall was torn down to

allow the river to run through rather than having surrounding buildings get flooded.

"We left none too soon for about twenty minutes
later the road between Nawiliwili and Lihue was washed
away by a landslide. All roads to Lihue were either
washed away or flooded.

". . . All afternoon the rain kept pouring down.
We kept broadcasting warnings to parts of the island in
danger. Speed limit on the highways was placed at five
mile an hour.

". . . When I came in the room at the hotel, the
floor was all wet. The water wasn't high. It had all
drained through the floor. All the windows on this side
of the hotel are broken. We're moving to the other side.
The rain came in so strong that it reached the opposite
wall in the bathroom—more than ten feet away.

". . . We're broadcasting all night long. . . . By
morning it's expected that floods will have wiped out
entirely several small towns near the ocean.

"Here's the story of Kapaia. This small town is
nestled in a valley. . . . At the upper end of the valley
about three miles from the town is a huge dam (reservoir) holding most of the water for this part of the
island.

". . . About twenty minutes after we arrived we
began broadcasting (by telephone from MS Carvalho
Store). Trucks filled with furniture were leaving for the
mountains as quickly as they could move—about six
or seven miles an hour. We couldn't see very much.
Luckily, the town of Kapaia was built higher from the
stream than at Nawiliwili.

"What we couldn't see we heard. And we heard
plenty. From up the valley came a rushing sound. We
believed the dam (reservoir) had broken. Cascading
down the valley, a huge wave of water was rushing
toward the sea. In its way was a small concrete bridge.

"Trying to cross the bridge was a Lihue Plantation car with three workers inside. They had been up
the Wailua Falls road to check whether the sides of the
dam (reservoir) might collapse. They felt it would be
okay because the water was pouring safely over one side.

"The road which they were traveling on coming down from the direction of the cemetery has a hairpin turn." (Later in the day after it was safe for a plantation *luna* to walk up the road again, he saw a gorge had been created through the road, measuring 150 feet across and 75 feet deep. Through it had rushed the water that the plantation car had been trying to ford.)

"One of the car's passengers heard the rushing water coming, opened the door and climbed to a high spot on the side of the road. The other two were trapped inside as the water quickly rose up to the middle of the door.

"The other passenger opened a door on the down side, fell into the raging torrent where he was carried toward a precipice. He managed to scramble to a small high spot in the middle of the river where he stood watching the car and driver slowly moving toward the cliff.

"The driver was unable to open the door on his side. As the car was swinging around, he climbed out the window but was pinned to the car by the force of the river. The wave hit the bridge splashing fifty feet into the air. The car turned, was swept to the edge of the bridge where it twisted.

"Water poured around the car. The pressure was so heavy the poor fellow couldn't get away. But after the first surge, the river went down and he climbed to the roof to temporary safety. A rope was thrown to him. He tied one end to the car and slowly pulled himself through the powerful current to safety.

"About a hundred yards from the bridge the water ran over a precipice to the main stream and on to the ocean. After about two minutes of terrific strain, the rope broke letting the strong current wash the car over the precipice where it landed upside down. We waited several hours in Kapaia while a landslide on the road to Lihue was being cleared.

"The head of the National Guard has broadcast a list of persons looking for their families. The National Guard Armory is housing all the refugees—hundreds of them.

"I'm terribly tired and sleepy so I'm going to bed. I'll write more tomorrow about the flood and the grand opening of the radio station. Good night.

"Love, Mike"

The rain continued in the Wailua/Waipouli/Kapaa area long after I had dropped off to sleep. During the night the Wailua River rose over its banks and surrounded the Vida and Alfred Hills home, where the Coco Palms Resort later was created. With several streams overflowing their banks within Kapaa town, a mammoth lake was created starting at the coconut groves and across Kapaa town to the rise in the roads leading to Kawaihau and Kealia. Hawaiian Canneries sent pineapple trucks into its camps to rescue some fifty families who were stranded and in danger. A second big lake was created in the area around the jail and golf course.

Some extraordinary rainfall readings included

On the evening of Lihue and Kapaa's tremendous cloudburst many families weren't able to re-enter the flooded areas around their homes. Sheltered overnight by the Red Cross at the Lihue National Guard Armory they returned home to begin the depressing task of searching for anything that might be of value. Some families were devastated with the loss of nearly everything they owned.

The next afternoon young Bill Alexander drove a family car down to KTOH to visit with Grampa and to talk about the previous day's deluge. It was easy driving into the station's unpaved parking lot because it had a slight downhill slope. But when it was time to leave, the squishy mud was still so deep, everyone at the station had to join in pushing the touring sedan out to the paved Ahukini Road where the wheels could gain traction.

25.43 inches at Lihue *mauka* Camp 9, over 19 inches at the Wailua *Uka* and Wailua *Kai* Camps, and more than 17 inches in Hanamaulu and Kealia.

Many people on the west side of Kauai didn't believe what was being broadcast. They thought it was some kind of a make-believe melodrama being produced in the KTOH studios. One Waimea resident, in a letter to KTOH, scolded the station for exaggerating the story in order to build up listenership.

It wasn't too much later that KTOH was over at the Waimea and Hanapepe rivers describing destructive flash floods that folks who were living on the sunny and dry east side found hard to believe.

6

Resetting Island Clocks as Time Marches Backwards

Before Kauai's first radio station, KTOH, went on the air in May 1940, most folks set their clocks according to plantation time. They could have asked the telephone operator for "time please" if they happened to have a phone. Very few people did. But it was easier for them just to listen every evening and early morning for the whistle of the nearest sugar mill or pineapple cannery siren. Then, if necessary, they could reset their timepieces.

All around Kauai each evening at 8 P.M., a penetrating signal announced it was time to get ready for bed. Then an early morning startling blast roused everyone to prepare for the day's activities. In very bad weather, the absence of a morning whistle meant "no work today" for field employees. Life was very simple. For the great majority of Garden Islanders everything revolved around a plantation and the only time they really had to pay attention to was plantation time.

Not all plantations, however, kept the same time. For operating reasons, some were a half-hour or a full hour different from Hawaii Standard Time. If you lived in Lihue and were invited to a party in Makaweli or to a Waimea school program, you'd better check their time against your own clock or you'd arrive on Hawaiian time plus or minus a half-hour or more.

To make it even more confusing, the Territory of Hawaii until WWII was two-and-a-half hours earlier than Pacific Standard Time. This odd arrangement had been made because the Hawaiian Islands are near the middle longitude of its time zone. Whoever made the rules believed it was important to make sure the sun would be directly in line overhead at twelve o'clock—as if it really mattered to anyone or anything, including sugar and pineapple plants.

Then along came radio station KTOH. From the first day we went on the air, time signals were given after every phonograph record during early morning hours and at least once an hour during the rest of the day.

Kauaians started buying radios. Soon the station's music, news and special events began appearing in people's kitchens and living rooms. (There were no portables or car radios, yet). Gradually the island's pocket watches, alarm clocks, kitchen clocks and trendy wristwatches were being zeroed in on KTOH as the official time source.

After a year or so of almost everyone converting to KTOH time, I happened to be down at the Nawiliwili dock when the interisland cargo and passenger vessel SS *Waialeale* arrived on its twice-weekly overnight voyage from Honolulu. One of the returning passengers, former senator Elsie Wilcox, came over to me and asked if I knew Kauai's time was different from Honolulu time.

I said I was aware some plantations did set clocks to suit their agricultural operations rather than following standard time.

She said that's not what she meant. She claimed that all the clocks on Kauai were different from those in Honolulu. She noticed it, she said, because she had set her watch to Kauai time before leaving for Town and when over there, she had to adjust it to match clocks on Oahu.

We compared watches and, sure enough, there was a difference of about seven minutes. My time was ahead of hers.

I assured her I'd check it out and later on that day I called Susie Dias who was the chief telephone operator at the Lihue phone exchange. I said, "Susie, you know every evening just before ten o'clock when KTOH goes off the air we call the telephone operator to check the time. And, if necessary, we correct our clocks." Susie said she wasn't aware of that.

Then I asked her how the Lihue telephone exchange verified the time for its clocks. Her answer was, "Oh, every morning about seven o'clock we call KTOH. And, if necessary, we correct our clocks."

Wow! We had a problem.

It had been like the blind leading the blind. For months and months people hadn't known what was slowly happening.

Susie and I both decided there was no way to get everyone on Kauai to change his or her timepiece seven minutes at the same moment. Besides, it would be terribly embarrassing if the world discovered how dumb we were.

So, between us, we made changes a minute at a time over a period of two months and no one noticed. After all, Kauai was a community where being nearly on time was just as good as being on time. If a person's watch was seven minutes off, who cared?

In this case folks were doing things a little earlier rather than a little later. And that wasn't bad at all. For more than a year people had been continually adjusting their watches believing their timepieces were junk— always running slow and needing to be corrected.

To make certain this didn't happen again we called on Jack Wada, local engineer for KTOH. Every week he then would tune his short-wave radio to WWV, a station whose time signals were broadcast around the hemisphere twenty-four hours a day. Jack relayed them to KTOH.

By solving this problem we could move on to doing other weird things that fledgling radio stations were inclined to do in the early days of radio broadcasting.

7

Charlie Fern and The Anna Gladys Debacle

The first time I saw Charlie Fern I thought he was an old man. A very old man. It was shortly after sunrise on a humid morning in spring, 1940. I was nervously pacing back and forth on the afterdeck of the interisland steamer *Waialeale* as it was drawing close to the pier in Nawiliwili.

There he was all alone on the dock—portly, neither too tall nor too short, a shock of dark-gray hair, ruddy complexion and in his customary fashion he was wearing a short-sleeve aloha shirt, starched white trousers and white shoes.

Here was my new boss: editor of the weekly *Garden Island* newspaper and primary architect of the publishing company's bold plan to establish a broadcast radio station on Kauai.

He really wasn't that old. It only seemed so. I was eighteen and he was over thirty, where "old" begins. At first glance that morning I'd have bet my bottom dollar he wouldn't survive another half century. He did. Plus five additional years.

Charlie Fern was only forty-eight years old on that momentous day when I walked down the gangway at Nawiliwili Harbor. Average life expectancy for American males in 1940 was 50-something. Would you believe I attended his funeral fifty-five years later, nearly 103 years after his birth, June 20, 1892?

He left the University of California in Berkeley during his junior year. America's participation in World

War One had just begun. Enlisting in the Army Air Service, he served as a second lieutenant pilot.

When the war ended he brought a World War One Army biplane called the "Jenny" to Hawaii on a Matson freighter, arriving on Oahu the week before Christmas in 1919. A few months later he is credited with making the Territory's first round-trip interisland land-plane flight between Oahu and Maui. For a while he made his living taking Oahu folks on short rides from the Kapiolani Park polo field.

Then on May 8, 1920, accompanied by two Navy seaplanes, he warily set down in a bumpy cow pasture in the middle of Kauai's Waipouli racetrack. This noteworthy event created Kauai's first landing strip. Even though it was just an open field lying about six miles from Lihue it became known as Lihue Airport.

Here he began barnstorming—charging adventurous Garden Islanders for wild sightseeing flights along the east and north shores. However, in just a matter of months the lack of spare parts brought an end to the risky venture and the aircraft was abandoned.

During the next two years he held several jobs, working initially as a timekeeper at Makee Sugar Plantation in Kealia and then as a salesman for Garden Island Motors in Lihue.

Folks say that one day in 1922, thirty-year-old Charlie Fern, former high school and college baseball star, told the editor of *The Garden Island*, J.C. Hopper, that his sports coverage was "lousy." (I'm sure he didn't say that brashly; he was too diplomatic. He would have made a sincere criticism intended to be helpful—a trait for which Charlie Fern was noted throughout his life.)

He was hired by Mr. Hopper to make an improvement. The paper's brief squibs covering sports events were expanded to a popular two-page sports section. Within two years the live-wire sports reporter became editor of *The Garden Island* and in 1929 publisher Hopper retired, leaving Charlie Fern in full charge of the paper.

In the meantime, the witty Irish bachelor had met an attractive Waimea schoolteacher, Mary Lucille

The Big-time Small-town Editor
that Everybody Called Charliefern

Kauai's twice-weekly Boat Days became a popular island-wide event when KTOH started broadcasting boat departures from the dock in Nawiliwili. Every Tuesday and Friday night at nine-thirty, folks all over the island tuned in to enjoy Hawaiian music and listen to Charlie Fern, or one of the others on the

station staff, interview Garden Islanders heading for the big city. The program was so popular that some people believed local politicians would make a special overnight trip to Honolulu just so they could get some free time to make a campaign speech.

One day a team of four or five young women arrived on the morning flight from Honolulu and fanned out to the population centers of the Garden Island. The attractive maidens, wearing blouses and skirts one size too small, were hustling magazine subscriptions that they announced would give them "points towards winning a college scholarship."

This picture of Charlie Fern was taken while a charming saleswoman was making her pitch in his office. He kept staring at the ceiling, lips tightly closed and feet on a chair so she couldn't sit down. After making her speech and getting no response, she slammed her briefcase shut and stomped out of the office. He then came to the group of us who were watching and advised us: "The best way to get rid of a salesman is don't say anything. Just keep your mouth shut and they'll disappear."

After he retired as editor and publisher of *The Garden Island*, Charlie Fern produced a weekly column called "From Where We Sit." Pecking away with just two fingers on his old Royal standard typewriter, he made observations of events affecting the island of Kauai. At every session of the Territorial Legislature in Honolulu, he sent back to *The Garden Island* his account of progress as well as behind the scene intrigues and many an individual politician's crafty schemes.

Gillespie. On June 30, 1922, when he finally had a good, steady job with the island's growing newspaper, they were married. Their only child, a son named Charles James Fern, Jr., was born in 1926. Choosing not to call him "Junior," they gave him the nickname "Mike." (And later upon my arrival, the boss decreed everyone should call me "Ashie" to avoid any confusion.)

I didn't know all this on the day I first walked down the gangway at Nawiliwili and it took me many years to learn it from others. Charlie Fern rarely talked about himself. He was too busy playing the role of Small-town Editor. He was constantly measuring the pulse of the public, protecting the people against government excesses, demanding improvements, and advocating everyone's right to life, liberty and the pursuit of happiness.

When he became editor, he made it a point to print as many local names as possible in news items covering every island happening: sports, religion, school affairs, parties, weddings, births and other social events. He often said it didn't matter whether a person was a laborer or boss, if his name was in the paper he'd buy a copy.

In addition to being a small-town editor and all-out volunteer public servant, he was someone extra special to me. He was my employer who required me to put in a good week's work every week. He was my boss who expected me never to make the same mistake twice. He was my father who tried to direct me into being a decent human being. My brother who had been there before and counseled me on life's pitfalls. My uncle who helped me understand the facts of life. My friend who made sure to be there when I needed someone to talk to. My educator who brought me together with learned luminaries. My matchmaker who tried to set me up with marriageable young ladies. He was a kindly, vibrant, spry, remarkable man who gave me access to the most interesting and fulfilling life a human being could wish for.

Those of us who worked for him at the newspaper or radio station always addressed him as "Mr. Fern." His close friends called him "Charlie" or "CJ." But everyone else on the island called him "CharlieFern," as if it were all one name. The only time I didn't call him Mr. Fern was when we were doing broadcasts together and I felt it was more professional to refer to him as "Charlie."

On one of those occasions we were broadcasting baseball from the ballpark in Hanapepe. Because of his earlier experience in baseball and his in-depth knowledge of other sports, he was a very fine play-by-play sportscaster. But on this day he almost cost KTOH its FCC operating license.

It was an important AJA (Americans of Japanese Ancestry) Senior Baseball game—bottom half of the last inning, two outs, the Lihue "Planters" ahead by one run. "Punchy" Furutani of the Makaweli "Indians" is at bat. A long, high fly ball is hit into center field. Charlie Fern's description is, "It's a long, high fly ball. Izuka is under it. Looks like the game is over. Boy, he sure hit a slow high Texas Leaguer . . . it's a can of corn. Izuka has it in his glove and Jesus!! . . . he drops it!!!"

We look at each other, our faces grimacing in anguish. There goes our license to operate the station. The FCC, in those days, was extremely strict about saying things like that over the air. Recovering quickly, Charlie says, "That's right, sports fans, gee whiz he dropped the ball and the runner's safe on first base." Whew! We never heard from the FCC.

Through the years, Charlie Fern served the island well. In 1940 and '41 as the Territory of Hawaii prepared for the remote possibility of war, and also continuing through World War Two, he mobilized the community into an effective civilian defense association. First, as chairman of the blackout committee he employed the newspaper and radio station's widespread influence to conduct two extremely successful practice blackouts. In the year prior to the bombing of Pearl Harbor, as the island was kept busy preparing itself for any possible emergency, Charlie Fern was coordinator for disaster relief. And on the morning of December 7, 1941, he was assigned complete control of civilian affairs as Director of the Office of Civil Defense.

From the day he arrived on Kauai he had been encouraging public participation in all kinds of sports. One of his many achievements was guiding the creation of Barefoot Football which allowed ordinary folks to enjoy playing organized football with just a minimum cost for equipment. Teams began to appear in the larger communities and on plantations. Leagues were formed and eventually the barefoot season became a Territory-wide major event.

The first large-scale promotions for Kauai as a visitor destination began in the mid-1940s. As the Kauai volunteer representative for the Hawaii Visitors Bureau, Charlie Fern initiated a publicity program trying to interest mainland tour operators and travel agents in seeing the little known attractions of the Garden Island. In the late 1940s he began arranging for a large group of members of the American Society of Travel Agents to spend several days touring the island. They made the journey to Kauai in 1950.

He also encouraged some twenty members of the Kauai Writers Group to prepare the island's first guidebook for visitors. The 85-page volume, about the size of a pocket book, included a map, as well as many photos and drawings. Descriptions of island cultural and scenic spots were featured along with chapters on Kauai's history, government, business, churches, birds/fish/flowers, and other subjects of interest to visitors. In 1951, the Garden Island Publishing Company printed the project as "Kauai, Hawaii's Garden Island"—now a collector's item. An updated and more detailed version was published a year ago.

Early in 1952, the long-time country editor turned over the reins of the newspaper to son, Mike, who then continued as editor until the paper was sold to Scripps League Publishers in 1966.

Stepping aside from the editorship gave Charlie Fern more time to promote Kauai as a tourism jewel. He also appeared at the newspaper office regularly to sit at his ancient Royal typewriter and, in his two-finger style, hunt and peck a weekly column, "From Where We Sit." In it, he didn't hold back on his observations of life as related to Kauai. Although the term hadn't been created yet, he was a top-notch "investigative reporter." Territorial legislators meeting in Honolulu often wished he had stayed home instead of coming to the territorial capital to pry into their machinations.

By 1956, the increasing number of visitors had made a substantial impact on the island's economy. The *Honolulu Star-Bulletin* and the *Honolulu Advertiser* invited Garden Islanders to join in honoring Charlie Fern with a recognition dinner at Coco Palms Resort. A special award for serving ten years as the island's active promoter of tourism was presented. He also was commended for his thirty-five years devoted to the Garden Island community.

Ultimately, in 1974, he received the local newspaperman's foremost recognition in being named to Hawaii's Press Club Hall of Fame.

Charlie Fern's political affiliation was never a secret. He was a true-blue, absolute, dedicated Republican. His newspaper editorials proclaimed this and his allegiance to the Republican Party often seeped into the paper's coverage of political affairs. (The radio station, on the other hand, was under strict FCC regulations and a colossal amount of Charlie Fern's adjectives were trimmed regularly before items written by him could be broadcast.)

At one election, when Democratic Party candidates failed badly, the newspaper's report on election results was sub-headlined, "Democrats Get Dirty Licking." This brought howls of protest. Subscriptions were cancelled. Democrats joined in boycotting newspaper advertisers. Charlie Fern claimed he had just used a very ordinary Hawaii expression, which simply meant, "sorely defeated."

The protest, while loud and heated, didn't last long. After all, there was only one paper for people to get news of Kauai and nearly all merchants had to advertise in its pages to remain competitive.

But the Democrats got their revenge in the next election.

Going back a number of years earlier when

The Birth of a New Era

In the mid-1940s, Charlie Fern appointed himself to be the volunteer marketing agent for Kauai's budding business of tourism. He was in a good position to do so since he was the boss of the island's only newspaper and radio station. Early on he recruited a group of Garden Islanders to write an in-depth guidebook for visitors.

In September of 1950 he invited a group of about 150 mainland travel agents to enjoy a familiarization trip to Kauai. Accommodations were hosted by the Kauai Inn which offered a room and all meals for five dollars a day. Newspaper and radio announcements drew hundreds of Kauaians to the airport to demonstrate the islanders aloha for visitors. Sisters Lani Higgins (right) and Sarah Kailikea along with Grampa serenaded the arriving guests.

Folks in Hanalei invited the travel agents to join in a *hukilau* to catch fish for a noontime *luau* with the community. *Kalua* pig, right out of the *imu*, was served along with a

complete menu of island foods including Hanalei's famous *poi*. As the visitors watched handicraft being made, Henry Tai Hook, the unofficial mayor of the North Shore, demonstrated how the *taro* root is pounded to make the delicious island staple called *poi*. The papaya, pineapples, *lilikoi*, bananas, sweet potatoes, grilled fish and chicken, chicken long rice, roast pork, and *haupia* quickly disappeared. There was a lot of leftover *opihi*, *lomilomi* salmon, and *poi*.

KTOH first went on the air, election nights found virtually all households tuned in to learn the results. After the polls closed, Charlie Fern and A.H. "Hib" Case would join as a radio forecasting team to predict probable results for each race.

Newspaper staff members were assigned to each polling place. They first reported to KTOH when ten percent of the votes had been counted and then again at twenty-five and fifty percent. The results were amazingly accurate. Charlie Fern and "Hib" Case were hailed as men of distinguished ability. (This was long before big-time network radio and television produced election-night predictions with massive computers using the same principle.)

For the election following the "Dirty Licking" incident, some still-angry Democrats gave Charlie Fern their "pay back." Their scheme was drawn up to embarrass the two eminent prognosticators.

The normal procedure for counting votes was for an election inspector to open a ballot and read off candidates who had checkmarks by their names. This time, in a number of precincts, the Democrats' plot called for checked ballots of certain candidates to be set aside temporarily as "questionable" and then be "rechecked" and counted after all the other votes were finished. This destroyed the radio team's statistical forecasts. By the end of the evening, the two wizards were thoroughly discredited. The following day smiling Democrats went around the island saying, "We gave 'em dirty licking!"

One day, when Charlie Fern was in his eighties, I stopped over in Honolulu for a few hours on a flight from the Orient to the Mainland. We hadn't seen or spoken to each other for more than twenty years. My call was to let him know how important he had been in my life. I wanted him to know how much I appreciated the opportunities he gave me.

He was living at Arcadia, an adult community in Honolulu, when I called about two-thirty in the afternoon. I said, "Hi, Mr. Fern. This is Mike Ashman." I thought he might say, "Mike who?" But his quick response was, "My God, Ashie, this is naptime!!" and he hung up. I never tried calling again but did write a let-ter (which he acknowledged with a postcard) thanking him for opening up the world to me.

In my attempted phone call I was hoping to rem-inisce about the many eventful and happy hours we had shared. There were so many episodes in our lives that were unforgettable.

One incident that we called "The Anna Gladys Debacle" brought us many laughs as we recounted it over and over again between 1940 when it took place and 1952 when I left Kauai.

Mr. Fern, in the role of matchmaker, always was trying to set me up with marriageable young women.

A week or so after the birth of KTOH, I received a printed invitation to a high society party to be given in the pavilion of the Lihue Hotel by a Garden Island maiden, Anna Gladys Stewart. It was to be a champagne punch evening reception and dance to introduce her houseguest, Merrie Pflueger, from Honolulu. Anna Gladys, whose parents lived somewhere near GP Wilcox's new home in Puhi (now Kilohana, the site of Gaylord's Restaurant), had returned to the island for the summer.

This was just the occasion my marriage broker/ mentor was looking for. When he learned I had an invitation he said, "She's beautiful. She has a pleasant personality. She's single. And she's an heiress!"

I told him I grew up in the Mission District in San Francisco and didn't know how to talk to a rich girl.

His reply was, "That's no problem. All you have to do is find some way to break the ice and everything from then on will follow naturally."

"How do I break the ice?"

"I'll tell you what you do. You get to the party about fifteen minutes after it's supposed to start and just hang around. She'll probably be a half-hour late. When she arrives and begins taking Merrie Pflueger around the room to meet the guests, you go to where she started. That'll become the end of the reception line.

"Then, when she gets to you, you ask her to dance and when you're out on the floor you say, 'You should always wear that color. It does something to your eyes.' I guarantee you she'll melt. From then on it'll be easy."

During the week before the affair I kept repeating, "You should always wear that color. It does something to your eyes." Sometimes I even said it out loud so I'd know what it sounded like when I had to say it.

The evening came. I put on my white dinner jacket. (All the *haole*s wore suffocating tuxedos or spiffy gowns to fancy parties.) I was living at the Lihue Hotel and kept an eye out for arriving guests. Fifteen minutes after starting time people began arriving and I joined about a dozen others entering the pavilion at the same time. (Nobody ever went anywhere on time. That was a rule.)

I wasn't acquainted with many people so, while a Hawaiian trio was making music, I tried to act very nonchalant. I wandered around inside the airy pavilion, examining the lattice-work walls, counting how many electric outlets were on the baseboard, analyzing spider webs, watching the rotating ceiling fans to determine which one was whirling the fastest, and trying to fill more waiting time by inspecting the array of daisies and amaryllis and by sniffing bouquets of fragrant gardenias, ginger and other tropical flowers displayed around the room.

Uppermost in my mind was that mystical phrase given me by my guru, Charlie Fern. I didn't want anybody to talk to me lest I forget it.

By the time Anna Gladys and Merrie Pflueger made their entrance there were about fifty guests—some standing around the bubbling punchbowl drinking champagne punch and others in small groups. A few couples had been dancing but the music ended just as the two young ladies entered the pavilion.

Both were very attractive. Anna Gladys was wearing a pale blue full-length gown. Maybe this was going to be easy. Once they had started making the rounds, I moved to the appointed spot and watched to learn how people shook hands with a rich girl.

As they approached me I became suave and

sophisticated, pretending to be engrossed in examining the tip of a potted palm branch. I wished I had a cigarette between my fingers so I'd look real cool.

When I turned to the two girls, the "on" switch in my brain started performing my well-rehearsed spiel. "I'm very pleased to meet both of you. It looks like this is the end of the line. Anna Gladys, would you care to dance?"

Halfway through the speech, I realized the girl in the light blue dress had been introduced as Merrie Pflueger. Anna Gladys was the other girl, wearing a white gown with a vest of multi-colored Scottish plaid. Now, what was I going to say out on the dance floor? I panicked!

I couldn't have stopped talking in the middle of what I had practiced. It would have made me look stupid. When I finished my greeting, I was hoping she'd say, "Thank you. Maybe later." But she said, "Yes, I'd love to" and we headed for the dance floor. I couldn't turn back. There was no hole in the floor to swallow me up.

As the Hawaiian group softly played a romantic island melody, my shoes clopped like they were heavy iron horseshoes. My knees kept banging against hers. My sweat glands pumped like my shirt was on fire. My tight-around-the-neck tuxedo shirt was sopping wet. I was positive Anna Gladys could feel perspiration seeping through my jacket. "How repulsive," she must be thinking. My mouth was full of cotton balls and my ears were burning, bright red. I wanted to say something but even though I opened my mouth nothing would come out. The musicians kept on playing the same song for a million years. I was miserable and I was sure she was sharing the agony.

From that moment on my mind is blank. I don't remember when the music finally ended. There's no recollection of my escorting Anna Gladys to the punchbowl or anywhere else. I don't know if I stayed the whole evening or ran off in embarrassment or sat in a corner and cried. Probably not the latter. My body was very low on liquid by that time.

Grampa is practicing how to appear nonchalant in preparation for sweeping Anna Gladys off her feet.

"Kauai is Truly a Remarkable Destination!"

With cameras and notebooks in their hands the travel agents were taken to just about every scenic and cultural spot from Kee Beach in Haena to the Kalalau Lookout at Kokee. They were pumped with names, facts and legends. Visits

also were made to a pineapple cannery, a sugar mill and a stop to watch the harvesting of sugar stalks from a recently torched canefield. Many agents expressed amazement at the clever laying of temporary train tracks through the field and the mammoth size of the loads of cane being dropped onto the small railroad flatcars. At Lihue Mill the visitors asked Grampa to stand beside a locomotive so they could take pictures to show clients how tiny was the little engine that could haul a seemingly endless line of loaded cars from faraway fields to the mill.

On the evening before the mainland guests left Kauai, an Hawaiian extravaganza was presented at the

Kauai Inn pool where blossoms floated on the surface. Under bright moonlight, as Miki Waiau, Ah Sau Ahana and Grampa played a collection of Kauai Island melodies, Kekaha's "Kauai Annie" *Hula Halau,* circling the pool, performed a medley of ancient and modern *hula.* A solo dancer, atop a bamboo raft guided by handsome swimmers, gracefully told of the Garden Island's waterfalls, flowers and *mokihana* leis. When they departed the next day, the travel agents were starry-eyed in love with the island. The leader of the group enthusiastically praised Kauai's "unparalleled scenery, strong culture and gracious people. Kauai is a truly remarkable destination! We will love you forever and ever."

I never saw Anna Gladys again.

Not too long ago I began searching for her, only to discover she is gone forever—leaving without answering a burning question six decades old: "Do you remember that certain evening in the summer of 1940 when a trio of Hawaiian musicians was singing a romantic ballad and you were held in the sweaty arms of a skinny, dumb city kid who was dancing like he had to go to the bathroom real bad?"

I'll never know if she remembered it. I hope she was able to forget it. I haven't. You know, as you get older you begin thinking more about the past than the future. There are some precious moments you just love to recall over and over again. There are other tormenting memories you wish you could forget. This Anna Gladys debacle happens to be one of life's bloopers that was caught on tape in my head and goes into reruns several times every season. When it's on, I don't seem to know how to switch channels. It's still highly embarrassing.

8

Preserving One's Culture and Going Night Fishing

What was it like living in a society where fixed barriers separated groups of people by nationality and by power structure?

Looking back sixty years from today's standards, it seems to me that it should have been awful. But, according to my recollection, it wasn't that bad. There were no sit-ins, no protest marches, no terrorist attacks.

I know there were workers and their families who wished it were different—higher pay, better living conditions, overseers who would be more considerate and less cruel.

However, there was a general acceptance of this imbalance. I think there was a widespread surrender to the way things were for several reasons. For one thing, most folks didn't know any better. Those at the bottom of the heap had no television or daily radio reports or newspapers to tell them that living and working conditions were different in the America away from Hawaii. For most immigrants, life was far better on Kauai and the opportunities seemed greater than in the land from where they had come.

In the early part of the last century there primarily were two classes of plantation society in Hawaii: the "haves" (people in charge) and the "have-nots" who were workers. In true Asian tradition of that time, workers appreciated having steady employment and they were willing to accept a humble role in the plantation hierarchy.

The first generation of contract laborers held extremely strong feelings about their own culture. They preferred to live in a community where their neighbors spoke their language, sang the same songs, ate the same foods and made sure their children married someone of the same nationality. In a sense they helped sustain their own segregation.

This was true of Japanese, Chinese, Koreans, Filipinos, Portuguese, Puerto Ricans and *haole*s. Each group had its own organization such as Buddhist Associations, Chinese, Korean and Fil-American Societies, Portuguese Welfare Association, and the others. For every nationality there were churches, sports leagues, picnics, movies, social clubs and holiday celebrations.

By the time I landed on Kauai in 1940, there was a large population of second generation and some third generation families. Many of them were continuing the family tradition of working for a plantation or related operations. Rumblings of discontent over wages, working conditions and housing now were becoming apparent.

One thing that hadn't changed though was the custom of always marrying within the family's cultural group. While a few young people ignored their parents' wishes, the practice was very strong and widespread, particularly among Japanese, Koreans and Filipinos. Some Chinese had ignored this custom and married Hawaiians. *Haole*s were among the most inflexible. For the majority of Hawaiians there was no restraint. Love for them knew no national boundaries.

In general, *haole*s perceived themselves as the elite. Rarely was anyone from the immigrant level invited to their homes or to live in their neighborhoods or to join their social organizations. Of course, there were some exceptions. There was little difference in this practice among other nationalities. Outsiders normally did not participate in Filipino fiestas, *Obon* temple rituals, welfare societies and even sports leagues.

That's the way it was. And that's the way it was accepted until World War Two when Kauai was inundated with *haole* GIs and Garden Island service men returned from duty in the *haole* countries of Europe and the mainland. Even immediately after the War, mixed marriages between a *haole* and a non-*haole* had a long way to go before gaining entry into high society.

Being with Radio Station KTOH, I was in an enviable position among the island's bachelors. Almost all the other *haole* single young men worked within the plantation community. They had to worry about being seen at a dance or movie or carnival with a non-*haole*. Plantation management still was frowning upon such conduct. But, somehow, my socializing with non-*haole*s didn't prevent me from being invited to Sunday lunch with Lihue Plantation's manager Caleb Burns or Grove Farm's manager Bill Alexander or Elsie and Mabel Wilcox, the two pinnacles of high society.

My boss Charlie Fern, editor of *The Garden Island,* was a man of the people. He didn't mind if I went out with a Japanese, Chinese, Portuguese, Hawaiian, Filipino or other non-*haole* young lady. I believe, though, he might have objected if it looked as if I had become serious about an Asian. This distinction was true, I felt, because he always was steering me towards eligible *haole* women and recommending them as great catches for marriage. I think even Charlie Fern was caught up in the widespread notion that a success-ful marriage required a bonding between hearts of the same nationality.

There must have been several dozen unmarried *haole* field *luna* and office personnel working for eastside Kauai plantations and other businesses. On the other hand only two eligible single *haole* young women lived year-round in the town of Lihue and one up at Kokee. Summertime brought a few girls home from college. The other year-round unmarried young women all were "spoken for."

So, when the Lihue Social Club or the Nawiliwili Yacht Club (both all-*haole*) held a party or dance there was a mad scramble for a partner. Local targets were the two Lihue librarians: Eleanor Harmon, a mainlander, and Irmgaard Horrmann, daughter of the Honolulu Lutheran minister who conducted services at the church on Lihue's German Hill each month. The other sought-after young woman, who lived in faraway Kokee, was Eleanor Weber, daughter of the Kekaha Plantation's water distribution supervisor.

These three were like queen bees. The librarians lived in a cottage just a short way down from the library (now the Museum) on what has been named Rice Street. That location was convenient when attending east side parties. Eleanor Weber's beehive, on the other hand, was such a long, long way to travel to pick up a date.

In 1940 there wasn't today's short, straight road between Hanapepe and Waimea. The County Belt Road beginning at Hanapepe turned *mauka* to the foothills and zigzagged around the Robinson sugar cane fields. Less than two lanes wide, this route was dangerous because of many curves and some uphill stretches where you didn't want to meet another car coming up or down. From Waimea to Puu Kapele in Kokee, the wandering car path again was narrow and winding, often covered with mud from heavy rain runoff.

At least three hours had to be scheduled for the drive from Lihue up to Kokee plus another three back to Lihue. That made picking up the Kokee queen bee an all-day undertaking. Fortunately, when the dance or party was over, she'd spend the night with her sister and brother-in-law, Dottie and Dan Foster in Poipu. Otherwise, it would have been something like a twenty-four hour trek for just a simple Saturday night date.

Because our boss Charlie Fern was so liberal, Bill Parsons, my KTOH partner, and I had unlimited opportunities for openly socializing with the island's other nationalities. And these other folks seemed to welcome us because we were different from plantation supervisors.

We were familiar voices that were in people's kitchens and living rooms every day. We weren't company bosses. Our broadcast relationships always were on a friendly, entertaining basis. Invitations came for *hekka* dinners, Filipino fiestas, Portuguese picnics, Hawaiian *luau*, Chinese Society banquets, and so many other local affairs.

In a letter written to my family, I wrote about a marvelous weekend spent with a Hawaiian family in Kalihiwai. Here's an eighteen-year-old coast-*haole*'s version of night fishing on a reef on the north shore of Kauai.

"September 16, 1940 . . . Dear Ma and Pa, Tonight is full moon. But so far the sky has had some gray and red shower clouds, so the moon came out for only a few minutes. Earlier tonight, about seven, the sun had just set and the moon was just rising. Boy, it was sure pretty. The clouds still had some of the color of the rainbow from the sun while the moon behind the palms and ironwood trees was big and red like a pomegranate. Everything was redder than May Day in Russia.

"Still, last night, when it was almost full moon, the sky was plenty clear. Bill Parsons and I went with the secretary of the station to her Uncle John Akana's shack over on the other side of the island by Kalihiwai. You pronounce it Ka-lee-hee-v-eye. One time you pronounce 'wai' W-eye and the other time V-eye. W-eye? I don't know.

"The islands aren't primitive or old fashioned or anything like that, but some parts are just a little bit behind the times. Maybe about a hundred years behind. No electric lights at Kalihiwai, or washing machines, or hot and cold automatic running water. The only running water I saw was in the stream not far from the house.

"Now, that part is a little ahead of my epistle. The three of us left the village of Lihue about five (P.M.) for the more-than-one-hour drive through the prettiest and greenest part of Kauai. After we arrived at the settlement, the sun was just enough to give us light to cut some bamboo poles for fishing rods.

"Lorraine (Fountain), that's the secretary of the station, her three girl cousins Adeline, Puanani and Kuulei, her boy cousin who is easy to call because his name is 'Boy,' Uncle John, Bill Parsons and I fixed up the rods with string, a hook, and a tiny lead sinker, then dressed for the fun of catching Opelu as in 'Johnny Opelu.'

"The beach at one spot is one of those well known coral reefs you read about in travel magazines. Only it isn't as nice as it sounds. Even the natives never walk barefoot on the reef because the coral is so sharp, and besides slicing your feet up, it causes blood poison. The fishermen wear tennis shoes or slices of rubber automobile tires for sandals. Then you still have to wear long pants and a sweatshirt (for mosquitoes).

"The reef isn't a smooth even piece of coral, as I found out. It goes out in one direction, starting out twenty feet wide, and ends up in a point. Then another section starts out like a needle and ends up like the day before payday—smooth and flat.

"Each of those sections is made up of smaller ones just like them, so you see if you don't watch your step you may land in a hole filled with eels and squids.

"Uncle John led us out for what seemed to be a mile or a little less right to the edge of the reef. All along the way we used our poles as canes to see how deep the next step was—sometimes one inch under water; sometimes only up to our knees. At one time I looked back while walking and slid into a hole. Nothing happened to me, but the eels and squid were plenty sore. They came up to give me the bum's rush but since I'm already Russian, I beat 'em to it.

"One of the cousins caught a squid, like an octopus, squeezed the black ink from his sac, and put him in the bag around her neck. Squid is supposed to be good bait.

"After walking, sliding and falling for about twenty-five minutes we came to the end of the reef where the water now was so deep the bottom couldn't be seen. Not even in the bright moonlight. There we stood about five feet apart, with our country-style fishing poles: just a piece of string tied to the end of the bamboo pole with a piece of lead and a hook.

"In the first five minutes, the youngest cousin caught a bag full of fish, about six to nine inches long, while the rest of us didn't catch as much. After the first eight or ten minutes the fish were a little more scarce, but by the time a half hour had passed all our bags were full. I think most of the fish were Opelu, though a few were tiny red fish with little points that stick into your hands. The smallest fish was five inches and the biggest more than a foot.

"Going back to the shore took a lot longer because a few clouds kept passing under the moon making it impossible to walk on the reef in the dark. We landed on shore safely with all our bags of fish still around our necks, even though sometimes the weight of the many fish threw us off balance.

"Down the road from the coral reef, we went swimming at Hanalei beach in the calm of the tropic moon. The bay is smooth as a lake on one side while on the other end the breakers were swell for surfing. We did both (ends) for a heck of a long time, until we were tired.

"While resting on the white coral sand, we cleaned the fish, and brought the rice and *shoyu* sauce from the car. The steamed rice was cold but it tasted good after all the exercise. The raw fish and *shoyu* was even better. If you asked me what raw fish tastes like, all I could compare it to is the taste of raw fish, for I never tasted anything like it before. After licking our chops for the last time we left for home, arriving real late.

"Today was work again, and tomorrow my day off. I'm expecting to sleep on the beach all day . . . luncheon served by nature: a coconut, some bananas, and papaya for a cold salad.

"Aside from being happy, gaining weight, and saving some money, I'm still the same. I'll try to write to everyone soon again.

"Your loving son, Mike."

9
Comfort Stations for Lonely Hearts

The population of Kauai in 1940 was about 33,000. The overwhelming majority was associated with sugar and pineapple plantations. Among Filipinos there was a ratio of seven males to one female. In the Japanese group it was two men for every woman. So, with that many bachelors it was no surprise to learn that scattered around the island were a number of small cottages with young ladies providing comfort for men who sometimes felt lonely.

In Kapaa Homesteads, alone, were two or three cottages somewhat separated alongside what today is called Kamalu Road. Built like plantation workers cottages, they had three bedrooms, a bath, and a combination kitchen/living room. Interior walls didn't reach to the ceiling so any cooling breezes could circulate amongst the rooms.

On the covered lanai in front was a long wooden bench where, on very busy nights, patrons waited their turn to be invited inside. It was handled something like in a barbershop: first come, first served. At the small kitchen table were about four chairs where the next batch of customers was served cold beer or soft drinks along with spicy *bagoong* and *kim chee*.

How come I know so much about this place?

Well, one summer I met Eddie who had returned home during his college vacation. He was the son of a plantation management employee and was a number of years older than I was. It took me a month to discover that Eddie didn't have many friends because he was considered to be "a wild one." I became his newest attempt at acquiring a crony. It lasted about one month.

One evening, early in our acquaintanceship, he asked if I'd like to visit the girls. Thinking he meant some librarians or schoolteachers, I said, "Sure. Let's go." He drove directly to the dark green cottages in the Homesteads. It didn't take long for me to conclude that these friendly courtesans were not librarians.

For Eddie, lingering with one of the girls was a freebie—just as long as he didn't come around on weekends or on payday. His father had arranged this complimentary service. (And based on the father's reputation he probably had worked out the same deal for himself).

I was solicited, maybe for free too, but politely declined for several reasons. I was deathly afraid of getting some kind of horrible disease that I couldn't explain to my family back home. Or, what if I had a sudden massive heart attack from excitement and the police report stated where it happened? I had a strong Baptist upbringing that didn't even allow going to the show or playing cards on Sundays. I knew that for an unmarried fellow doing THAT at any time was out of the question. And then there's the potential embarrassment—what beginner really wants to perform a duet with a professional?

So, while Eddie was being comforted, I had a nice long conversation with one of the girls and the house-mother/timekeeper. Even though their faces were plastered with a coat of paint they seemed so ordinary, talking about things like home and family.

Without thinking I asked whether they were part of a "white slave ring" I'd read about in the Sunday paper. They both laughed out loud and the house-mother patted me on the top of my head.

"This is business," they said. "We're here to make a lot of money and then go back home with a nice nest egg, get married and raise a family." Most of the girls, they explained, were *haole*s from the mainland, a few were locals, and some were Polynesians from the South

Pacific. During our friendly conversation, we sometimes giggled as we overheard comments flowing over the walls of the bedrooms.

This scheme of young women offering consolation to the Territory's lonely men wasn't limited to cottage visits. There were other techniques. What these professional sweethearts were carrying out in or near plantation communities was illegal but it was accepted. Everyone just pretended it didn't exist.

A racially mixed couple appeared on Kauai one day. She was a tall, slender, stately Samoan who looked like she might have been a high school beauty queen. He was a handsome, husky Afro-American who claimed to have been a boxing champ. Both had likeable personalities.

She went to work for Von Hamm Young Company as a part-time outside saleswoman, walking through plantation camps selling household appliances and bicycles. He was glib and witty, with an extensive knowledge of popular music. When he volunteered to work free as a disk jockey for KTOH, he was accepted eagerly.

Early every afternoon he would drop her off at some plantation camp with her demo bicycle where she began making calls on homemakers, displaying her appliance catalog and taking orders. Later, as the men returned from the fields, she peddled her bike to their cottages and dormitories to make her sales pitch. If they desired something other than electric frying pans or bicycles, she'd sell at full price early in the early evening and later on at half-price as a closing out sale.

Meanwhile each afternoon, after having delivered his companion to a camp, the popular disk jockey came to KTOH to conduct a request program from 2:00 P.M. to news time at 6:00 P.M. Later, when the plantation whistle blew at 8:00 P.M. she'd close her display case and wait for him to pick her up.

After a number of months, the police called KTOH to tell me the couple was to be arrested that day and shipped off to Honolulu. I asked if that could wait until the popular disk jockey's program was completed because we had no replacement. "No strain," replied the officer. The real reason for requesting a delay was that we knew the arrest would make a great lead story for our evening news.

When the time came that afternoon it all went on as scheduled with an officer handcuffing the transgressor and leading him away as his closing theme song was ending. KTOH had a news scoop about the capture of a suspect being described just as it was happening.

Kauai wasn't the only island with attentive therapists for men with heartaches. On Lanai, where years later I worked as personnel director, there lived a plump middle-aged woman named Mary who rented a cottage from Plantation Housing. She was affectionately known as "Mary *Puka*." Month after month, for years, she invited male friends to shoot craps, play *Pai Gow*, or spend a few minutes alone with her. On payday weekends, young, attractive female houseguests came from Honolulu to visit her. No one ever complained.

Well, not exactly every single patron was pleased with her. One day a tractor operator came into my office and asked if I could get his hard-earned five dollars back. His complaint was that during all the time she was comforting him, she was just lying there eating an apple. I told him there's nothing I could do because she really wasn't a company employee, even though he might have thought so.

Also on Lanai, a plantation electrician was carried off to the hospital with several fractured ribs. He had been up on a utility pole outside of Mary *Puka's* bedroom window where he had no business to be. He became excited, lost his grip on the pole and fell about fifteen feet. He claimed this was an industrial accident because it happened on company time. He won.

This surprising decision led to the blossoming of another employee's grand idea. A shop mechanic demanded the company pay for the care and education of his youngest child. The mechanic claimed he sneaked home during working hours one day to visit his wife. Nine months later a son was born—conceived on company time. Before this matter was settled, I was transferred to Wahiawa Plantation. But, I believe, this time the company was the winner.

Laborers at Wahiawa Plantation found female companionship more readily available in the nearby town and in Honolulu. Still, hustlers were seen making regular calls around payday. One common routine was for the girls to buy tiny ten-cent bottles of perfume from Kress or Woolworth in Honolulu. They then would come up to the plantation and go from room to room in a dormitory selling perfume for ten dollars a bottle. It was a legitimate transaction. The girls couldn't help it if they suddenly fell in love with the customer and spent extra time with him.

This came to my attention when an equipment operator came into my office asking if I could get his money back. He said the *wahine* came into his room, took his ten dollars, gave him a bottle of "medicine for smell da body" and then suddenly left because her "husband" was out in their big Cadillac honking the horn. She explained she had to go home to cook dinner for their children.

Later the worker learned the couple drove directly from his dormitory to another where she continued peddling perfume. I recommended the disappointed lover tell his story to the police. He was hesitant. Didn't want to get in trouble because "da husban' stay beegah den one giant black bull." All he wanted was his money back.

One other means for enjoying female companionship on Kauai before World War Two was at the two taxi dancehalls in Kapaa. Here lonesome men bought tickets allowing them to dance with pretty hostesses for three minutes per ticket. At the one called the Rialto, music was provided by a pianist, drummer, guitarist, mandolin player, and an all-around trumpet-sax-clarinet musician.

Twice I filled in for the sick piano player. It was not fun. It didn't matter if the song was written as a fox trot, two-step, march or polka. It had to be played in slow three-quarter waltz time because that was the best tempo for snuggling. No lonely fellow wanted to spend his meager earnings just to hold hands with a partner hanging out there someplace jitterbugging.

Every song was played in the same key. Not only that, it seemed there never was a break to rest. Each musician took a turn playing melody with the piano leading off. We'd do exactly five choruses for each song with the mandolin player shouting out the name of the next song during the fifth time around. If I didn't know the tune, I'd holler "Not me" and then fake an accompaniment until the fourth or fifth chorus when I could pick up the melody.

Every once in a while the dance hall manager rang a bell and the dreamy client gave his romantic partner another ticket to continue waltzing. If he wanted to have one of the girls spend the evening alone with him a "fine" was paid. The amount would equal what the manager determined the girl would have collected from clients if she had stayed.

Sometimes, while dancing, a poor soul would run out of tickets and cash. No problem. The young lady would continue cuddling on credit. The next day she'd meet her partner at the company store after work where he had an almost unlimited charge account.

He felt so proud as he walked into the store arm-in-arm with a beautiful blonde. His compatriots stood aside with envy. And then the axe would fall. For the couple of dollars he might owe her, she'd select a $10-dollar dress or $15-dollar suitcase or a bottle of very expensive perfume. She couldn't be challenged. That would have been a terrible loss of face.

Some of the taxi dancers seemed to be a different breed from the ladies of the night up in the Home-steads. According to Phyllis Horner, wife of the Hawaiian Canneries manager, more than one disillusioned young lady appeared at the doorstep of the Horner home on Wailua Beach.

The bewildered girls explained they had answered mainland newspaper ads seeking young women "to entertain servicemen in Hawaii." Not fully understanding the significance of the message, they found themselves without much money in a small town on an outside island dancing with laborers who couldn't speak English. Mrs. Horner was known as a compassionate and generous woman—a constant source of gifts for boat transportation home.

One afternoon, shortly after my Kapaa Homesteads adventure with Eddie, I was in Kress Store in Lihue buying a spool of thread. I was having a conversation with another shopper, Alice Alexander, wife of the Grove Farm Plantation manager.

She was a very sweet little woman—the loving sort of manager's wife who knew the names of wives and children of plantation workers. A daughter of the early Bond missionary family, she knew all the words for all the verses of all the hymns in the book.

Quite often she invited me home after church for Sunday dinner. And sometimes there was an invitation for dinner during the week with the luxury of staying overnight in the plantation manager's huge white mansion. Her three sons, close to me in age, were away at school most of the year and my being around, she said, eased some of the pain of their absence. I wouldn't have done anything to spoil that image.

It was easy to see everyone standing in Kress Store because there weren't any shelves. All the items were spread out on long, low counters with extra stock stored in cabinets below. The waist-high counters made it possible for a person to see from one end of the store to the other.

As Mrs. Alexander and I were talking, someone came into the shop. We both glanced over and saw the Kapaa Homesteads housemother who had patted me on the top of my head. I wasn't concerned until Mrs. Alexander waved and said, "Good morning, Sharon" and the woman replied, "Hello, Mrs. Alexander." I went into shock. Suppose she looked at me and said *"Howzit?"* Or even worse, spoke my name? In less than one second I was out of there without my spool of thread.

I was utterly astonished at that time and over the next sixty years often have wondered how come respectable Mrs. Alexander knew a bimbo like that?

10

Hollywood Comes to Kauai and Everybody Wants to Get in the Act

When Metro-Goldwyn-Mayer arrived on Kauai in the spring of 1950 to film *Pagan Love Song,* Garden Islanders by the hundreds showed up for casting calls hoping to see their faces appear on the silver screen. In just one scene alone at Ahukini Harbor an estimated 400 to 600 people appeared in the film. Only the MGM paymaster knew for sure how many there were. His was the job of handing over a ten-dollar bill at the end of the day to each budding movie celebrity.

Hollywood brought Howard Keel and Esther Williams to star in the movie about an Ohio schoolteacher "Haz Endicott" who had inherited a Tahiti coconut plantation. This hero meets and falls in love—out of love—in love again with a *haole* mermaid "Mimi Bennet" vacationing in Tahiti and whom he believes is a Polynesian *vahine.*

Little known to moviegoers a half century ago were supporting members Rita Moreno as "Terru" and Charles Mauu as "Tavae." They acted as a young sister and brother, housekeeper and right-hand-man team, for Howard Keel. These two, along with Minna Gombell as Esther Williams' Tahiti-resident aunt, completed the cast of imported Hollywood headliners. But there were other prominent supporting actors and actresses recruited on Kauai, all with principal speaking parts.

When the finished movie premiered on Kauai a year later, Lihue Theater was mobbed. The four showings on that glittering April Sunday and the three other sold-out shows on Monday turned into controlled chaos. Once the movie started everybody stayed in his or her seat but the clamor by the audience often was louder than the soundtrack.

During the opening scene hundreds and hundreds of Kauaians, mainly those who resembled Polynesians dressed island-style, trotted along the road down the hill to Ahukini Harbor. They were supposed to be hurrying to greet an arriving interisland steamer. As this mob begins to appear on the big screen, there are shouts from all corners of the theater: "That's me!" "There's Miki!" "Look Mabel folks!" And when Kapaia's "Big Bill" Kaliloa, in the role of a jalopy-taxi driver, pushes his way through the crowd and begins talking to "Haz," the audience cheers as if he had just scored a winning touchdown.

After "Big Bill" delivers "Haz" to his new South Sea Island home (fabricated in a corner of the Coco Palms Hotel grounds), other Garden Islanders begin parading through the motion picture, scene after scene. Each new face is greeted with screams of recognition.

Little Leilani Isaacs, Phillip Costa and Charles Freund show up in major speaking roles as "Haz's" *hanai* children. Phillip was taken to Hollywood to finish his role. Seven-year-old Larry Ramos distinguishes himself as a professional in one of the film's major musical numbers, playing the ukulele and singing "House of Singing Bamboo."

Getting big laughs every time a bathtub gets shattered are Sam Maikai, the plumber, and Helen Rapozo as "Angel," the plumber's wife, who carries the plastic tub around the set on her back.

Dozens of young local swimmers perform in the water ballets with cameras focused close enough to identify faces. Again the excited audience drowns out the full orchestral ballet music.

Working every day of filming but not appearing on the screen were the "doubles." It was their role to stand in front of the crew as lights and reflectors were adjusted, camera angles practiced, microphones hung in

"The Longest Party I Was Ever At!"

To produce just a few minutes of the *Pagan Love Song* movie, an all-day-long shoot takes place on the lawn of the Wailua Beach home of Phyllis and Albert Horner. As the story unfolds, Howard Keel, as "Haz," thinks Esther Williams, as "Mimi," had invited him to a hang-loose Tahitian *tamaraa*. He arrives barefoot, wearing a baggy shirt and *pareu* wrap-around.

In this photo, "Mimi" tries to coax an embarrassed "Haz" to stay for the formal lawn party. In the background are Gramma and Grampa along with Karen Everest (center) snickering at the sight of "Haz's" inappropriate outfit. The face seen at the upper right is that of hungry *Garden Island* reporter, Barlow Hardy, staring for about eight hours at a large platter of tempting fried chicken that only a swarm of pesky flies was allowed to touch.

Before "Mimi" notices that "Haz" has joined the elegant gathering, he is coerced into meeting many of the Kauai folks who are acting as "Mimi's" Tahiti dinner guests. Standing at the left rear is Gladys Brandt, Kapaa High School principal, carrying on a conversation with an Oahu gentleman extra. Beside them is a group of Kauai musicians softly playing island melodies.

At the left table Albert Horner, Hawaiian Canneries manager, extends his hand to greet "Haz" who is being introduced by Hollywood supporting actress Minna Gombell, in the role of "Mimi's" aunt "Kate." Seated with Horner are Al Giles from the Kauai Fruit Packers pineapple cannery in Kapahi and Virginia Brandt, an employee of the Bank of Hawaii branch in Lihue.

At the lower right table, Gramma, Grampa and Karen Everest make small talk with Lee Abrams, wife of auto sales manager Louie Abrams. While the three of us, sitting, are earning our daily ten dollars for saying nothing important, Lee is being paid thirty-five dollars for a legitimate speaking part. When "Haz" is brought to our table, Lee gives him an "I'd like to see you later" look, flutters her eyelashes and sensually whispers, "Why, hello." That was it. Seventeen dollars and fifty cents per word.

place and tested, and all the other time-consuming fine-tuning that had to be done before the real actors began performing. For the 6′ 4″ inch Howard Keel, director Robert Alton chose Charlie Schimmelfennig. Given the coveted role as stand-in for Esther Williams was Jessie Rapozo. Petite Anna Maglinte was perfect for Rita Moreno and Eddie Kaleohi was a close match for Charles Mauu.

Charlie Schimmelfennig is no longer with us but Jessie is on the staff of an optometrist in Lihue, Eddie works at the airport, and Anna lives up in Kapahi with her husband, Alex, who was the popular bartender at Coco Palms for decades.

The casting director, with his sharp eye for what people really should look like, chose *kamaaina* Eric Knudsen to appear as the interisland freighter captain and then decided real-life Admiral Keleher didn't look any higher in rank than second mate and navigator.

As the ship entered the harbor, my part was to look like a returning resident standing at the rail along-side Howard Keel, pointing to interesting landmarks of his future island home. But the best part was yet to come. Hurrying down the gangway, I was greeted by my movie "wife" (a nurse from Wilcox Hospital) who jumped up, threw her arms around my neck and smoth-ered me with kisses. For this they paid me ten dollars? Behind us in the harbor were my buddies earning their ten dollars struggling in their canoes and tiny sailboats trying not to get smashed by the ocean-going hippohulk freighter.

Here's how that gangway moment was described by *The Garden Island* newspaper columnist Matsuo "Sidelines" Kuraoka: "TAKE A BOW, GANG! Ahukini, the little town that Captain Jack W. Bertrand looks after with paternal interest, suddenly came to life. The whole MGM crew plus some 400 extras went there to film the arrival of the Matson freighter Hawaiian Forester on Thursday.

"First man off the ship was Mike Ashman, who was greeted with a kiss by his 'wife'—played by pretty

Florence Pirnie. They shot this scene over about a dozen times before it took . . . and both hams certainly did retakes with gusto!

"Didn't know why Mike Ashman should get all the breaks. Sidelines would have been just as good in that role. I made a kick to Bob Alton, the director, and Al Jennings, his assistant. They assured me that they were saving me for greater things. 'Give us a little time' they said, 'and we will have you with Rudy Valentino.' That satisfied me as I could always see myself as the great lover. However when I got home the little woman, who is a suspicious soul, informed me that Valentino is dead. Now I am just wondering . . .

"Other 'tourists' in the movie were Diohne, Margy and Gail Teall, Eric and Hazel Knudsen, Henry Wedemeyer Jr., Darrow Watt, Fred Brandt, Kenny Baker, Duke Cunningham, Bob Morton, Sam Wilcox, Dick Sloggett, Dwight Mossman, Paul Story, Rhea Ehlers, and Bruce Wichman.

"Quitting time found all of the extras in line to receive pay for the day's work. Saw Mary K. Au, Georgiana Haumea and Alfred K. Au, all of Hanalei. One of the youngest in the cast was Frances Kaawai, 5, of Anahola.

"Other Hanalei-Haena actors and actresses were: Francis Chandler, Agnes Ching, Spencer K. Peters, Elizabeth J. Jones, Rachel Mahuiki, Myra Maka, Nancy Puulei, Jeremiah Kaialoa, Rosalina Chandler, Hilda Maka, Annie Tai Hook, Sarah K. Rubin, Louisa Haleakala, Jane Kerr and Mary Kauo.

"Among those who rode to sea in the outriggers were: Stanley Kaluahine, Abraham Kawaihalau, Joe and Eugene Kahaunaele, Norton Malina, Joseph Goo, Joseph, John, William and Abraham Kaauwai and Walter Kahai.

"Walter and Abel Wood, Neil Schimmelfennig, Hiram Kaleohi, Alapai Kolo, Raymond Kauai, Harold Telles, Ernest Lovell, Leslie Nunes, James Panui and Sam Pa. Sam Kai helped me pick out names.

"Mermaids out to meet the freighter were:

Garden Islanders Perform with the Best of Them

Seeking to buy household items for "Haz's" new House of Singing Bamboo, "Haz," along with his new housekeepers "Terru," and "Tavae," bargain with the shrewd Wong Fo who really is G.M. Shak, bookkeeper at Hawaiian Canneries. Standing behind the counter in the background is Wong Fo's handyman who in

real life is George Kondo, the proprietor of George's Sodaworks just down the street where Kauai's fizzing creme soda was bottled for all the island's *luau*. (Above) Hazel Knudsen enters the shop pretending to be a tourist looking for souvenirs while local extras keep the background in motion.

During a break in filming, G.M. Shak (left) and George Kondo talk story with nineteen-year-old Hollywood starlet Rita Moreno appearing in the role of "Haz's" lively housekeeper "Terru."

Mervlyn Kahaunaele, Annette Holt, Pauline Kaneakua, Anne Maglinti, Edna Hurley, Lily Bender, Peggy Becklund, Harriet Montgomery and Maureen West."

("Sidelines" never overcame his mock envy. As long as I lived on Kauai, he never did stop complaining about his missed chance at romantic stardom.)

Meanwhile in Kapaa town, a small store down the street from the Hee Fat building was turned into a Chinese merchant's shop with G.M. Shak (Hawaiian Canneries bookkeeper) as the inscrutable shopkeeper and George Kondo (proprietor of nearby George's Soda Works) as obedient clerk. As cameras are rolling, "Terru" (Rita Moreno) and "Tavae" (Charles Mauu) go through a dozen retakes of a bargaining session for "Haz" who is standing by ready to buy items for his new home. Hazel Knudsen, portraying a lady tourist, is seen browsing through the shop.

Here my role is to stand in the doorway, dressed in a French policeman's uniform, pretending to be keeping peace in the village. A background of wandering Polynesians and others dressed in *muumuu* and aloha shirts walk back and forth along the street during retake after retake. Among them are Cy Maier (Lihue Theater manager) in the costume of a French soldier, Roy Becklund (Lihue Store assistant manager), as a maritime officer, and *kamaaina* Eric Knudsen, dressed as a tourist, also strolling through town.

In one of the early major scenes, "Haz" shows up at a *haole* garden party thinking he's been invited to a local folk's *tamaraa*. Wearing a brightly-colored Tahitian *pareu* wrap-around instead of trousers, and with great embarrassment, he's forced to meet the high-fashion guests. All the party-goers are standing around making cocktail conversation or sitting at small tables set up on the lawn of the imposing Wailua Beach home of Hawaiian Canneries manager Albert Horner and wife, Phyllis.

Barlow Hardy, a heavyweight *Garden Island* newspaper reporter known for having a voracious appetite was given a role standing alongside the long buffet table loaded with tantalizing, mouth-watering party food. In his newspaper account of the filming he wrote: "Moviemaking lost all its glamour for some 20 or 30 island residents who were cocktail party guests Sunday at the Albert Horner home for MGM's *Pagan Love Song*. The 'party' was located behind a bamboo fence on the edge of the lawn overlooking the ocean.

"Working for pay enjoying yourself at a party sounds like an ideal occupation but try it sometime. The table was loaded with baked ham, fried chicken, two great big cakes, salad, and other things to eat. 'It's good casting having you in this scene,' Mike Ashman told me, but the 'guests' couldn't touch a thing. There was some nibbling, of course, but it was definitely not the thing to do . . . even the punch—orange—was poured back into its original container when the sampling got a little too enthusiastic.

"Most of the 'guests' sat at little tables while a few stood at the buffet table loading—and unloading—their plates. In the latter category were Budde Crabbe, Lou Eckart, Camille Scura, yours truly, and in some of the takes, Esther Williams.

"Sunday's all-day-long scenes—which will probably flicker across the screen in a couple of minutes—show Howard Keel showing up at Esther's aunt's house clad in a *lava-lava*—or something like that—and no shoes, not realizing there's a party on, being hauled by auntie, with him telling Esther 'You've had your little joke, I'll be on my way!' stalking off with Esther chasing him. Then the two of them making up—or something— outside the garden where the party takes place.

"At the party all the 'guests' are having the time of their lives with Director Alton telling them 'Now act hilarious! You're having a wonderful time! Lots of talk and laughter!' Then lots of talk and laughter ensued, although there was some comment to the effect that it would have been little more realistic if there had been some refreshments forthcoming.

"The next shot showed auntie introducing Howard to various guests sitting at the little tables. This took at least a dozen tries, with the sun getting hotter and hotter and the lights adding to the temperature and the guests keeping up the gaiety.

"A halt to the moviemaking was finally called somewhere around 5:30. Things had started off fairly soon after 8:00 . . . '8:00 to 5:30,' someone commented, 'that's the longest party I was ever at!' 'Never,' said somebody else, 'have I stood in line so long for so little!'

"Somewhere along in the taking—and retaking—was an hour's break for lunch: creamed chicken salad, vegetable, cake, bread and butter, and beverage . . . all on MGM . . . and, of course, the long breaks in between shots while the boys were getting the camera and lights set up again. But the newcomer's interest in the technicalities of moviemaking seemed to wear off as the day wore on."

Looking back now from the year 2000, filming in 1950 was relatively simple. Today with all of filmmaking's special effects we see that Hollywood's early trickery was very elementary—no computerized backdrops or animation, only homemade imagery. The scenic viewpoint you see today above Lumahai Beach was just a barren road shoulder until a movie crew brought in a truckload of *hala* and *ohia* trees along with a variety of bushes and vines, turning the spot into a romantic bower of tropical greenery. The movie's moonlight scenes were shot during bright daylight with blue filters over the lights and camera lenses.

When the movie ultimately was shown on Kauai, howls of laughter erupt in Lihue Theater as scenes beginning in one part of Kauai suddenly shift to another part of the island. "Haz," riding a bicycle, is shown crooning "I'm a happy troubadour just singing in the sun." Starting out at northshore Haena, he falls into the pond at faraway Kalapaki Beach just as the chorus ends.

In another scene, "Mimi" drives her convertible along a road that takes viewers from a Kealia canefield road to the Waipouli coconut groves, about five miles away, in just a few seconds. When "Haz's" pig runs out of his house at Coco Palms on Kauai's east shore, he's seen racing out of his home, down the steps and chasing the porker along Haena's Tunnels beach on the north shore. Again the crowd roars.

The scene in which "Mimi" and "Haz" fall in love is taken on the beach at Lydgate Park in Wailua as they gaze enraptured northward at the Spouting Horn which is twenty miles south of them in Kukuiula.

At the time moviegoers hear Larry Ramos singing "House of Singing Bamboo," they don't realize the audio track of him with his ukulele was recorded in the living room of my family's rented plantation house. Producer Arthur Freed seemed to think the acoustics of this old Lihue Plantation supervisor's residence (on the site of the present Chevron gas station across from the Museum) must have sounded like the interior of a bamboo house.

So, one afternoon a sound truck backs up to our front door, sound equipment is brought in and set up, and young Larry sits on our kitchen stool singing, "Got a place in the sun, a particular one, on a tropical avenue. Far away from it all that I happily call the house of singing bamboo."

During the course of seven weeks of filming, interviews with three of the stars were tape recorded and later broadcast over KTOH and the other three stations of the Territory's Aloha Network. While Charles Mauu declined to record a conversation about his pathway from Tahiti to Hollywood, the others told extremely interesting stories of their travels along the entangled and wearisome uphill climb to stardom.

Interviewed in his ordinary single room at the Kauai Inn one Sunday morning, Howard Keel told me that after his coal miner father died, his mother packed their few belongings into the family's old car and headed for the West Coast. She had found life difficult in the small mining town where her meager income came from cooking and cleaning house for the community's affluent residents. Howard, whose real name was Harold Leek, had just entered high school and he remembered being an unpopular, skinny kid who was so shy his life was miserable.

Their 1934 journey westward ended when their

Kapaa Becomes Tahiti for Hollywood's "Pagan Love Song"

A small store along the County Road in Kapaa is decorated to become the general mercantile shop of Chinese merchant Wong Fo. Curious Kapaa onlookers stand around all day fascinated by the filming. There's no interference from

passing cars because in those days there were only about six thousand registered vehicles on the entire island and hardly anyone ever drove through Kapaa town.

To create an authentic island atmosphere in some of the shots, dozens of local extras continuously walked back and forth in front of Wong Fo's shop. Among them were Grampa as a French policeman

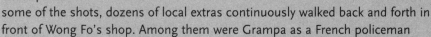

shown here flanked by Lihue Theater manager Cy Maier, dressed in a French military uniform, and Eric Knudsen, *kamaaina* businessman and teller of legends, who was supposed to be a French businessman, or an American tourist, or a local doctor, or whatever the moviegoer imagines he is supposed to be.

jalopy broke down in Southern California's Palomar Hills and without money for car repairs the two settled in. Here he began to blossom, playing on the high-school baseball, basketball and football teams, and taking part in student body shows. His goal was to become a doctor.

Eventually he and his mother moved in with an uncle in Los Angeles where his mother found employment as a live-in servant. Young Harold moved from job to job as parking lot attendant, dishwasher in a boarding house and whatever else he could find in an economy recovering from the Great Depression.

This was during the age when live amateur shows were popular attractions in neighborhood theaters. Making the rounds of movie houses he'd sing one of the day's top tunes and occasionally was able to pick up cash as a winning contestant. This led to his being hired as a singing waiter and the beginning of his extraordinary musical career.

His first full-time business position came just before the start of World War Two as a clerk with Douglas Aircraft. At the same time he continued taking voice lessons and appearing as a casual artist performing for anyone who wanted to hire a singer. Recognizing his talent, the aircraft manufacturer assigned him to travel around the country to raise the patriotic spirit of the company's workers and customers. After a while Douglas Aircraft offered him a responsible, steady position as a production supervisor in a Midwest factory. Following much thought about the insecure and unpredictable nature of show business he chose to turn down the aircraft company's offer.

Instead, he auditioned at playhouses. He toured college campuses. He sang at luncheons for women's groups. To improve his bookings, he reversed the spelling of his last name, changing it from Leek to Keel. In Chicago he won second prize at the city's annual music festival. He continued to hustle singing opportunities wherever they appeared.

Recalling the struggle to survive, he told the radio audience the big break came when he received a message that famed producer of Broadway musicals, Oscar Hammerstein, wanted to hear him sing. Soon he replaced John Rait in the lead of the Broadway show *Carousel.*

Appearing in London he received congratulations from the Queen for his stage performance in *Oklahoma.* A master of ceremonies unintentionally introduced him as "Howard" instead of "Harold." It sounded nice and Howard became his new name.

Returning home after a successful eighteen months in England, the new Howard Keel was given star billing in the movie *Annie Get Your Gun.* The film's producer, Arthur Freed, immediately offered a contract for Freed's next production, *Pagan Love Song,* bringing Howard to the Garden Island and this room at the Kauai Inn where he contemplated his future: "The public is fickle," he observed that day. "I wish I knew how they'll treat me."

During the following fifty years he has continued to be one of the public's favorite musical stars and dramatic actors. A string of successful movies, frequent stage appearances, recording contracts, and ten years as a headliner in the TV series *Dallas* is the answer to his early speculation over his uncertain future.

(Staying at the Kauai Inn room next to Howard Keel were Honolulu newlyweds Lois and Dudley Dambacher. Not knowing who was their neighbor, they recalled later that they complained to each other about "the guy next door who got up every morning before sunrise and stood in the shower for hours and hours singing as loud as he could. It wasn't exactly what we had hoped for on our honeymoon.")

Esther Williams was interviewed on a Sunday morning in her rented home at the far end of the Kauai Inn's spacious lawn. Today the Lihue Court Townhomes development has replaced the lawn and the few single-family houses that were there in 1950. Because her husband Ben Gage, a prominent radio network announcer, and their toddler son, Benjamin, had accompanied her to Kauai, a house was considered more appropriate than a hotel room. Besides she already was one of the top box office attractions worldwide. The other Hollywood members of the cast, still waiting to be recognized as special people, were given rooms at the Kauai Inn.

Esther Williams' rise to stardom came quickly. But it had a heartbreaking beginning in the rubble of an athlete's biggest dream completely crushed.

The Hollywood celebrity told the radio audience that swimming always was part of her life. As a youngster she spent her spare time at beaches and public swimming pools around Los Angeles. By the time she was sixteen she had won three national swimming championships. In 1940 she achieved the ultimate honor of being chosen to represent America in the Tokyo 1940 Olympics—games that were cancelled because of the war in Europe. Her long-held dream of representing the United States on the winners' podium suddenly became a dismal nightmare.

However, it wasn't long before legendary showman Billy Rose, seeing photographs of Esther in newspapers and magazines, invited her to audition with about a hundred other beauties for a role in a lavish water-oriented musical production going on tour around the United States. Famed swimmer Johnny Weismuller, an Olympic champ and movie star, chose Esther to be featured as the show's leading "Aquabelle."

This was the beginning of her successful performing career. MGM executives reviewing the Aquacade offered her a screen test in which she did a scene with Clark Gable. A contract was offered and she made her film debut with Mickey Rooney in an Andy Hardy film.

On the Sunday morning of the interview on Kauai she laughed as she revealed that whenever MGM wanted to test a prospective female leading lady they'd place her in an Andy Hardy movie. Before her had been hopefuls such as Judy Garland and Lana Turner. "If you didn't make it, that was both the beginning and end of your movie career," she said.

The film with Mickey Rooney was a smash hit. With World War Two underway, she became a pinup favorite—her bathing beauty photos ardently carried by GIs overseas to all war theaters.

Midway through the war she was paired with Red Skelton in a comedy to be called *Mr. Coed*. The screenplay was written as a funny film about a songwriter who enrolls in a girls school to be near the swimming teacher with whom he had fallen in love. Because this was Hollywood's first swimming movie, the cast and production crew began making up all kinds of elaborate water scenes on the spot. When the film finally was released Esther Williams had taken over top billing and the movie title was changed to *Bathing Beauty*. For that year, 1944, the film was runner-up to *Gone With the Wind* in box office receipts.

By the time she arrived on Kauai in 1950, she had completed eight major films with leading men such as Spencer Tracy, Van Johnson, Peter Lawford, Frank Sinatra, Gene Kelly and others.

"The folks on Kauai," she said, "should be so grateful that God placed them on this beautiful, peaceful island."

Although Esther appeared at the Kauai Yacht Club several times for dinner, she didn't make the rounds of the many parties as Howard Keel did. For one thing she had a family life at home. Another reason, not disclosed until after filming was completed, was that she was pregnant with her second child. Care had to be exercised. She did appear, though, at the Annual County Fair where she presented a new Pontiac to the Fair's grand prize ticketholder.

During the next ten years she starred in more than a dozen motion pictures. An active businesswoman for more than thirty years, she's associated with construction of swimming pools bearing her name and the Esther Williams Collection of swimwear. Fifty years have gone by. Her name still is recognized around the world.

For Rita Moreno, interviewed during a break on the set at Coco Palms, being a dancer was her only ambition as a child. Born in Puerto Rico, little Rosa Alverio came with her mother to New York City where her mother began working in a clothing factory to earn

Hollywood Loves Kauai and Vice Versa

It seemed that just about everybody on the island must have appeared in *Pagan Love Song*. Scene after scene included mostly Kauai faces and voices. In one setting alone there were from four hundred to six hundred local people appearing as extras. On the day that beautiful Hollywood leading lady Esther Williams and her husband, network radio announcer Ben Gage, with son Benjie, were greeted at Lihue Airport, hundreds and hundreds of Garden Islanders gathered to see the arrival of the famous couple. For many Kauaians this also was their first look at the island's new interisland airport.

Albert Horner, seen here on the lawn of his home where several scenes were filmed, is regaling members of the movie production staff with his fascinating memoirs. One eye-catching room of the Horner home contained a full-size pipe organ where the pineapple executive noodled away in his spare time. The crew also took delight in walking through his house to examine trophies of his occasional African safaris—many wild animal heads gracing the walls along with skins of jungle beasts covering the floor. The standout trophy was the preserved hollow elephant leg by the front door where umbrellas were stashed for use on rainy days.

Charles Mauu was just nineteen years old in his homeland of Tahiti when he appeared in his first movie, *The Coral Island*. The talented Polynesian singer

with his famous coconut ukulele eventually reached the nightspots of Southern California and was cast as "Tavae" in his first Hollywood film, *Pagan Love Song*. The next year he was an Indonesian warrior in the Bing Crosby-Bob Hope-Dorothy Lamour comedy, *Road to Bali*. The tall, dark and handsome islander not only continued being cast as a Polynesian but also as an American Indian, Asian and Latino as well as an African native in Tarzan movies. Quiet and soft-spoken, he often said that if he could make a living on Kauai he would stay on the Garden Island forever.

enough money to bring the rest of the family to the States.

She said she could remember as a child growing up in a tenement neighborhood. She was very shy, couldn't speak English, and didn't do well in school. In order to gain acceptance by her classmates, she always was volunteering to do the Mexican Hat Dance for every school occasion. At age seven she began taking dancing lessons and by age thirteen was appearing with her stepfather in a nightclub act.

Taking her stepfather's name, Moreno, she went out on her own—being billed as "The Mexican Spitfire," "Rosita the Cheetah" and similar catchy stage names. Eventually, a Hollywood talent scout brought her to MGM where she was given a standard juvenile contract of seven years and her name changed to "Rita."

She was still a teenager when she arrived on Kauai and already was worried that she'd be typecast into the pool of bit players who always found themselves filling Hollywood's need for Indians, Asians, Latinos and other minorities.

This didn't happen. At the present time she's the only female performer to win all four of the most prestigious show business awards: the "Tony" for Broadway stage, an "Emmy" for television, the "Alma" for outstanding actress in a dramatic series, and the ultimate tribute—an "Oscar" for best supporting actress as Anita in the movie *West Side Story*. Not a year has gone by without her name being billed somewhere as a star attraction.

The most exciting moment during the filming on Kauai was not caught on film. It happened one day at a Haena beach in a scene where "Mimi" is paddling an outrigger canoe away from shore after returning a pig to "Haz" who's sitting on the sand.

The scene ends and cameras are cut as "Mimi" is seen paddling out to sea. An unusually large swell rolls in, capsizing the canoe.

Spectators on the shore anxiously look for "Mimi" to surface. It seems like an eternity before local swimmers finally dive into the surf to begin searching underwater for her body. It's feared the outrigger arm has struck her head, knocking her unconscious.

In the meantime the swimming star, worrying that she'll be hit by the tumbling canoe, dives to the bottom and skims along the undersurface a good distance down the beach where she surfaces unnoticed. While the distressed crew and cast are nervously watching the rescuers, she walks up behind the group asking, "What's all the fuss about?"

The visibly relieved director, Robert Alton, tells her if she'll do it again they'll rewrite the script so "Haz" can save her life and they'll live happily ever after. The pregnant movie star's quick answer is, "No way!"

11

When "Haole" Was Just Half of a Word

There was a time when the word *"haole"* was just an ordinary Hawaiian noun or adjective describing what a person looked like. If you had round eyes and pink skin you were called a *haole*. That word, alone, meant nothing more than "paleface" or "Caucasian." If you had narrow eyes and darker skin, you probably were called Japanese, Chinese or Korean, even if you were born in Hawaii. A darker, browner skin usually meant you'd be termed Filipino. If you had brownish skin and always had a happy face you, no doubt, were Hawaiian.

There really was no difference when you looked at the faces of a Portuguese and a so-called *"haole."* The only way you could tell they were supposed to be unlike would be to look at a census or other government form which required Portuguese to skip the box marked "Caucasian" and check the box titled "Portuguese." Can you believe that?

In everyday conversations and in newspaper reports it was acceptable to refer to yourself or to others by what a person's face looked like. There was no disrespect associated with being described by your parent's nationality. It was just another word such as tall, short, fat, skinny, ugly, beautiful.

In San Francisco, where I grew up, I was a German kid who played with Jewish kids, Polish kids, Irish kids and others. When I started kindergarten, German was my first language with a smattering of

Russian. Many of my classmates also spoke only their parents' native language or limited English with their parents' foreign accents: Yiddish, Polish, Italian, Swedish, Chinese, Norwegian and more . . . even Irish and Scottish brogues were difficult to understand among children associating with others for the first time.

Way back in the early 1900s, when so many adults on the mainland were immigrants, their offspring commonly were identified with the parent's nationality. So, it was easy for me, as a newcomer to Kauai, to accept the same pattern that existed here. Not only did some locally born young people speak with Japanese, Filipino and Chinese accents, there were many adult *haole luna* and businessmen, born and raised on Kauai, whom you'd swear had just arrived from Germany, Portugal or Scotland.

In most cases today, referring to a person by his ancestry is considered not very nice. That's especially true of the word *"haole."* The friendliness and innocence of this term now is tarnished. If you're called a *haole* today, you're probably sensitive about it. You're wondering, "Is that good or is it bad?"

You didn't have to wonder about it sixty years ago. *"Haole,"* at that time, was really only half a word. Every *haole* was known as a specific kind like a rich *haole,* fat *haole,* cute *haole,* and so on.

At the top of the ranking were "nice *haole*s" like Elsie and Mabel Wilcox who were devoted in their service to people. Alice Alexander, wife of the Grove Farm Plantation manager, would be called a "nice *haole*" because she cared about laborers' families, showed concern and offered help when needed.

Then there were "good *haole*s." This would be somebody like your supervisor who was fair, considerate and respectful to you. He sensed when you weren't feeling well and was tolerant. He gave explanations when you didn't understand something and didn't try to make you feel stupid as some others did.

There were "okay *haole*s" whose lives were rooted on Supervisors Hill but who joined workers in fishing contests, played inter-department baseball, or just drank beer with the gang once in a while on paydays. If he brought the beer, he'd be an "*ichiban* (number one) *haole*."

Then there were "local *haole*s." These were *kamaaina* who could tell the differences between the faces of Japanese, Chinese and Koreans.

The occasional mainland visitor to Kauai who described what a lovely picnic she had at "Key" (Kee) beach over at "Hyena" (Haena) would be a "coast *haole*." (Anyplace in North America was known as "The Coast.")

The resident *haole* who comes into a store and expects to be waited on before everyone else would cause mutterings of "that damn *haole*."

If you couldn't tell the differences in the faces of Japanese, Chinese and Koreans, you'd be labeled a "dumb *haole*."

The ones who attend their first *luau* and throw up on the table when they see a live *opihi* crawling around on their paper plates, would be described as "stupid *haole*s."

If you were a local guy who took a girl to a Saturday night dance at the plantation gym and some *haole* guy asks her to dance, he'd be a *"pilau haole."*

If she says, "Yes," he becomes a "stink *haole*."

Then at the end of the evening as the band plays a slow, romantic last dance—where the couples are snuggling—and he's dancing with the girl you brought, he has earned the title "*pilau* stink *haole*."

That was about as low as you could get.

12

Mike Fern and
The Tryst at Hee Fat's

I've never met anyone who didn't like Mike Fern. Mike was a pleasant fellow, extremely forthright, never became angry, was friendly in a reserved manner, was interested in everyone (and everything), and had many other virtues.

He also was a genius, had an instant recall photographic memory, wore very thick glasses, and was very shy in most social situations. He didn't start many conversations but if the subject was something in which he had an interest, he'd join freely in the discussion.

Sometimes he'd communicate with just a grunt to indicate "yes" or "okay" or "hello" or "see you later." That also was his normal response when someone told an off-color story and everyone else was laughing. The grunt attested to the fact he had been listening and thought the joke was a waste of precious conversation.

The son of Charlie and MaryL Fern, he was christened Charles James Fern, Junior, when he was born in 1926 but nicknamed "Mike" to avoid confusion with his well-known father. Just as everyone called his dad "CharlieFern" (as if it were one name), folks all referred to the son not as "Mike" but as "MikeFern."

At the time he was a toddler, there was no question he was someone special. Mrs. Fern told me his first words were spoken in sentences. If she read him a children's story once and didn't repeat it exactly the same the next time, he'd correct her.

He had the same problem in school when he'd

Likeable Mike Fern possessed a limitless gigabyte hard drive somewhere in his head. Everything he ever perceived was permanently archived for downloading as needed.

innocently and eagerly correct his teachers. I spoke with some of his former elementary school instructors after I moved to Kauai in 1940. They told me, "We loved Mike Fern but he was exasperating. He knew everything about the subject being taught. He always was correcting us and he was always right." One teacher said that while she was helping the other students learn to read primary grade stories about "Dick and Jane," little Mike was hunched over at his tiny desk reading *Time Magazine.*

Everything he saw, heard, felt, smelled or tasted was entered into his mega-gigabyte memory. In addition to fervidly reading (memorizing) books and magazines that everyone else enjoyed, he loved registering into his mind the data from State, County and private business reports.

"Hib" Case, chief financial officer of Grove Farm and corporate secretary of *The Garden Island* Board of Directors, told me a tale of Mike's fabulous memory. He said that one evening he and Charlie Fern were sitting out on the Fern's lanai, just chatting. The Cases lived down the road from the Fern's home. That night they were talking about automobiles.

Mike, not yet a teenager, was sitting over in a corner shuffling through the pages of a book, subconsciously memorizing its contents. At one point in the conversation "Hib" said to Charlie, "The so-and-so automobile was the first American car made for sale to the public."

Mike lifted his head and said, "I'm sorry, Mr. Case, it was the so-and-so." And he mentioned a different carmaker.

"Hib" replied, "I'm sorry, Mike. You're usually right but this time I know I'm correct."

Mike answered, "If you'll go over to that stack of magazines and look at page 48 of the February 21st *Saturday Evening Post,* in a middle paragraph of the first column there's the name of the first American car manufactured for sale to the public."

"Hib" said Mike's data transfer was accurate with the exact magazine, date, page, column and paragraph.

"Hobey" Goodale, retired Kauai rancher and auto dealer, has his own favorite anecdote. In a small gathering along with Mike Fern and Bob Englehardt, "Hobey" asked Mike if he remembered the license plate of Bob's father's truck of an earlier year, some five years back. Mike rattled off some letters and numbers. "Hobey" and Bob drove down to the Ahukini warehouse where Bob's father was manager of Ahukini Railway. Here the wall was plastered with Bob's dad's old license plates. They found exactly what Mike Fern had extracted from his incredible zipdrive.

Want another example? Takeshi Gokan was *The Garden Island*'s bookkeeper. All day long his nimble fingers hopped around over the keys of a comptometer as he worked with numbers. Mike did his calculations in his head.

One afternoon when the boss wasn't around we set up a contest to see who was the fastest. Takeshi and Mike were given a lengthy column with identical sets of numbers—three digits per number. They started together and finished about the same time. Both sums were the same.

I asked Mike how he did it. He said it was simple. You round off the top number and remember how much you rounded off. You add the rounded figure to the next number and add or subtract the amount rounded off. And you just keep going like that down the column. He said "simple." Yeah, right! Very simple.

There's one thing he did that must have been a habit because many Garden Islanders have reminded me about it. This was when Mike would drive to the Post Office after lunch to pick up the company's mail. Engrossed in sorting through the envelopes, he'd walk to the newspaper office and someone else would have to be sent to pick up the car.

He was the newspaper's and radio station's walking research library. One day I was doing a story on Kekaha Sugar Plantation. I called Mike and asked him if he knew Kekaha's sugar production for a previous year. He answered, "For which field?"

When I returned to work at KTOH after World

War Two, my family lived in a house just behind the publishing company. Many times we'd be surprised by seeing Mike Fern sitting in our living room reading one of our magazines or books. We hadn't heard a knock on the door or an "Anybody home?" This was his version of paying a friendly visit.

At one time my wife was noticeably pregnant and Mike was carrying around a copy of L. Ron Hubbard's book *Dianetics*. He appeared in our home, relaxed in a chair reading his book, and when my wife greeted him he grunted, tucked the book under his arm, knelt in front of my wife and talked into her belly-button as if it were an intercom connected to the unborn baby, saying over and over again, "You will remember this when it is necessary. You will remember this when it is necessary." We've been asking our son about this for half a century, but evidently it hasn't become necessary yet.

It always seemed Mike Fern was completely content with being a loner. He never was seen walking around with his arm around a girl, or a boy either. His closest friends were numbers and the letters of the alphabet.

For his twenty-fifth birthday a group of us fellows decided to take him out to dinner and then see that he had a memorable celebration.

At that time I was playing piano at Ben Ohai's Club Blue Lei in Kapaa on weekends. Across the road, upstairs in the Hee Fat Building, was the reception room and living quarters of a professional woman who provided comfort and therapy for lonely men. For several obvious reasons she was known to us as "Lani Moo." When her business was slow, this young belle sometimes came over to the club for refreshment and maybe to hustle a patient.

We fellows chipped in to compensate the young lady for an evening of physical therapy for Mike. I told him a very nice woman had arrived on Kauai and was living in Kapaa. She was complaining she hadn't yet met anyone who could carry on an intelligent conversation and that she had invited him to stop by some evening for

If you delete all of today's images of cars, the hanging advertising and the dotted white line, you'll see Kapaa's Hee Fat Building as it appeared a half-century ago. You'd also see a lot of giant potholes on what was then called the Belt Road.

a cup of coffee or tea. He grunted, which meant he agreed to a visit with her.

After our dinner at the Coco Palms Lodge, he followed me in his car to Kapaa. I took him to Hee Fat's and introduced the two of them to each other.

The next weekend "Lani Moo" came over to Club Blue Lei and gave the money back, saying she never had so much fun in her life. I didn't ask and she didn't say what happened that night. Today, I wish I'd been a little more inquisitive. It's assumed he felt he was with her to enjoy her conversation and that's exactly what he did.

On the day his father stepped aside as editor of the paper in the early '50s, Mike Fern took over the position. He did a credible job until the paper was sold in 1966.

As you might guess, he moved on to working with computers on the mainland. When old-timers ask me, "Whatever happened to MikeFern?" I tell them he's still a genius, still a bachelor, and living contentedly in Southern California. Last year I learned he's writing a book on the subject of how to raise children. I want a copy.

13

Whatever Happened to *Da Kine* Stuffs?

Everyone knows a living language undergoes continuous change. New words are created, trendy expressions come and go, and once-familiar words fall out of usage.

Over the past sixty years, the every-day language of Kauai has undergone a noticeable evolution. It seems the grammar and inflection, and sometimes local pronunciation, have remained about the same. But most of the common pidgin words and expressions of yesterday have been replaced by English dictionary words learned in schoolrooms.

Early in this past century in Hawaii, pidgin English was a necessary creation enabling people of a half-dozen languages to speak with one another. Some words were Japanese, others Ilocano. A few were Korean or Portuguese and many came from Chinese dialects. It was a real chop suey lingo with most of this non-English vocabulary coming from the Hawaiian language.

Once in a while today you'll hear folks saying, *"pau"* or *"mauka."* It seems the Hawaiian word most widely used now is *"mahalo"* which has replaced "trash" on rubbish cans. "Suck 'em up" at one time was *"okole maluna."* "Hang loose" is the current expression for the once common *"hoomanawanui."* *"Pehea oe?"* now comes out *"Howzit?"* *"Komo mai"* is "try come." *"Aole pilikia"* is "no strain." Some of the favorite, almost overworked, expressions today are *"ohana"* for "family" and the terms *"maka ainana"* and *"kanaka maoli"* for "common" or "native" person. Where are phrases like "bull hash" or *"bulaia"* or *"hoomalimali"* which all meant someone had just made an unbelievable statement?

Pidgin was so ingrained in everyone's language that you couldn't adequately express yourself without relying on pidgin words. The loftiest plantation manager and his Vassar-educated wife would carry on conversations with others that today would require translation.

For example, someone today tells you a story about his good friend in Lihue who takes the storyteller's station wagon without permission and goes for a joyride towards the Waimea side of the island. While passing through Puhi he skids on mud that was carried onto the highway by trucks hauling cane to the mill.

The car rolls down an embankment and lands upside-down across an irrigation ditch close to where a crew of poison-spray workers is eating its mid-morning meal. Lunch boxes fly all over the place. A supervisor is nearby and yanks the door open, pulling the driver out of the car. Nobody is injured or killed. The work crew is so shook up it can't work the remainder of the day.

The storyteller says he always considered his friend to be intelligent but now thinks the driver is crazy. He adds that his friend is a loony pumpkin head and should be locked up in the State mental institution in Kaneohe. The car owner explains he's really very angry about this inconvenience and is out of luck because the car is out of commission and the stupid driver is stubborn about paying for damages. "My big-mouth friend," he adds, "claims it's the plantation's responsibility because its truck drivers left the muck on the road."

With a sigh of capitulation, the car owner says he's very tired, wants to lie down on his couch and get some sleep. "Maybe tomorrow I'll feel better about this."

A half-century ago, the same story told by most folks on Kauai, including a college educated *haole*, would have sounded something like the following. It would all be spoken with correct grammar and proper sentence structure, but dotted with pidgin.

"My *aikane* cockaroached my banana wagon and went *holoholo* towards Waimea. When he was near Puhi the car went *pahee* on *lepo* left by canehaul trucks going to the *hale ko*. The car went *huli* down the *pali* and landed *kapakahi* across an *auwai* right where a *sabidong* gang was having small *kaukau*. Their *bentos* and *kaukau* tins went *lele* all around. A *luna* was nearby to *hemo* the door and *huki* the driver out of the car. Nobody was *manu kina* or *make*. The gang was so *weliweli* they couldn't *hanahana* for the rest of the day.

"I always thought this bugger was *akamai* but he's really *pupule*. He's a *bakatare bobura* and should be sent to Room 13 in Kaneohe. I'm really *huhu* over this humbug. And now I'm *poho* because the car is *hana make* and the *lolo* bugger is *paakiki* about paying for it. The *waha* claims it's the plantation's *kuleana* because their drivers left the *mea* on the *ala loa. Auwe!* I'm really *luhi*. I just want to lie down on my *hikiee* and get some *moemoe*. Maybe *mahape* I'll be *pololei* again."

How many young folks growing up in Hawaii today know the meaning of phrases and sentences like these, so common two or three generations ago?

Sure, I'll *kokua*.

The frustrated mother told her *keiki* to *kulikuli* while she wiped his *hanabata* with the hem of her *palekoki*.

I'll give you these *pua, manuahi*.

Don't pass around that *pilau* cheese . . . it's *hauna!*

I *kapu* this seat on the school bus.

I'll meet you *pau hana* by that giant *ulu* in front of the post office. I'll be wearing my *papale niu*.

The *pake wahine* is *hapai* again so her *haole* side-kick has to raise another *hapa keiki*.

I saw that it really was you who made *da kine*, so—Wop your jaw!

If you don't stop being so *niele* somebody goin' broke your head.

She's so *momona* because she's *hoito* around food . . . everything she puts in her *waha* is so *ono* she just has to *hana hou*.

I stay so *huhu* I tell the *luna* "you one *salalabit*" and he stay put my *bango* in his *botoboto* book. Then I go home, drink up until I stay *pio*.

The whole thing was just a *shibai*.

Don't be so *hilahila* . . . go over and *wala au* with him.

One more time you *kolohe* . . . I give you good licking!

Ever since she thinks I gave her *ukus* she keeps giving me *da kine* stink-eye.

That darling *keiki* lying over there on the *punee* has the cutest *piko* in its *opu*.

What he's saying is right on the *kinipopo*.

The girls don't like him because he's not only *manini* he's real *s'kebei*. And his brother is real *ham sup*, too.

When she went to the *benjo* she accidentally walked into the *kane lua*.

That horse was so *makule* that when it lay down last night it went *make*-die-dead.

He won't go *hee nalu* in anything but *palaka* shorts even if there's a *puka* in the *okole*.

A significant change over the years has been the pronunciation of the name of Kauai's beloved last king, Kaumualii. A half century ago everyone was speaking it as *"Ka—umu—ali,"* meaning "the royal oven"—the same pronunciation that appears in Hawaiian dictionaries. Today it comes out as *"Kau—mua—lii,"* meaning "your little something or other." It's probably impossible to change it back to the proper pronunciation.

In recent years, while I was making a living as a tour escort, I often heard the characteristic lilt of voices from Hawaii on all continents.

One day there was a group from Kauai taking pictures of each other on Glacier Point in Yosemite. Another time I ran into a gathering of island golfers overwhelming a hotel in Reno. A busload of island folks hopped out of a tour bus at Churchill Downs for the Kentucky Derby. They were chatting with enchanting island accents. In a castle in Germany, I heard a voice saying, "Try see if there's a *benjo*." A couple stood before me at the desk in Zimbabwe's Victoria Falls Hotel and the wife tells her husband, "They said try wait." Hawaii voices were perceived while journeying through countries all over Asia. Even on the Great Wall of China, twice I took pictures of tourists from Hawaii who wanted to be photographed together.

As soon as any of these globetrotters began speaking, you easily could tell from where they came. Always I greeted these travelers and then asked, "Aren't you from Hawaii?" Very surprised, they'd answer with something like, "Yes. How in the world did you guess?"

14

Plantation Camps and Opting for Segregation

Distinguished son of Kauai, Eric Knudsen.

Being invited to Charlie Fern's home for dinner in the early Forties was a very special treat. For me, it was like attending an exclusive small banquet featuring a brilliant after-dinner speaker.

Charlie Fern and his wife, MaryL, often hosted well-known local and off-island guests. Visiting dignitaries, whether from the mainland or other Hawaiian Islands, or just from the other side of Kauai, frequently stayed overnight with the Ferns rather than taking a room at the decent but plain Lihue Hotel. Being included for dinner always was a rewarding educational experience.

On one evening the houseguest was a son of Kauai, Eric Knudsen, who was spending the night at the Fern's following a late-afternoon meeting of stockholders of the Garden Island Publishing Company. After dinner it was the custom for the men to unwind and talk story in the coolness of the screened-in lanai of the Fern's home.

Their plantation-style house was on the old road to the high school, just down from the Grove Farm homestead museum, close to where the road curves up to Kauai High. In a way, being out on this veranda was like relaxing in a perfumery with fragrances of gardenias, stephanotis, tuberose, ginger, *honohono* orchids, and more. All year 'round evening breezes carried the scent of fragrant blossoms.

It was remarkable how unassuming and friendly

such a notable as Mr. Knudsen could be. Born at Waiawa, West Kauai, in the 1870s, his grandfather had been the last President of Norway when it was under Danish rule, and his mother was the beloved Annie Sinclair of Niihau.

A Harvard Law School graduate, who at one time had practiced in Massachusetts, Eric Knudsen chose life on Kauai as rancher and sugar planter. In the early 1900s he was elected to the Territorial House of Representatives and later served as President of the Senate as well as Kauai County Chairman and member of Kauai's Board of Supervisors.

Now he was here with just Charlie Fern and me, talking about the early days of Kauai. I was interested in why sugar and pineapple plantations segregated workers into ethnic camps. I said it was somewhat like San Francisco where I grew up.

That major mainland city, in the early part of this past century, was dotted with many immigrant groups living in ethnic neighborhoods. Mine was a German cluster within a larger Irish community. Russians lived on nearby Potrero Hill. Jews had a large settlement in the Fillmore district. Italians chose North Beach. The Swedes and Norwegians congregated in the Upper Market Street area. And, of course, there was the famous Chinatown, plus so many more European and Asian boroughs.

In the case of San Francisco, new arrivals were able to choose where they wanted to live. "But here in Hawaii" I asked, "why do you make them stay in isolated camps?"

That was a vexing dilemma the plantations have faced for years, Mr. Knudsen explained. On one hand the Planters wanted to have mixed camps. It would help produce a second generation that would be more American than kids growing up where a single foreign tongue was the primary language. Also, housing employees of different nationalities in the same camp, it was thought, might make it more difficult for laborers to band together in work stoppages. If you can't communicate, how can you join in a revolution?

On the other hand, there were two basic reasons for keeping nationalities separated. One was the employees' own wishes. The other was plantation operations.

Workers preferred living where neighbors spoke the same language, ate the same foods, sang the same songs, joined in the same religious worship services, and in so many other ways carried on treasured traditions of their homeland. Housing them together was con-

During July and August each year, the entire island joined the Japanese community in celebrating *Obon* Festivals when the souls of the dead are believed to return for three days. Each of the island's Buddhist Missions took its turn during the summer *Obon* season in constructing a temporary wooden tower where Taiko drummers played. Bright lanterns were hung everywhere. As special recorded *Obon* music played over a loudspeaker, men and women dressed in yukata kimonos circled the tower dancing *"bonodori."* Non-Buddhists often joined their Japanese neighbors in dancing. The bright lanterns illuminated stalls where Mission members sold a wide variety of Japanese foods and sometimes offered games of skill to raise funds for the Mission.

sidered an important means to enhance lives and reduce demoralizing feelings such as homesickness and loss of identity.

Secondly, most plantations organized their field gangs by nationality to make it easier for workers to understand instructions. A kindred group also provided a sense of comradeship and team effort.

Because of limited transportation, homes for these closely-knit field gangs often were located as closely as possible to the area in which they worked. This created tiny scattered villages with addresses like Chinese Camp, Japanese Camp, Filipino Camp, Mixed Camp, Puerto Rican Camp, Korean Camp, etc.

The advent of World War Two along with the organization of workers into a labor union brought an end to nearly all company-owned housing. Plantations began allowing employees to buy the houses in which they were living or giving them the opportunity to build their own new homes on tracts of company land being set aside for larger communities.

One of the early major housing developments was created when Lihue Plantation expanded the small camp across from Lihue Theater into a large new subdivision. That piece of land on the *mauka* side of what is now called Kuhio Highway, between Wilcox Hospital and Lihue's main intersection, once was the border of a mixed camp and its adjoining canefields.

Today it's a long wall of business buildings behind which are countless single-family homes. In early 1941, Lihue Plantation offered houselots 50 feet wide and 150 feet deep at seven cents per square foot—a total of $525 for a houselot of 7,500 square feet. Other housing projects followed, notably around Hanapepe, Kalaheo, Eleele and Puhi as well as in the pineapple and ranch-lands in and above Kapaa and Wailua.

The word "camp" still is heard when some old-timers are referring to newer subdivisions, estates, and other residential areas. There's a pleasant, nostalgic feel-ing when I meet old friends and they say they live in "The Kalapaki Villas Camp" or "The new Ka Lepa

Villages Camp they just built by the County Road in Hanamaulu." It always has meant an area where someone's home was located.

Today when talking with old-timers who grew up in Kauai's camps I've sometimes asked what is the first thing they think of when I say "plantation camp." The answers seem to overlook hardships and usually bring recollections of pleasant times.

Some of the immediate responses have been—

A retired electrician said, "I remember in Filipino camp we had string orchestra with about twenty guys playing all different kind sizes *bandorya* and guitars and string bass. Every Sunday they practice on one low platform where they get programs and meetings. I sit down on the ground with other kids and we talk about which instrument we are going to play when we grow up. I like the *bandorya* because they play it fastest. Sometimes on Saturday nights they put on program playing marches, some popular songs and songs from the Philippines. Everybody in camp is there and old people they sometimes laugh or cry when they hear songs from the P.I. After the war I stay on the mainland for a while and then come back. The camp is gone and I never get to play anything like I wanted."

A great-grandmother remembered, "When I was little I hate firecrackers in Chinese Camp. Every time somebody celebrate something they burn firecrackers. Maybe it was New Year's or somebody who's old had birthday or somebody had something good happen and they want to celebrate. I hate it maybe because my ears was smaller than now and I couldn't stand it so good. I used to hide and stick my fingers inside. But today I never mind when kids burn firecrackers. I like watch them get excited when they see fire and hear noise. I buy them firecrackers and stuff like that."

A retired school cafeteria worker said, "It seems funny but the first thing I think of is a pair of black shoes. My mother died after she had four kids. I was oldest. My father never married again. He gave us to other families in Korean Camp to watch daytime. At night I help him with housework. One day when I was in high school some guy asks me to go to a dance at the gym. Nobody in our family had shoes except my father. I did not want to wear man's shoes. There was a lady in camp who had nice shoes and she let me use them. I shove paper inside so my feet never slide around. That was the most excitement in my whole life—dancing in the gym with a big orchestra and first time I ever kiss a boy. I married the guy. If it wasn't for black shoes we never find each other."

A grandmother, former pineapple cannery worker, laughed as she told of some unpleasant moments. "I lived in the Japanese Camp where we had a big iron *furo* for the people to soak in after they washed themselves. Every day in the afternoon somebody built a fire under the *furo* to heat the water. After *pau hana* each family took turns going into the little wash house where we scrubbed ourselves clean. Then we went to the *furo* where we took turns soaking. When I was a young teenager, I didn't want to go in the *furo* because it had all kinds of stuff floating on top of the water. I always thought it came from the men and that I might get pregnant. My mother made me go inside. I was the fastest getting in and out of the *furo*. I always kept my knees pushed together tight."

A retired truck driver recalled the days he grew up in a mixed camp with many Portuguese families. "What I remember best is shindigs we get in camp. Somebody would want to celebrate and we get big party. I don't remember who paid for all the *kaukau* but there was *huli-huli* chicken, barbecue beef meat, sausages, and all kinds macaroni salad. Some ladies made *malasadas* and *pao duce*, you know *da kine* sweet bread, and we all get some. Sometimes the old people would sing *fado* from Portugal and they dance *chamaritas*. The best entertainment always was some guys who play guitars and sing cowboy music. They get cowboy handkerchief on their neck and wear cowboy hat. Some even get those thick cowboy pants that movie cowboys wear when they ride horses. I think every Portuguese boy thought he was born cowboy. If he didn't get job as *paniolo* then he would get guitar and sing songs about riding the range. They don't show things like that in TV or movies now. The kids think they are born to be hot-rods and join gangs. In camp it was one big family. We watch out for each other. Not like today. Everybody separate."

15

When "Ring the Operator" Meant "Turn the Crank"

O nce upon a time, in a faraway, strange, hidden land called "The Garden Island," people had telephones that were wooden boxes attached to a wall—

that operated by your turning a crank,
that caused a bell to ring at the local phone
    exchange,
that summoned an operator,
who connected you to another wooden box,
way on the other side of the island,
where people got very excited because they could
    actually hear somebody talking through a skinny
    wire.

All the happy people living on this magic island— well, almost all of them—thought being able to talk into one end of a wire to someone hearing you at the other end was real cool and outrageous!

That's the upside.

Here's the downside. Imagine being awakened every workday morning at five o'clock by four loud rings on the telephone. And the call never is for you. It's even worse if you don't want to wake up till seven.

That kind of suffering was the plight of Kauai folks on a party line that had crank-style instruments. As late as the mid-1950s some areas of the island still were being served by old-fashioned wall telephone boxes. Instead of being able to dial a number, these callers had to spin a crank to alert (wake up?) the operator at the local exchange who then manually completed the connection to another phone somewhere else on the island.

Before WWII, Kauai's Mutual Telephone Company had only two automated exchanges: Lihue and Waimea. In these distinguished districts, callers could dial others directly—but only to those in their own district.

Telephone subscribers in Hanapepe, Koloa, Kapaa, Kilauea and Hanalei districts weren't so lucky. They had to call the operator first.

In those exchanges, if your call was for someone in your own district, the operator then plugged your phone line directly into the *puka* connected to that person's house. If the call was for someone living in the island's other exchanges; your line was plugged into a slot that was connected by cable to the other far-off exchange. There the operator, sitting in front of a big PBX board with slots for all her area's phones, would patch your call into the called party's *puka* and then push a switch to ring the bell.

It was a complicated, slow, but user-friendly network with pleasant operators standing by around the clock. Outside of Lihue and Waimea, no one really needed to remember a phone number. Calls usually were placed by name. Sometimes before connecting your own line to the other party's line, the neighborly operator would say, "She's over at So-and-So's house. Do you want me to ring there?" Or, she might say, "Nobody's home. They're having dinner at So-and-So's. They usually get home about nine o'clock. If you like, I'll check after nine and then call you back. Okay?"

Doctors always let the local operator know where they were. People expecting a call but having to leave their home or business for a while advised operators when they'd return or sometimes asked them to just take the message. Non-human answering machines still were nearly a half-century away.

On the entire island, there were only 1,432 telephone subscribers in 1940. Today, in the year 2000, with only twice the population, there are 40,000 sub-scribers. (Even as late as 1955 only 546 dial phones existed in Lihue and 272 in Waimea)

Phone numbers in the Lihue automated exchange were easy to remember—only three digits. In fact, so easy to recollect that I still recall KTOH's two phone lines sixty years later: 261 and 361. The Garden Island newspaper's was 312. One of KTOH's biggest advertis-ers was Garden Island Motors: 275.

If you check through advertisements in *The Garden Island* prior to World War Two you'll discover no merchant listed a telephone number. It just wasn't necessary.

Business telephones in the early '40s were com-mon. Residential phones, on the other hand, were lim-ited. For one thing, much of the island's population lived in scattered sugar or pineapple plantation camps where phones were considered to be not really neces-sary. Plus, they were relatively expensive. Long work days and six-day weeks didn't allow much time for phone conversations with others. Moreover, almost everybody that a laborer might know lived within walking distance of his home.

In the larger communities there were business-men, some government employees and plantation super-visors whose homes had telephone service. The standard home connection was one line shared by at least four families. If one party was on the phone, the other three couldn't call out or receive calls. When it was you on the phone, it was irritating to have someone on your line keep lifting up his handset to check if you had finished your call. Always there was the suspicion that someone was listening in to your conversation.

In the 1950s, many rural homes still had wooden telephone boxes fastened to a wall in the kitchen or bed-room. You spoke into a cone-shaped black tube sticking out of the front of the box. On one side of the case was a cradle holding the earpiece and on the other side was a crank. To call the operator, turn the crank once and hang loose until she's able to patch into your line. If she's busy handling another call, try wait.

Whenever there's an incoming call for someone on your line, the operator sends a specific number of very loud rings that clang inside every single box the entire length of the party line. Everybody stops whatever he or she is doing, listens, and counts out the number of rings. If you lived at telephone number four, you answered four short rings. Five was one long ring. Seven—one long, two short. Our home was number twelve: two long and two short.

This system was exasperating. Not only did everyone hear every ring that your neighbors made going out to the operator for their outgoing calls, there were annoying incoming calls at all hours of the day and night. You were forced to listen and count every time to see if the signal might be for you. Although bothersome, it still was better than no telephone at all.

The early morning hours during the first few weeks our family lived at the end of the cable in Poipu were miserable—four annoying rings at 5:00 A.M. daily except Sundays!

I'm sure they were for someone who worked on a plantation. Who else would want to be awakened at that god-awful hour every day? I know I easily could have discovered who it was and politely or impolitely told him to do several things including buying an alarm clock. One morning, in a combative brave moment, I did pick up the phone but no one came on the line. These certainly were just routine wake-up calls.

I figured this disturbance must be for someone really important because no one else along this multi-family chatterbox system had complained. So, in a gesture of peaceful compliance, every night before we went to bed I unscrewed the wooden cover of the box and stuck a piece of thick cardboard between the bell and its clapper.

This reduced the penetrating sound to a mere buzz—quieter than the croaking *bufos* out in the garden, allowing us to listen to waves dashing against the rock wall in front of Dr. Brennecke's house, and keeping the night so still we could hear the occasional sounds of

Night Marchers traveling from Boneyard Beach to Polihale.

And so it came to pass, the bell-ringing monster living in the noisy wooden box on the bedroom wall was slain. And all the members of our family in the little hamlet of Poipu on that faraway, strange, hidden land called "The Garden Island" lived happily ever after.

16

How Much Do You Tip for A Nickel Bowl of Saimin?

There was a time when people actually bent down to pick up a penny seen lying on the ground. That was when one cent had some real buying power.

In 1940 you could go to the Post Office and buy a penny postalcard that included both the card and the stamp. You'd just write your message on it and for that one penny it would be delivered to anywhere in the United States.

When you sent a one-ounce first-class letter from Lihue to someone else in Lihue all you needed on the envelope was a one-cent stamp. Three pennies would pay first-class postage for a letter that went by boat mail to the other islands or to the mainland. The newly established and rarely used airmail service via the Pan American Clipper was an enormous 25¢.

A penny also bought a large-size candy bar or a hard rubber pocket comb or an imported Sunkist orange or a giant dill pickle out of a barrel or a half-inch-thick slice of baloney or so many other precious items.

A nickel was an even bigger piece of change. Barbeque Inn, down the street from Kress Store in Lihue, offered a bowl of savory, freshly made *saimin* for a nickel. Most of the items in the nearby Kress Store were of the five- and ten-cent variety. Tip Top Café's coffee and pastry combo was five cents for the regular morning businessmen's coffee klatch. An ice cream soda at Ota's Sweet Shop by Lihue Theater was just five pennies. Kids paid a dime to go to the movies next door.

The Dang family's Sun Kwong Sing Store, by the bridge in Hanapepe, in 1940 advertised a pound of sugar or rice for five pennies. For six pennies you could have a pack of cigarettes or a package of Jell-O. Eight pennies bought one can of Campbell's Soup, Van Camp's pork & beans, Vienna sausages or Pet evaporated milk or a roll of Scott Tissue. Sun Kwong Sing, located where the NAPA Auto Parts store now stands, announced a summer clothing sale with a rack of dresses for 25¢, 50¢ and 75¢.

Not to be outdone, Lihue Store's manager, Herman Grote, promoted what he advertised as "the largest retail market in the Territory" with prices such as Mayflower Kona Coffee 22¢/lb., Delicious apples and Bartlett pears from the mainland for 12¢/lb. and 13¢/lb. Leg of lamb was 31¢/lb, Princeville beef chuck roast 22¢/lb. A 25-ft. garden hose cost just $1.25. And in the clothing department a ladies slack suit went for $1.98, Arrow fancy dress shirts just $1.55, Haynes underwear only 28¢ per item, and fancy percale yardage 19¢ per yard. If you were planning a June wedding, a man's McGregor 3-piece dress suit was $5.95. An extra pair of pants 99¢. At the island's three H.S. Kawakami Stores the nationally famous "Mitzi Dresses" were only $1.00.

Cigarettes, in 1940, were $1.20 per carton. Schenley's Cream of Kentucky Straight Bourbon was advertised at 94¢ a pint, $1.84 for a quart. To attend a Saturday night dance at the gym with a live orchestra men paid 40¢ and women just 25¢. A full year's subscription to *The Garden Island* newspaper was only $2.50. That's right—one full year!

A four-route bus service was offered by Nawiliwili Transportation Company from Nawiliwili to Kealia and from Nawiliwili to Koloa, also between Koloa and Hanapepe, and from Eleele to Kekaha. Tokens, used to pay the fare, were 7½¢ from Nawiliwili to Koloa or Kealia and 15¢ for the longer trips. When Nawiliwili Transco ended its bus service in 1941, Yoshida Service

Station in Kapaa inaugurated a cruising taxi service. Riders paid a dime to go from Lihue to Hanamaulu and 20¢ between Lihue and Kapaa/Kealia. A monthly commute card for the taxi cost $6.00.

Overnight travel to Honolulu on the Tuesday and Friday inter-island steamers was $7 per person for a 3-person cabin, $10 each for a 2-person stateroom, and just a couple of dollars for passengers who didn't mind sitting around all night or sleeping on deck. Inter-Island Airways scheduled round-trips to Oahu daily. The fare: $27 roundtrip.

These prices before the war may seem low. But relative to people's earnings they're probably in line. Fifty-five percent of Kauai's population worked in sugar in 1940 with paychecks from around $26 to $40 per month. Another very large percentage of employment was related to pineapple with a similar rate of pay. Elected County supervisors earned $100 a month while the County Chairman and County Attorney each received $350 per month.

My home for the first month on Kauai was the lone room above Jack Wada's appliance sales and service shop in Nawiliwili. Rent—$5.00. Across the road was the small ten-room Kuboyama Hotel, also available for $5.00 a month for a long-term resident. Both catered to traveling businessmen who arrived and departed on the interisland steamer that docked nearby. Off-island businessmen were soaked around $2.00 a night at the Kuboyama.

Wanting to be near all the action in Lihue and close to where meals were served, I moved to the island's only authentic hostelry—Sheriff Willie Rice's Lihue Hotel. This was a collection of a single small two-story building and a number of one-story cottages of four rooms each on what is now called Rice Street. After the war, the hotel was remodeled into the Kauai Inn and now has been become the site of Kalapaki Villas.

Here at Lihue Hotel, for five dollars a month, I had a room with weekly maid service and a view of what I considered to be fabulous tropical gardens. Fragrant *honohono* orchids and gardenias were blooming every-

A porte cochere sheltered guests entering Lihue Hotel's main building with its tiny reception desk and dining room. Most of the cottages were on the left of the driveway, amid tropical foliage reminiscent of a Tarzan movie.

where. When picked and spread out on all the flat surfaces in my room, the sweet-smelling blanket of gardenias made San Francisco's finest funeral parlor pale in comparison.

The Lihue Hotel had two dining rooms. The fancy one was entered through the lobby of the larger building. It had tablecloths, candles and waitresses. The other (nicknamed "The Rose Room") was a screened-in lanai behind the kitchen where I dined along with *luna* from Lihue and Grove Farm Plantations, *paniolo* from Kipu, hotel staff members and a few other local folks. The *luna* and cowboys tethered their horses on a telephone pole nearby.

Food was the same in both places but the price was more reasonable out in the kitchen *lanai*. All-you-can-eat breakfast was 25¢, lunch 35¢ and dinner 40¢. Five dollars a month for a room and a dollar a day for food was pretty good for someone like me earning $80 a month. High-priced meals in the dining room totaled an exorbitant $2.50 per day.

I don't remember the daily or weekly room rate for Lihue Hotel off-island guests. Virtually all travelers

On Fort Street looking *mauka* from Honolulu's Aloha Tower was the extraordinary block-long Alexander Young Hotel. Shops lined the ground level, including the Young Hotel Bakery with its toothsome pastries. Above were three floors of offices and exceptionally large hotel rooms. In the forties, a room with a bath went for $2.50 per day, with a discount for *kamaaina*, and an evening of romantic dinner dancing on the roof totaled $2.50 per person.

to Kauai in 1940 were businessmen. Tourists still were a decade away. But, I do have a 1940 newspaper ad for the Alexander Young Hotel in downtown Honolulu where most Garden Islanders stayed while in Town.

Visitors to Oahu in 1940 could choose among several major hotels in Waikiki or two multi-story properties in the business section of Honolulu: the Alexander Young Hotel and the Blaisdell Hotel. Both were located in the neighborhood of Hotel and Bishop Streets. Another popular, very inexpensive lodging was the YMCA near Iolani Palace.

The Young Hotel, four stories high and almost a block long, was a popular setting for moonlight dancing on the rooftop to the music of the Gigi Royce and Alvin Kaleolani orchestras. Before the war, dancing cost $1.00

per person. Dinner and dance $2.50. A room with a bath was advertised at $2.50 per night with a special discount given to island residents.

After the war and until the mid-1950s *kamaaina* outer-island residents enjoyed a five dollar rate for any available room in just about every hotel on Oahu, including the Royal Hawaiian where I once spent four nights in the Diamond Head Suite for a total of twenty dollars.

Kauai had its own five-dollar-a-night hotel after the war. Alfred and Vida Hills turned their home at the mouth of Wailua River into a 22-room riverside lodge called Wailua Beach Hotel. During the war it had been turned over to the USO to provide an entertainment spot for servicemen. The Hills' post-war five-dollar rate included use of a common kitchen while a small café also offered three meals a day. In May of 1950, Grace Buscher (later Guslander) took over the hotel, enlarging it into the sixty-room Coco Palm Lodge. By 1953 it had expanded into the widely acclaimed Coco Palms Hotel and Resort.

Thinking back to 1940, I sometimes wonder if we ever tipped anyone. I recall haircuts, given by the *Mama-san* whose shop was between TipTop Café and Senda's Photo Studio, cost 20¢. Did I give her two pennies or a nickel tip? Who knows? There was no real taxi service on the island so there was no tipping there. Hotels didn't have bellboys. Henry Hoshide, Lihue Hotel's bookkeeper and desk clerk, would carry someone's bags if the visitor couldn't handle them alone. Was he tipped?

Whenever I felt the need to save money, I'd skip a hotel meal and head for Barbeque Inn for a stomach-filling nickel bowl of *saimin*. The Inn also was where young people hung out to pass away idle time. Teenager Ann Akiyama, who was a Hollywood-type beauty, waited on the few tables. She, alone, was an attraction. But she was strictly "hands off." Nobody had to tell us. Her boyfriend, whom she later married, was "Yasu" Yasutake, the Territory's featherweight boxing champ.

I wonder if I ever tipped her? Did I leave just one

solitary penny lying on the table? It certainly wouldn't have been a nickel because that would have been a 100% gratuity. Even just one penny would have been 20%.

I called Ann recently and she can't remember either. Could I have been such a dork that I left her only one penny? Would she have gratefully picked up a penny and dropped it into her apron pocket?

I just can't imagine that the two of us would do that. Or, did we?

17

What Do You Do After They Roll Up the Sidewalks?

Until GIs began arriving on the Garden Island in the months prior to World War Two, this island was somewhat like many small communities on the mainland where it's said, "They roll up the sidewalks early every evening and store them away for the night."

On Kauai there was very little to do during the week after the 8:00 P.M. mill whistle or cannery siren suggested it was time to get ready for bed. Actually not many people on weeknights were really interested in finding the answer to "Where's the action?"

Plantation workdays beginning around 6:00 A.M. were long and the labor very exhausting. Those offices and businesses directly associated with sugar and pineapple started work at seven o'clock or earlier. Doors at other businesses opened around seven-thirty or eight. So, for most folks, it usually was early to bed and early to rise.

From time to time there was a reason to stay up past eight—church choir practice, Lions Club, American Legion, PTA, ethnic societies and other community gatherings. There were planning committee conferences for carnivals, other fundraisers and similar group meetings.

During the week most families, however, stayed home in the evening. School kids did homework as older children and mothers made lunches and completed other chores for the day. Mothers and fathers who worked on the plantation made preparations for the next day.

The two Honolulu radio stations along with KTOH filled the early evening hours for the vast majority of Garden Islanders. KTOH's popular evening Filipino and Japanese language programs topped the ratings. There were no all-night radio stations in the Territory.

For those who really did want a weeknight out on the town, most communities had a friendly pool hall, an entertaining moving picture show, or a quiet spot where you could buy a drink. Four towns, Waimea, Hanapepe, Kapaa and Lihue, welcomed night owls to their roller skating rinks which remained open until ten. Each plantation community had its own theater showing one Japanese and one Filipino movie each week plus Hollywood films on the other evenings and weekend matinees. Sometimes Portuguese movies were featured. That was it. Not much.

But on Saturday nights, people could go for broke. Carnivals and dances were big attractions. Almost every weekend, somewhere on the island, a community group, athletic league, ethnic association, church or school presented a festive carnival. Games of skill and food booths, especially those serving cone *sushi* and *malasadas,* were the primary enticements. Stage shows by sponsoring members often were added to attract more big spenders from other parts of the island.

A few large organizations brought in E.K. Fernandez' carnival rides—a Ferris wheel, roller coaster and more. The big brotherhoods like the Lions Club and American Legion presented the mothers of all carnivals: a colossal circus that ran daily for a week to ten days. Just about all 33,000 Garden Islanders attended, many even on work nights.

About two or three times a month, a Saturday-night dance was given somewhere around the island at one of the plantation or high-school gyms. Men paid 40¢ and ladies 25¢ for admission to an evening of music by live dance bands ranging in size from about eight to twenty instruments. There were the Lamplighters, the

Ambassadors, the Joyland Serenaders, Al's Troubadors, Dickie Hamada and the Starlighters, Billy's Snappy Pickers, and others including the two big bands: Charlie Kaneyama's Merry Melodiers on the Waimea side and the Rapozo Brothers Reliance Orchestra which played at the major dances on the Lihue side of the island. These latter two bands became the mainstays of KTOH's Saturday night remote dance broadcasts in the 1940s and '50s.

With several thousand servicemen on the island during the war, country music and songs of the South Seas flourished at bars and nightclubs. Hawaiian musicians prospered at nightspots in Waimea, Hanapepe, Kalaheo, Nawiliwili and Kapaa.

The island's larger private business companies always had a group of employees who joined in singing and playing island music for company affairs. Now, with an island full of visiting GIs, the musicians had second jobs entertaining in the evenings. Members of Slim Holt's Kauai Terminal Hawaiians and Sam Peahu's Nawiliwili Transco Hawaiians were in big demand.

Some of the nightclubs continued after the wartime servicemen left the island. Most of them carried on live entertainment on Fridays and Saturdays.

After the war, when I returned to Kauai, I joined Sarah Kailikea, her sister Lani and brother Henry in playing Hawaiian music at Nawiliwili's Luau Garden on weekends. This island-music group also included Ili Waalani, Frank Castillo and Ah Sau Ahana, a well-known steel guitarist.

Although Sarah and Melvin Kailikea's Luau Garden became a very popular hangout, there always was a search to attract more and more of the night-people who wanted to party. One day the Kailikeas decided that in order to increase business, photographs would be taken of lighthearted customers dancing in the dimly lit nightspot. The idea was to print the pictures as advertisements in the weekly *Garden Island* newspaper.

The photos weren't a success. Every week for months, Ray Sasaki, *The Garden Island* photographer, took a series of photographs of happy faces sitting

Typical of nightclubs in the middle of the last century was Luau Garden in Nawiliwili. Placed around a good-size dance floor were tables often decorated with tropical flowers. Just about every nightspot would have wooden poles trimmed with colorful crepe paper to resemble the royal *kahili*. Glass balls in nets customarily hung from ceilings. There were lots of palm fronds lining walls as well as a small stage where musicians played mostly Hawaiian music.

Occasionally Filipino and Japanese popular songs answered requests from patrons. Very few mainland tunes were heard until GIs appeared during World War Two and then western music was added. Live entertainment after the war usually was limited to Friday and Saturday nights while a jukebox played Big Band recordings the rest of the week.

Other nightclubs were very similar to Luau Garden in appearance. A few gathering spots, such as Club Jetty, served a full menu of food but at most of the nightclubs just a bartender and waitress served drinks and *pupu* such as *sashimi, kim chee, pipikaula, lomilomi* salmon, *daikon, hana ebi, namasu, poke,* and *laulau* with *poi*.

It's interesting to note that men wore slacks or jeans and leather shoes—no shorts or *zoris*. It was the custom both day and night for men to wear long pants. Shorts were worn only when puttering around the house or going fishing or such occasions when you're roughing it or not going to be out in public. Some *kamaaina* today still are never seen wearing shorts. It wasn't colder then. There hasn't been a shift in the climate. People have changed.

around tables and romantic couples snuggling on the dance floor. No picture ever could be printed because always there was at least one person shown cuddling up to someone he or she shouldn't be seen with.

The musicians, though not all related, were like family. We all played at Luau Garden mainly for our own pleasure. If people wanted to dance, that was okay with us. We valued the fun of making music together and eating as many *laulau* as we could scarf down at the end of the evening. Sometimes, I'm sure, they lost money on us.

Sarah and Ah Sau still are with us. Ah Sau lives in Lihue where he's retired with wife, Mary, after three decades of hosting guests at the Ahana Family Motel down the street from today's TipTop Cafe. Sarah's devoting her time to saving a huge and ancient banyan tree slowly embracing her Nawiliwili home in its expanding, air-root arms.

The Manji Ouyes, who had been operating their successful Hale Aina cafe in Nawiliwili, relocated to a spot on the harbor's edge, renaming it Club Jetty. The Mike Ashman Quintet was the first group to offer entertainment there, being paid five dollars each for five hours of music on Fridays and Saturdays. Besides my piano, there was Ah Sau Ahana's steel guitar, Miki Waiau's Spanish guitar, "Big Bill" Kaliloa's string bass and George Boiser's drums.

Nearly all Club Jetty patrons were local folks. Tourism had not yet given birth. In those days Japanese and Filipino ballads were almost as popular as Hawaiian songs and, when I sang them, folks began calling me "The Albino Hawaiian," "The Japanese Troubadour" and "The Filipino Mystery Singer."

The latter nickname originated during a guessing contest over KTOH's Filipino Radio Hour. A string of Visayan, Tagalog and Ilocano love songs was recorded by me as part of a contest to identify "The Filipino Mystery Singer." Grand prize was a used car from Garden Island Motors. The contest was the idea of the station's new Filipino program director who followed Abe Albayalde and Leonora Currameng.

Often on plantation payday weekends, big name show-people were brought over from Waikiki's nightspots. Entertainment-starved Garden Islanders gathered for the rare pleasure of seeing and hearing the singers and musicians who were featured on the day's hit phonograph records.

Across the road from the Roxy Theater in Kapaa was Club Blue Lei, foremost in presenting Waikiki's talent. It was standing room only for an evening with famed composer/singer Johnny Almeida and his companion songstress Genoa Keawe. As part of the show, Kauai's Aggie Waiau was invited to sing along with a classic hula performed by Kapaa's Eileen Smith, dressed in a shimmering white *holomu*. To the left of Aggie is Johnny Almeida (dark glasses) plucking away on his famed mandolin and on the other side is Genoa Keawe peering around Aggie's shoulder.

The producer of the program drove the clunker around the island for half a year promoting the contest. Then after the six-month guessing game was over and no one had mailed in the singer's name, he kept the car for himself. (A few years later he took the same recordings with him to Oahu where he ran a similar contest on a Honolulu station. Again he wound up with the grand prize. Eventually, he served time in prison for fraud in another matter.)

From Club Jetty we musicians went home with some money in our pockets rather than an *opu* full of *laulau*. After every session, the Ouye's would hand me five $5 bills to be distributed among the five members of the band.

Many years later, while living on Lanai, a letter came to me from the State tax office saying it finally had tracked me down and a huge amount of taxes, interest and penalties was owed for all the $25 payments recorded in my name in the Ouye's books.

Although I explained the situation and proved the taxes were paid on my share—and claimed the others probably already paid the income tax owed on theirs—the bureaucrats advised me that was not the tax department's problem. It was mine. I should go back and collect from the others. I didn't. Tax collectors haven't changed a bit.

When Ben Ohai refurbished Club Blue Lei in Kapaa, then billed as "Kauai's Biggest and Finest Nightclub," our five-piece group moved over to play for weekend dancing. It was a successful nightspot for a

Popular singer/songwriter Andy Cummings was mobbed at Lihue Airport upon his arrival for a weekend of concerts at Club Blue Lei. In front of a KTOH microphone, he wowed the crowd with his signature composition, "Waikiki–At night when the shadows are falling, I hear your rolling surf calling—calling and calling to me." It seemed most of the Club Blue Lei's sell-out crowd were his sisters, brothers, cousins, aunts, uncles and *calabash* cousins. Andy grew up in Kapaa.

long time. Sometimes on payday weekends, Kauai's own entertainers who had gone on to fame in Honolulu, came back for guest appearances.

Among them were Andy Cummings and Johnny Almeida with Genoa Keawe. Andy grew up in Kapaa. His relatives, alone, filled up half of Club Blue Lei. Johnny Almeida always told the audience he was happy to be back on Kauai because the people here made him feel as if he had just come home again. He often cautioned the audience to be careful when gathering *mokihana* and *maile*. At the time of his birth, his mother was up in the mountains gathering *maile*. Juice of the fragrant vine found its way into his eyes causing a lifetime of blindness.

I'm glad I wasn't on Kauai when the new Nawiliwili Road was built right over the top of the Kauai Yacht Club covering its restaurant, bar and swimming pool. Many glowing memories now are lying under the macadam where the road begins to rise by today's Hale Kauai. The Yacht Club formerly had been Papalinahoa, the Wilcox family's plantation-style beach home at Niumalu.

It was at the Kauai Yacht Club that folks partied

Papalinahoa, the Wilcox family home near the shore of Nawiliwili Bay, was turned over to servicemen for recreation during World War Two. Later it became the Kauai Yacht Club where the island's sailors and landlubbers gathered for dinners during the week, Saturday night party time, and Sunday family day. The few members who actually went sailing competed on Sundays with a small fleet of one-person Star Class boats.

on Saturday nights and on Sunday afternoons taught our youngsters how to swim. Every few months brought a moonlight dinner dance with the Rapozo Brothers Reliance Orchestra, featuring "The Happy Haole" as vocalist. That was real cool! I bet I'm the only kid on my block in SF to grow up to sing with an orchestra doing imitation Big Band arrangements. And during the Big Band Era, at that!

The Reliance Orchestra led by "Mac" Rapozo and featuring nearly all of his seven brothers, was the choice of east side groups who could afford a full-size dance band. It always attracted a good crowd—except for one distressing episode.

For a while, the Valley House above Kealia was turned into a hilltop restaurant, cocktail lounge and ballroom. The former home of Makee Sugar Plantation founder, Colonel Spaulding, was bought by Helen Luscher in 1948 and renovated to become a high-class nightclub, featuring the locally celebrated Reliance Orchestra and "The Happy Haole" every Saturday night.

The opening was a smash. Then for a while attendance was fine. Then just okay. The following weeks looked pretty bad and eventually business became terrible. Several beautiful dance hostesses were brought to the island with little success.

With no one on the dance floor, the musicians would sit quietly on the bandstand hoping someone would drive up the long, winding road from Kealia to the elegant Valley House. We listened for cars to arrive. Sheet music for the next song was ready.

At the entrance to the spacious grounds, a wooden bridge with loose planks rumbled each time a vehicle crossed over. Whenever we heard that sound, "Mac" gave the downbeat and the music would begin with our hope that whoever was driving by would like the sound and stop. That didn't always work. The Valley House restaurant and nightclub had a short life. It was just too far away from civilization.

I wish I had at least one photograph taken of me alongside my two musical buddies, Ah Sau Ahana and

Miki Waiau. But there isn't any. The three of us managed to wander from one spot to another, singing and playing our collection of Hawaiian classics. I don't think our trio was the greatest, but we were dependable. And that counted.

If Tommy Gage or Fay McKay, managers of the Kauai Inn, suddenly wanted a show for visitors staying at the hotel, they'd call us and we'd be there performing on the lawn of the hotel that evening. The setting was magnificent—a broad, green lawn stretching as far as the eye could see with Mount Haupu accenting the background.

When large groups of visitors were registered at the hotel, "Kauai Annie" Holt and her Hawaiian troupe traveled all the way from Kekaha on the west side to carry on the program after our trio finished its performance. Mainlanders came to the Garden Island for a Hawaiian experience and Kauai Inn, the only tourist-class hotel on the island, tried its best to accommodate them.

On many evenings, seven-year-old Larry Ramos would be featured in our program. His mother, Pat, was manager of the hotel gift shop. Larry wowed the mainland visitors. His ukulele solos were awesome. The talented second-grader didn't just strum while he sang. He also performed his own solo ukulele arrangements of Hawaiian songs, of Broadway hits, of classical music.

Upon winning the 1949 Territory-wide ukulele contest he was brought to New York City by Arthur Godfrey to appear on his top-rated national telecasts in 1950 and '51. When Metro-Goldwyn-Mayer came to Kauai to film *Pagan Love Song*, Hollywood producer Arthur Freed noticed little Larry from Kalaheo performing in our show. The youngster was added to the script.

Shortly after reaching twenty years, Larry Ramos became an international entertainer as "Pineapple" with the New Christy Minstrels. In the late '60s he joined The Association, a group of six performers of which he now is director and part owner. Today they're still circling the world, appearing at theaters, nightclubs, and with leading symphony orchestras.

Imagine how much fun and how exciting it would be if you were little Larry Ramos and you had to ask your second-grade teacher for permission to skip school so you could travel to New York to sing and play the ukulele on the top-rated Arthur Godfrey TV program. When he returned after a week in the big city, it seemed like every kid in Koloa School had bought or borrowed an ukulele and was asking Larry "for show how you make *da kine*." He returned to the Arthur Godfrey Show a second time—staying away from school two months. Back home again, as Larry was performing for a small group of tourists staying at the Kauai Inn, Hollywood producer Arthur Freed was so impressed that he wrote Larry into the script of the movie, *Pagan Love Song*.

In the meantime at the mouth of Wailua River in 1950, Alfred and Vida Hills first leased and then sold their former home that was serving as the unpretentious Wailua Beach Hotel to a *hui* including Grace Buscher Guslander. Ah Sau, Miki and I were hired to do the cocktail hour at what she first called Coco Palms Lodge. Evening entertainment for weekends and for special occasions brought singers and dancers from Henry Sheldon's Kapaa Mormon Church Choir.

At dusk each evening as the sky slowly turned to shades of red and purple, and the happy guests sipped *mai tais*, Ah Sau, Miki and I softly sang, "Twilight in Hawaii when the lights are low, brings me thoughts of someone on a distant shore . . ." Guests ooh-ed and ah-ed with pleasure at the sight of bartender Alex Maglinte casually strolling around the palm-fringed lagoon lighting tiki torches. For the guests it was a last-ing memory of ancient Polynesia.

As evenings went by, Alex began to move a little faster around the lagoon because of pesky, aggressive mosquitoes. Then, because it didn't look quite right to see the handsome, bare-chested, macho torchbearer keep swatting himself during such a mesmerizing moment, he began to jog faster and faster and faster.

Eventually he sprinted as quickly as he could without missing any torches and we had to change our slow-paced song to a sprightly Tahitian melody that sounded very much like the cowboy chorus "Yippee, Yippee, Yippee Yea." And that impromptu Coco Palms innovation, some fifty years ago, may have been the beginning of today's popular torchlighting ceremony celebrated each evening at hotels and resorts through-out Hawaii.

Within two years the Coco Palms Lodge became the Coco Palms Hotel and there began the illustrious professional career of Kauai's Larry Rivera. Like Larry Ramos with his ukulele, this Larry with his guitar also was born to be a top-notch entertainer.

As an early teenager he loved to hang out around KTOH. In those days cowboy music had great appeal. Skinny little Larry would stand in front of the broadcast

In 1954, the US Army Pacific sent out a call for the best entertainers from all its thirty-five installations in the Territory of Hawaii to take part in an All-Army talent contest. From Kauai came a trio calling them- selves "The Beach Boys" (long before Hollywood's "Beach Boys" became the "Beach Boys.") At the close of the intense competition, the first place winners were Kauai's Larry Rivera along with Josiah Pua, at the piano, and Ernest Shey, bassist. For Larry Rivera, it was the foretelling of his dazzling future.

microphone, along with his two sisters, singing away with his young, high falsetto voice. His tone was in true pitch and vibrant with showmanship.

While a student at Kapaa High, Larry Rivera had told his social studies teacher he wanted to become an entertainer. The disgusted teacher counseled him, "What do you want to do that for? You can't make a liv- ing and raise a family on Kauai by singing!" Well, Larry worked hard and he did reach the top of his profession.

He was with Grace Buscher Guslander from the very beginning. From busboy on up in the dining room, he then headlined the hotel's spectacular Hawaiian entertainment until the day the world-famous resort was closed by Hurricane Iniki nearly four decades later. It was the longest-running show in all of Hawaii.

Larry not only is known today as the personable composer/singer/guitarist "Mr. Kauai," he has written over fifty Hawaiian songs, recorded seven CDs, thirteen cassette releases, two video tapes, and with his wife, Gloria, has produced a large family of fellow entertain- ers. Last year, in 1999, he was honored as "One of Kauai's Living Treasures."

One of the funniest stories about an island boy who made it big as an entertainer was told by Garden Islander E.C.S. "Budde" Crabbe during a party at the

It Was So Much Fun, He Just Couldn't Quit

It wasn't enough for Grampa to be the vocalist for the Raposo Brothers Reliance Orchestra, spending many Saturday nights entertaining at dances in the island's plantation and high school gymnasiums & the Yacht Club & the Valley House. . . .

Or, with accompanist Greg Valdez, crooning Ilocano, Tagalog and Visayan love songs while making the circuit of Filipino camps and the stages of plantation movie houses on evenings when Filipino films were being shown. . . .

Or, at events like Sharon Sue's Ladies Fashion Show at Lihue Plantation's Isenberg Gym when he pretended he knew what he was singing when he warbled Japanese pop tunes like "Kan Kan Musume" and "Tonko Tonko." . . .

Or, spending Hawaiian nights at Nawiliwili's Luau Garden with a family of musical cousin-sisters and cousin-brothers (from left) Ah Sau Ahana, Lani Higgins, Grampa, Ili Waalani, Sarah Kailikea and Fred Castillo. . . .

Or, teaming up with Miki Waiau (Spanish guitar) and Ah Sau Ahana (steel guitar) in starting the entertainment at the Kauai Inn, at Manji and Emma Ouye's Club Jetty in Nawiliwili and at Ben Ohai's refurbished Club Blue Lei in Kapaa, and in pioneering the sunset Hawaiian ceremony at Grace Buscher's early Coco Palms Lodge. . . .

Then one night at a YMCA annual dinner Grampa thought he'd bring a touch of class to Kauai by singing arias from German and Italian operas. By the time he decided to quit . . . everybody was asleep.

Crabbe family's coconut plantation home in Waipouli, near the site of today's Coconut Marketplace.

Budde and his brother "Buster" were raised in Hawaii. Their grandfather, Clarence Linden Crabbe, after whom Buster was named, was known as "The father of the GOP in Hawaii." Their father, Ned, was a Territorial Prohibition Agent. The two brothers' leisure-time home was in the waters of Hawaii where both became excellent swimmers.

After Buster went on to win a gold medal for the 400-meter free-style swimming event at the 1932 Olympics, America's movie-makers called on him to swing from tree to tree as one of the early Tarzans in Hollywood films. His first "Tarzan the Fearless" Saturday matinee serial ran for thirteen weeks at Kauai's movie houses.

Budde knew Buster must have had a hand in the script because the name of the African chief was *"Kukae."* That's Hawaiian for excrement. On Saturday afternoons when the serial was shown, kids delighted in hearing someone saying out loud, "Me Tarzan," "Me Jane," *"Me Kukae."*

Every weekly episode ended with a cliff-hanging crisis. Either Tarzan or Jane or one of their pet animals was about to be killed by a native warrior, a wild animal or an accident. The youngsters in the theater loved to hear expressions such as Jane's entreaty, "Oh, Tarzan! We need help! Go find chief! Tarzan, you go *Kukae* . . . go *Kukae* right now!" The kids would howl with laughter. They'd stamp their feet, punch each other's shoulders, roll around on the floor.

On the way home they could be heard taunting each other, "Me Tarzan. You *kukae*," with the rejoinder, "Not!!! Me Tarzan. You one big *kukae*."

18

Terms of Endearment and "Aloha–I am Pig Slop Man"

I have a theory that the friendliness of a community can be measured by the percentage of nice nicknames in relation to total population. In other words, the more friendly nicknames that people use, the greater the comradeship, fondness for each other, and good-fellowship in a neighborhood. Maybe someday this measurement will be endowed with an awesome title like "Geniality Index."

A half century ago, this important index level ranked very high on the Garden Island. Thus it would help to confirm that the community was strong in camaraderie, kindness to each other, a concern for one another and a feeling of kinship. As a result the crime rate was low because there aren't many people who really want to commit crimes against members of their families. Kauai was like one big family.

The nice nicknames I'm talking about aren't those generated from given names, like Hank, Chuck, Mickey, Liz and Becky, but sobriquets such as "Tootsie," "Butch," "Chicken" and "Bunny."

Kauai's nickname cup in the mid-1900s runneth over. There were obvious handles such as those for local baseball great "Lefty" Hirota, union leader "Slim" Shimizu, car rental pioneer "Slim" Holt, mechanic "Shorty" Rapozo, and airline official "Fat" Takamiya. You'd think "Fat" would be one of those ugly nicknames that is subtracted from the list of nice ones to compute the Geniality Index. But, not so. He'd turn around when you hollered "Hey, Fat!" without getting mad. He even signed off on some reports as "Fat."

"Mormon" Nakamura evidently was a member of the Latter Day Saints Church but does anyone know why he was singled out for the byname. Perhaps he was the only Mormon Church member on a team where all the other players were Buddhists.

Matsuo "Sidelines" Kuraoka acquired his name in the 1950s through his newspaper column just as Dennis "Happy Camper" Fujimoto has his today in the year 2000.

"Mustache" Watanabe, as a small boy playing marbles, had the habit of holding a dirty finger under his nose while contemplating his next shot. Only one play-mate ever made the mistake of telling him he looked just like Hitler. When Henry Uchiyama graduated from Kauai High and joined *The Garden Island* pressroom staff, he already was known as "Grandpa" Uchiyama. How come? He joined the likes of "Tootsie" Miyake, a fellow worker bearing a strange but warm-hearted nickname, and "Turk" Tokita, the newspaper's sports reporter.

The origin of Coca-Cola distributor's "Butch" Yamaski is understandable. His given name was Buichi. How did baseball player "Punchy" Furutani and his brother, "Chicken," earn their designations? How about others like Kapaa's brother service station operators "Big Mice" and "Small Mice" Yoshida, disk jockey "Needlenose" Dougie Pratt, and storekeeper "Chicken" Sadamitsu. Everybody identified sugar plantation man-ager Wilfred Baldwin as "Bunt" long before the days he entered plantation life as a horseback riding field luna. His nickname began in the cradle that his Scottish mother had decorated with "wee baby bunting." Over time it metamorphosed through "Buntie" to just plain "Bunt."

If the AJA Baseball League had a Hall of Famous Nicknames you'd be sure to find, "Honky" Mineshima, "Chunky" Mizutani, "Lippy" Higuchi, "Duke" Nataya, "Wimpy" Nitta, "Bucky" Tanaka, "Radish" Amaki, and so many more.

There's a lot I can tell you about "Rubberman" Higami, a controversial Territory of Hawaii professional wrestler.

One Saturday evening Charlie Fern and I were at front-row ringside doing a broadcast of professional wrestling matches from Isenberg Gym in Lihue. ("Sad Sam" Ichinose was the sports promoter who brought boxing and wrestling to outer island fans.)

"Rubberman's" signature hold was an arm-choke around the neck during which he pressed a couple of fingers into his adversary's throat. This caused his antagonist to collapse, seemingly lifeless on the mat. Many fans throughout the Territory believed this "Japanese armbar" hold was fake. So, towards the end of the main bout that evening when he jabbed his fingers into his opponent's throat and wrapped his arm around the neck, there were resounding boos.

When the knocked-out wrestler recovered and booing continued, "Rubberman" strode around the ring challenging anyone to step in for a demonstration of his nefarious technique. There were no takers. However, two fellows sitting near Charlie Fern and me suddenly picked me up and handed me over the ropes into the outstretched arms of the brutal heavyweight wrestler. (I only weighed 137 pounds.)

I could remember standing in the ring for just a moment and then lying flat on my back on the mat looking up at the gymnasium roof. Spectators later told me that in between those recollections "Rubberman" had done the neck job on me, dropped my limp body to the mat, grabbed my curly hair and dragged me around the ring three or four laps, bouncing the back of my head onto the mat several times. He was no fake.

Now, let's suppose you're a very sensitive teenager. You answer the phone one night and someone asks to speak to "Stinky" or "Dummy" or "Screwy." And you know that the caller is talking about your very own impeccable, intelligent, wise, loving father. You're supposed to feel insulted and hostile. Right? But you're not because those actually were commonly used, friendly nicknames of prominent Garden Islanders.

"Stinky" Davis was on the staff at Hale Kauai. His mother had named him Richard. But when he telephoned, he didn't use "Richard" or "Dick." He'd just say, "Hello, Ashie? This is Stinky." Just like that.

"Dummy" Turqueza worked on the plantation and from time to time played his guitar and sang on the KTOH Filipino Radio Hour. His real name was Domingo but over time it must have been corrupted from Domi to Dummy. He didn't mind. He was very proud when he heard the announcer proclaim, "And now ladies and gentlemen, for a very special treat here is one of Kauai's favorite singers, Dummy Turqueza. It's all yours, Dummy." Perhaps he never knew the unrefined nature of his nickname.

"Screwy" Achor needs some explanation. Art Achor was appliance department manager for Lihue's Von Hamm Young Company store. He was a very intense, driven person who followed through on everything he set out to do.

Art was one of about nine or ten Kauai Yacht Club members who raced around Nawiliwili Harbor buoys on Sundays. Their Star Class sailboats were big enough for only one person. If he didn't win the Sunday morning race, he'd spend the rest of the day fiddling with the rigging to make sure he'd win next time. Folks used to say, "Art's really screwy about his boat."

He had other ideas that people thought were somewhat screwy. For example, he often rented his family car to visiting salesmen. He'd take a half-day off from work to make the two-hour drive to the Mana inter-island airport, pick up a client, drive back to Lihue and turn the salesman loose with the car.

His, also, was the screwy notion that Kauai should have a full-time taxi. So he bought a car and hired a driver to make the airport run. After the one daily flight, the taxi driver hung out at Lihue Store hoping for fares. When someone not near Lihue Store wanted a cab, he or she would call the Achor house around the corner next to the post office. Mrs. Achor would dash over to the taxi to dispatch it. If she wasn't home, folks knew they could call the Lihue Store manager's office and a store employee would pass along the message.

When the airport was moved to Lihue, Art's screwy inspiration was to lease more cars and have them waiting for arriving visitors who might need transportation. Then when Hertz made the decision to enter the Kauai market, the guy everyone called "Screwy" Achor was awarded the franchise.

The last time I saw him was at a travel conference in Bali. He promptly turned around when I called, "Hey, Screwy." He presented me with his business card that listed him as a Hertz vice president for international marketing. The back of the card was printed in Japanese. I was disappointed. Nowhere did it show his nickname.

In addition to "Slim" Holt and "Screwy" Achor there were two other Kauai princes in the realm of rental cars in Hawaii. Each one also had a pet name.

Close friends of Wailua's Bob Iwamoto called him "Rabbit." Don't really know why. Maybe it was a take-off on his name "Robert." When he expanded from u-drives to coaches and guided tours, a cute bunny rabbit became part of the company logo and still is seen promoting Roberts Tours of Hawaii.

"Willie" Duarte, from Kalaheo, became a popular international tourism figure with his Hawaiian entertainment promoting his u-drives and tours at travel shows around the world. When he was in grammar school the fairy tale of Snow White and the Seven Dwarfs was among the top stories taken out of the school library. Each morning, when Willie and his young siblings joined in crossing the road to the school, kids would tease them with, "Here come the seven little Duartes."

My wife and I first heard the strangest of all local nicknames late one afternoon when we answered a knock on our back door. Standing there was a giant of a man who softly spoke, "Aloha. I am Pig Slop Man." (That ranks right up there with Batman, Wonder Woman, Superman and Spider Man—"Aloha, I am Pig Slop Man.")

At the time he appeared we had just moved from the "Horikawa House" to the "Andy Gross House" in Lihue. (After Lihue Plantation employee relations manager Andy Gross had moved to another area, we were the fortunate family to rent the supervisor's cottage near the post office, directly across the street from the library, now Kauai Museum. On that site is today's Lihue Chevron service station.)

We didn't remember being notified to separate our rubbish into wet and dry garbage—the dry to be picked up by the county. He wanted us to know he was the grateful pig farmer who would stop at our house once a week to pick up the wet garbage to be used as "pig slops" for his swinery.

We agreed to place a pig slops metal bucket right next to the rubbish can at the beginning of our driveway (where Lihue Chevron gas pump #3 stands today). This is about as far away from the house as we could put it. In the pail would be tossed papaya, banana and potato skins, rotting avocados and mangoes from under our trees, things like leftover spoiled rice and gravy, and any other foodstuff ripe for disposal.

A board was laid on top of the bucket to help keep flies from entering, plus a heavy rock to keep the wooden cover from flying off on windy days. Our resident flies, however, found access easy. They swarmed in thick clouds waiting for their turns to enter and enjoy a meal. When the cover board blew away, every fly in the whole neighborhood rushed over for a mammoth *luau*. It seemed that after every meal each fly would deposit an egg in the decaying mush.

From time to time the contents of the pail would be thrashing with squirming white maggots. It looked like a boiling, bubbling porridge of worms. But every week without fail the contents were picked up by someone who appreciatively dumped them onto his truck and hauled them away.

To show his gratitude for the weekly supply of pig victuals, "Pig Slop Man" always left a gift during the week between Christmas and New Year's. There, lying on the wooden cover next to the rock, was an un-wrapped present—a large, jiggly chunk of pork fat.

After carrying it into the house the first time, my wife plopped it into the kitchen sink and we just stood there looking at the quivering blob. There was a hint of meat on the underside but what held our attention was the glistening top of a greasy-looking lump of pig fat. There's no way to describe the turbulence in our stomachs as we wondered what are we going to do with it? We couldn't bear to cook it and eat it. Heck, we had a hard time just looking at it.

It shouldn't be given back to "Pig Slop Man." It was his sincere "thank you" gift. To do so would be like telling him, "We didn't like the Christmas present you gave us. Take it back and don't ever do that again." That wouldn't have been a nice thing to do.

We knew some people would love to have it to prepare a tasty treat for a New Year celebration. But we also were aware that eating animal blubber would pack a person's heart with solid fat that would kill him. We didn't want that on our consciences.

Now that half a century has gone by, it's probably okay to tell others what we did. We wrapped the thick slab in newspaper, put it in a paper bag that was then wrapped in more newspaper and placed in another bag, and so on until it was well disguised. Then we hid it in the middle of the dry rubbish can. "Pig Slop Man" was one of the County's garbage crew. We wanted to make sure that if he happened to be the guy standing in the truck bed shoveling rubbish around to make it level, that he wouldn't accidentally rip the bag open and discover our ingratitude and deceit.

Years later this incident was discussed at a party where the group couldn't agree on the proper way to have handled it. I offered to seek professional advice on the matter and wrote a letter to Dorothy Dix who was at that time the counterpart of today's Miss Manners and Dear Abby. Neither did I receive a letter in reply nor did I find it mentioned in a Dorothy Dix column. Maybe she thought someone was pulling her leg (what-

When the county truck was *pau* hauling rubbish for the day, "Pig Slop Man" and other workers would be assigned to additional tasks. Here a crew becomes part of the road maintenance gang sweeping away cigarette butts, twist-tobacco cigar stubs, flattened dead *bufos* and fallen leaves.

ever that means) or more likely, after having wrestled with this perplexing question, she realized it was too difficult for any human to answer.

Pig Slop Man, Grandpa, Tootsie, Big Mice, Small Mice, Turk, Bunt, Jiggs, Chicken, Needlenose, Chunky, Lippy, Duke, Bucky, Wimpy, Butch, Mustache, Mormon, Sidelines, Bunny, Lefty, Slim, Fat and Shorty along with Dummy, Screwy, Honky, Punchy and Stinky were all terms of endearment at a time when a fondness for each other was a soothing force on this island.

When looking at the year 2000's Geniality Index for Kauai it seems something distressing must have been taking place over the past five or six decades.

I don't know as many Garden Islanders now as I did then. Today, if that group of old timers who have retained their bynames is set aside, the somber result is that except for "Happy Camper" I really don't know anybody on the island with a nice nickname.

Kauai today is only one notch above zero on the Geniality Index scale? What happened?

19

Land of No Addresses and The Mystery of the Missing Picture Bride

Try to imagine what it must have been like living in a community of 33,000 residents where no one's house had a number by the front door and if the streets had names, nobody knew them.

Because Kauai didn't have home delivery of mail until the 1950s, there really had been no need to go to the bother of numbering houses and putting up street signs. Most of the time, everybody's home address was a house described as being close to somebody else's house or near a prominent landmark.

Normally, an individual's home was identified by the name of the family living in it or the name of the owner if it was a recent rental. Nearly all businesses were on a main drag with a sign near their front doors so they were easy to find. Who really had to have a number?

It was just as mellow when it came to street names. Garden Islanders called the island's common roads according to where they happened to go. The main one circling the island from Mana to Haena simply was called the Belt Road or, sometimes, the County Road or the Government Road.

There were other important side streets, lanes, and assorted car paths referred to as the road to Kokee, to Menehune Ditch, to Hanapepe Valley, to Numila, to Kukuilono, to Hawaiian Fruit Packers (Lawai), to Koloa, to Poipu, to Puhi, to Nawiliwili, to Ahukini, to Wailua Homesteads, to Kapaa Homesteads, to Hawaiian Fruit Packers (Kapahi), and to Kealia. Also, each of the narrow one-lane side roads to a plantation camp plainly bore the name of the camp. Strangely, today's Rice Street was known as the road to Nawiliwili and today's road to Nawiliwili was High School Road.

If you were living on Kauai at that time, just how would you reply if someone asked, "I'll drop it off at your house. Where do you live?"

It wasn't easy. When my new family moved to Kauai in early 1948 we rented "The Horikawa House." The owner was the fellow who ran the dining room and kitchen at Lihue Hotel. Nearly everyone in Lihue knew where this dwelling was. Today it's 3156 Ekahi Street. Now, that's what you call easy to find.

But fifty years ago, for people planning to visit my family from other parts of the island, our address would be strung out with people's names until the prospective caller could recognize one of our neighbors.

Usually we started out with, "We live in the yellow house on the road behind Lihue Theater" and then added:

> "Across Dr. Yoshimura" — the eye doctor
> "Across Mike Ota" — the proprietor of Tip Top Café and Bakery
> "Next door Sam Peahu" — tour driver and popular musician
> "Next door Umemoto-san" — Circuit Court clerk
> "In front "Mac" Morinaka" — Garden Island Publishing linotype operator
> "Down from Jack Wada" — appliance sales and repair tradesman
> "Up from the Dias Family" — popular Hawaiian household
> "Halfway down the road across Dr. Wallis" — Lihue Plantation physician
> "Up from Ah Sau Ahana's place" — well-known musician and County employee
> "Half-way down from the Schumacher's" —District Highway Engineer

and so on until someone's name rang a bell.

With such a rigmarole, how in the world would anybody possibly address a Christmas card to your family?

That's where each town's postal clerk served the community well. He or she was the human conduit through which cards, letters and packages flowed in an orderly fashion to everyone's house.

On Boat Days, every Tuesday and Friday morning at about seven o'clock, U.S. Mail was the first freight to be off-loaded from the interisland steamer from Honolulu. A truck waiting at the Nawiliwili pier quickly delivered the precious cargo to the Lihue Post Office where it was sorted for transfer to the post offices scattered around the island.

Once the rural area mail had been sent on its way, the Lihue staff of two to three persons set out to sort through the enormous heap piled in the middle of their workroom. Some items were shoved into small, individual wall boxes rented by the few residents and businesses lucky enough to have acquired one. The remainder, the vast majority of correspondence and packages, then had to be alphabetized before the eleven o'clock lunch hour when people stopped by to pick up their mail.

Supervising the Lihue operation was Martin Drier, Kauai Postmaster during the '40s and '50s. No one was sure where he came from. Nobody asked. It wasn't important in those days. Because of his strong Polish-Yiddish accent, some people today think he must have come from some place like New Jersey after emigrating from Europe. Others speculated that he was perhaps a nephew or other relative of a Lihue sugar mill engineer named Drier, or of August Drier who, at one time, had operated a small sugar plantation near Kalaheo.

This not-very-tall, slightly-built public servant was here, married locally and was raising two lovely daughters, Mary and Hermine, and son Richard. The family's home was just down the road from the post office towards Nawiliwili in one of the dozen plantation-style cottages lining the Kapaa side of today's Rice Street.

During the hectic Boat Day lunch hour, while the

No Wonder They Decided to Put Up Street Signs and House Numbers

In the simpler days a half-century ago when Garden Islanders wanted their mail they had to travel to the nearest post office. Folks in Hanalei made this Federal Post Office Building their town center.

Gramma & Grampa's first home was this "Horikawa House" on the road behind Lihue Theater. Today it looks almost the same as it did in 1948 when this picture was taken. But, across the road from

the "Horikawa House" this neighboring grand mansion, belonging to the TipTop Cafe's owner Mitchell Ota, now has been replaced by the popular Tip Top Hotel and Restaurant.

The National Guard, in

1940, marches down "The Road to Nawiliwili" now named "Rice Street." At right is the same intersection in 2000.

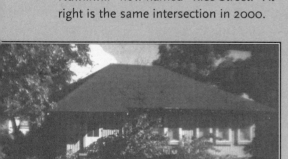

Behind the small grove of trees in the center of the left photo was the "Andy Gross House."

This Lihue Plantation supervisor's cottage, known as the "Andy Gross House," was Gramma and Grampa's second Kauai residence. This former home for our family of five has become today's ten-gas-pump Lihue Chevron Service.

Just a little way down the road towards Nawiliwili stood the Lihue Hotel (up to the 1940s). It expanded into Kauai Inn in the '50s with a spectacular view of Mount Haupu. Where once there was a sweeping hotel lawn there now is this new community of some 174 family residences called Lihue Court Townhomes.

No wonder the island now needs street signs and house numbers. They say, "You can't stop progress." And they tell us, "Progress is really good for people." GET REAL!!!

Lihue mail clerk was handing out letters and packages to persons standing at the counter, Martin was eyeing the next patrons walking towards the postoffice. His recollection of faces and names was amazing. By the time the approaching individuals reached the counter, the postmaster would have located the mail and put it in the clerk's hands before the addressees could speak their names. This knack of knowing everyone in the community by sight was true of all the island's longtime postal clerks.

His ability to figure out poorly addressed envelopes seemed uncanny. During my first month on Kauai in 1940 a letter from a close friend in San Francisco appeared in the Garden Island Publishing Company mailbox. It bore only two words: "Ashie / Lihue." This envelope had passed through the mainland postal service all the way to the proper addressee two thousand miles distant. About a month later another was delivered with just three words: "Smiley Mike / Lihue." No company name. No box number. No zip code. No Territory. They both probably would wind up in the dead letter office today.

"Special Delivery" mail cost a lot more and was intended to be delivered in person as soon as the item arrived at the final postal station. In Lihue it was set aside until after the noontime surge. Then, if the addressee had a telephone, he'd be asked to come pick it up—unless he didn't mind waiting until someone from the post office brought it by after work. If there was no phone, Martin and the clerk kept an eye out for a neighbor who'd be asked to drop it by on the way home. If all that failed, the clerk would hop on a bike or drive a car and set out looking for a house that had no address.

Whenever the clerk knew someone was sick or otherwise unable to get to the post office, the mail would go home with a friend or neighbor. Most likely this was not according to regulations but on Kauai it was the thoughtful thing to do.

Martin was a regular in the coffee klatch that gathered just about every workday morning at TipTop

Café for a nickel's worth of pastry, coffee and fiery debate over solutions to the world's problems. You could tell he was accepted by the elite Lihue businessmen because, just as they did, he had his own personalized shaving mug on the shelf of the barbershop next door.

Young boys getting haircuts dreamed about some day being so famous that they'd have a mug up there with dignitaries like Sheriff Willie Rice and his two brothers, rancher Charlie Rice and Judge Phillip Rice, newspaper editor Charlie Fern, Lihue Store manager Herman Grote, bank managers Frank Crawford and J.B. Corstorphine, auto dealer J.C. Plews, insurance broker Dwight Cunningham, and about a half-dozen other local notables. For Kauai, that row of shaving mugs was the equivalent of Hollywood's Walk of Fame.

The klatch members roared in unison one morning when "Red" Hessian, a neophyte *haole* businessman running for public office, walked into the café and announced his candidacy. Martin, as the only Jewish resident of Kauai, assured "Red" in his strong accent, "Don't vorry. I guarantee you'll make it. I control the entire Jewish wote for the whole island."

One of Martin Drier's favorite stories was about a plantation field worker who came to the postoffice window one day at *pau hana* with a small, open package and a rumpled mail order catalog. He kept asking the clerk, "Where da *wahine*? Where da *wahine*?" The clerk, not sure what the problem was, called Martin.

Using hand gestures and pidgin they eventually learned that the agitated man some months earlier had come across a catalog like those sent to rural customers by Sears Roebuck and Montgomery Ward. In it the bachelor had seen several sketches of women's torsos, each displaying a brassiere for sale. There were no heads in the drawings or anything below the waist. That did not matter to him. He liked what he saw and with the help of a friend he filled in the order form, bought a postal money order and sent away for his picture bride.

After hearing the solicitous explanation by the post office people, the disappointed intended-groom began to understand the reality of his situation. Not only was he brokenhearted but also distraught because he had paid out a large part of his meager earnings for something he wasn't going to receive. Feeling very sorry for the fellow, Martin bought the bra.

Then, as Martin Drier's story went, he wrapped the bra as a gift and gave it to his Hawaiian wife, Mariah,

The Wailua-Waipouli-Kapaa coastline has shown a tremendous change over the years. The hub of Kapaa town was Hawaiian Canneries and American Can Company surrounded by workers' camps along with some private cottages and an assortment of small businesses. Hawaiian Canneries was one of three on the island. Hawaiian Fruit Packers, known as the "Up Cannery," stood on a hill above Kapaa town. The Kauai Pineapple Company fields and cannery were in the Lawai valley near Kalaheo. American Can Company supplied containers for all three canneries. All four companies disappeared in the 1960s as the result of intense competition from pineapple grown in foreign countries.

Spread out below Kapaa's Sleeping Giant mountain are pineapple fields with a group of harvesting machines seen criss-crossing rows of ripe fruit. During canning season the sweet fragrance of fresh pineapple being processed sometimes was overpowering. *Pono* was the brand name of Hawaiian Canneries "fancy" pack and because of its high quality it appeared on the shelves of America's gourmet shops. Today the former cannery site is Pono Kai Resort that is part of a seemingly unending row of hotels, condos, restaurants, shopping malls and other tourism-related businesses.

An aerial view from the Kealia side of Kapaa shows the Kealia to Lihue sugar mill railroad track bordering the shoreline. The straight stretch of that Belt Road today is part of the exasperating Kapaa traffic bottleneck. In this fifty-year-old photo can you believe there are only five, count 'em, five cars traveling between Kealia and Kapaa town? And nobody is heading up towards Kawaihau.

for a wedding anniversary present. It didn't fit but she said she wanted to keep it as a treasure from "her wonderful, extravagant, romantic, lover husband." He then smiled, winked and said no more.

In November of 1950, the U.S. Postal Service offered to inaugurate home delivery in the town of Lihue. The Kauai Chamber of Commerce called an evening public meeting so folks could hear a Postal Service representative make the far-reaching proposal. A good crowd of businessmen and others attended to hear about all the benefits of home delivery.

The Postal spokesman explained that in order to have home delivery all streets would have to be named and given markers, all houses numbered, and every householder would have to provide a mailbox at the front of his property. At the end of the meeting a vote was taken. The only person who voted in favor of home delivery was the representative of the postal workers' union.

20

A Final Serving of
The Leftovers

For a young man raised in a neighborhood of paved streets and three-story flats that were standing side by side in one of America's biggest cities, the island of Kauai was an eye-opener. It wasn't only the majestic beauty of an unspoiled garden island that was so fascinating but also the unbelievable way of life led by the folks who lived here.

Some observations of what I saw as peculiar situations are recorded in letters sent in 1940 and '41 to my family back in San Francisco.

In 1940, the county jail at Wailua was known as "Montgomery Hotel," named after jailer Kalei Montgomery. The little two-story building on a small plot of land across from the county golf course was the temporary home of only 170 prisoners in all of 1939. Last year, in 1999, there were over 900 inmates. Although Kauai's population has less than doubled, the tiny lockup has grown to the current 9.5-acre correctional institution. In sixty years, the work of jailer Montgomery has mushroomed to a staff of sixty-three. Food cost per prisoner was 43¢ per day in '39. Now it's close to $4.00 a day.

During the day, in Jailer Montgomery's time, prisoners were allowed to sit on the bench outside the tiny lockup where they could wave *shakas* at friends driving by. No fence closed off the property. There are stories about convicts wandering off and not getting back to the jailhouse before the doors were locked at night.

They'd have to wait outside until morning or go home for the night.

One prisoner, very thin in stature, was able to squeeze between the iron bars, permitting him to burglarize nearby homes and businesses for a long period of time before being discovered.

In my letter of April 29, 1940, I wrote, ". . . The company has five cars that we can use anytime we want. Incidentally, the keys are always left in the car. Some homes have no locks on the doors. The door (at KTOH) from the outside studio to the main studio has no lock either. Everyone is trusted here. Sunday morning early we passed the county jail. Some of the prisoners were sitting by the side of the road. The other one was chasing chickens."

———————

My starting pay at KTOH was $80 a month. When I first arrived on Kauai, I stayed in a room above Jack Wada's appliance shop in Nawiliwili for five dollars per month. Charlie Fern talked Sheriff Willie Rice into letting me have a room at the sheriff's Lihue Hotel, also for five dollars a month. After a week at the hotel I wrote:

"May 7, 1940 . . . Living isn't so high here. So far, my laundry bill has been 35¢. All my white shirts were washed, along with three polo shirts, lots of underwear, stockings, and handkerchiefs.

"Mr. Fern couldn't swing the deal with the 'Bachelors' Club' (Lihue Plantation *luna* quarters). But, he did get me a big room with private bath (at Lihue Hotel) for a low price. And the food at the hotel is only a dollar a day (in the 'Rose Room' behind the kitchen) instead of the regular $2.50 (in the dining room). So I'm getting along swell."

". . . It may sound silly on the mainland but the men here wear orchids. There are some growing right outside the window here by my room. Right next to it are seven big bushes of gardenias. Boy does it smell pretty here at night. In the garden are some African tulips more than twenty feet high. I'm taking some pictures so I'll send them home."

———————

"September 8, 1940 . . . In almost two weeks, I'll have been away from home for five months, almost a half-year. It seems like only a week to me. In that time, the only clothes I've had to buy were my tuxedo ($23 tailor-made) and another slack suit costing me three dollars and a half. Didn't have to buy stockings or underwear or even have my shoes resoled. They'll still last for another year.

"I go to the show only about once or twice a month, so most of my money is spent buying Coca Cola to keep cool. My dentist's bill (to Dr. Justin Smith for a molar extraction) was ten dollars, and that's about all. Still the money goes and goes.

"The island is still the same, except that streetlights are being strung up, a sidewalk is being laid, and fire hydrants were just put in last Saturday. I don't know why the Supervisors wanted the hydrants. I've never seen a fire engine on the island, or even a volunteer fire department. Whenever a fire occurs, the people rush

It wasn't until World War Two that the County of Kauai established a proper fire department. Before that, fire emergencies usually were handled by the nearest plantation. Some community "fire trucks" were plantation fertilizer spray equipment taken off a job to fight a blaze. Lihue Plantation had a real fancy fire engine—a Packard sedan rebuilt in the Hanamaulu Shop to bring a tank of water and a hose to wherever it was needed.

out just to watch the place burn." (A County Fire Department was organized later during World War Two.)

———————

[After having spent one day in bed with a bad cold] "October 1, 1940 . . . This morning I got up at seven to eat breakfast at the hotel. My eyes were a little bit red and my nose stopped up so *Mama-san,* the wife of the cook, Jimmy Yoshioka, said she'd fix something for me . . . something like tea and ginger. In Japan it cures almost everything. When she brought in the drink she showed me part of a root she had cut up and put in the tea. I asked where she found it and she said outside someplace. It was just an ordinary root of a plant but it helped."

———————

"October 14, 1940 . . . On Friday a young guy from Oahu—pronounced O-Wahoo-yipee-hi-yo-ky-yay—paddled ninety miles on a surfboard from Kaena—Ka-ena—Point to the Lihue side of Kauai. He did it all in only thirty hours. When he arrived we broadcasted his story and he revealed that seven years ago, when he was on the mainland, he was told by specialists that he had an incurable case of tuberculosis. During the past seven years he has lived on the beaches, eating mostly fruit and vegetables, and in general doing nothing but letting nature cure him. Now he's probably one of the healthiest persons in Hawaii. Aside from being a beautiful land, this is a healthful Zion."

———————

County and Territorial elections held every two years consistently generated tremendous public interest. In 1940 the turnout of eligible voters was over 90%. Two years earlier 90% also had cast their votes. Participation still was high through the 1950s when from

89.1% to 91.7% of Kauai's registered voters showed up at the polls. (Today it's less than half that percentage.)

There was no question that for Garden Islanders the election campaign every two years was as much fun as the Annual County Fair which usually counted around 30,000 admissions. After my first encounter with the widespread enthusiasm for campaign rhetoric and music I wrote:

"October 31, 1940 . . . For the past month everybody on the island has been excited about the coming election. The other night we broadcasted the big campaign rally in Lihue where each politician brought along musicians and *hula* dancers to warm up the crowd before describing what a bum his opponent was and reciting his own list of promises.

"The music was loud and the *hula* rhythms very catchy. Many politicians joined in singing with some even dancing. Among the most popular was Jacob Maka from the Hanalei side of the island who wins lots of votes because he really is swell in electrifying the crowd when he sings 'Ka Wai o Na Molokama'—a song about the waterfall behind Hanalei town.

"Others, like Abraham Kaulukou, the County Attorney, get reelected because they know how to talk seriously about problems and can convince voters they know how to fix them. A few like Sheriff Willie Rice, who has been sheriff since 1900, and two brothers K.M. and K.C. Ahana, the County Auditor and County Clerk, just get reelected term after term as if they own the jobs.

"From time to time during the evening people in cars belonging to the opposition party drove by honking their horns so loud that the speakers couldn't be heard. They're either paying back for what was done to them at their own rally or paying in advance for the disruption they know is coming at their next one.

"It's swell to hear so many challengers tearing their opponents apart using pidgin English. The sentences come out of their mouths upside-down and sideways with pronunciations not found in any dictionary. I'll bet if Miss McGloin, my high school English teacher, heard this she'd throw an apoplectic fit."

"November 12, 1940 . . . Friday is a big holiday here in the Islands. It's the Philippine Commonwealth Day, celebrating the fifth birthday of the Commonwealth. Almost every Filipino has been brought to Hawaii by the plantation companies to work for two years as a laborer and very few are American citizens, so a day like Friday is better than a New Year celebration. Every plantation will close down, very few stores will remain open, and all day the station will be Filipino. Starting Wednesday night we're going to be busy with programs from all of the plantations' Filipino camps, so every minute will be taken up."

"January 15, 1941 . . . The circus has come to Kauai and I went to the first circus I've ever gone to in my whole life. Seems funny I have to travel two thousand miles from home before I see one.

"I'm sure this E.K. Fernandez Circus isn't as big as the P.T. Barnum one but it has a little bit of everything from animals and acrobats to zany clowns. There are some weird people in the side shows, plus a Ferris wheel and other exciting rides, games of skill where people throw money at a barker who lets them throw baseballs at a row of milk bottles or toss wooden rings over prizes—lots of food booths, and a tent with all kinds of entertainers including some Hootchie Kootchie girl dancers.

"One of the most popular performers is a fellow from Honolulu named 'Howdy' Reynolds with his puppet called 'G-Man Joe.' His act is like Edgar Bergen and Charlie McCarthy. The kids think it's swell because 'G-Man Joe' is sassy and talks back to 'Howdy' Reynolds. The kids on Kauai aren't allowed to get sassy with their parents or other older people so seeing someone else doing that gives them a big charge in the funny bone.

"I made friends with the Turkish belly dancer

who can wiggle and shake every inch of skin on her body. She's a nice lady who was raised in Los Angeles and has never been to Turkey. But she said she's been doing the belly dance ever since she learned how to walk and now she makes a good living at it. She talks like she dances—very fast and the words come bubbling out of her mouth. In my wildest imagination I never dreamed I would ever meet a belly dancer who knows more Bible verses than I do.

"The piano player makes me feel funny-kind inside. At first I thought he was a woman. When we first met he tried to kiss me like society people do when they greet each other. He also likes to put his arm around me if we're walking in the same direction. He's an excellent pianist and must be pretty lonely traveling all the time from place to place without making any good friends. Even though I feel sorry for him, whenever he's eating in the Rose Room I always check where he is and sit at another table.

"All the rest of the circus people are like our neighbors were in San Francisco—friendly and quiet. The performers all eat at the Lihue Hotel in the Rose Room in back—you'd call it the back house—and they've been very friendly. So, everything at the circus is free for me including hot dogs and pineapple juice."

———————

"January 31, 1941 . . . We are bound by the forty-hour a week law and Mr. Fern has often reminded me of it. He says that he is liable to prosecution for any violation. But no one can get him for breaking the law unless the employee complains and I don't want to bring any charges because I'm getting a college education from this extra work.

"Most of the extra work has to do with gathering and writing news. That way I get my geography, history, present world affairs, spelling, composition, and plenty of brain exercising. The few extra hours of work are well worth it. It doesn't give me much time to myself, working straight through from five-thirty in the morning until six-thirty at night, but it keeps me busy doing something good, and after all a farmer doesn't kick when he has to work all day, so why should I?

"I like to go to bed about nine o'clock. Monday nights we have a Japanese men's chorus. Tuesday nights the men build sailboats. Wednesday there is the *haole* men's glee club. Sometimes on Thursday night I help Lorraine Fountain train the Japanese (Christian Church) junior choir as it practices. Friday nights are the nights I usually go to bed early unless I'm playing music or the community is having a celebration of some kind. Saturday nights I have been working most of the time. And, Sunday nights I go to the show or sleep. All day Sunday is my day off so I sleep until nine, go to church and in the afternoon go to the beach. That's how I spend every day, with sometimes a few exceptions."

———

"March 17, 1941 . . . Last week I observed a good example of how successful radio advertising can be. I was in Don's Drug Store in Nawiliwili when the customer ahead of me said, 'I want a tube of Colgate. Give me the Ipana kind.' I thought everybody knows Colgate and Ipana are competing brands of toothpaste so I asked Don what that was all about.

"He said that for many, many years, Colgate had a super duper salesman who came to Kauai several times each year to take orders from merchants and set up displays in all the stores on the island.

"While here, he went around to all the elementary schools to teach children how to Colgate their teeth. He gave each kid a small Colgate toothbrush and a tiny tube of Colgate toothpaste. He then showed them how to Colgate up and down on their teeth as well as how to Colgate from side to side. He explained that if they Colgated every day, they wouldn't get cavities. They were urged to Colgate regularly so they wouldn't have to go to the dentist. Colgating, he assured them, made teeth stronger. Colgating made people beautiful. And so on. So, for years people haven't been brushing their teeth, they've been Colgating them twice a day. Now along comes KTOH with one of its advertisers being Ipana toothpaste and slowly people have been deciding to Colgate their teeth with Ipana, instead.

"Don also said Kauai people have been asking for Sal Hepatica, the powder that is mixed in water and cures all sorts of ailments. I'm sure all this is the result of our reading commercials on KTOH each day reminding listeners, 'Ipana for the smile of beauty—Sal Hepatica for the smile of health.'

"He said he has to listen to KTOH because customers sometimes can't remember the name of the product but they know the slogan or can sing part of the jingle. He said that he's had to order all kinds of new things like Vaseline Pomade that men want to make their hair shiny and sticky so it will lie flat on their heads. People want Eno salts to take after eating too many *laulaus*. Ladies are asking for Halo Shampoo because it 'glorifies your hair' or, as they say it, '*da kine* shampoo that makes it squeaky clean.' And there's been a rush to buy Carter's Little Liver Pills to cure all their backaches. I wonder if people ever will get tired of hearing so many commercials over and over again and decide not to turn on their radios."

———

"June 2, 1941 . . . I am still well except for my right arm which is all blistered. The Mokihana Serenaders who come down to the station every Saturday night often wear *mokihana* leis and when they're through they give me the leis because I like them so much.

"The *mokihana* is the flower lei of Kauai—this is the only island that grows these berries. I always knew that the green berries burned the skin, but two Saturdays ago I carried about six leis on my arm. It was so warm that I perspired and the acid juice from the berries went through my shirtsleeve into my arm and ate its way up past my elbow and down to my wrist.

Among the most popular Hawaiian music groups was the Mokihana Serenaders (from left) Harry Jim, Charlie Kaliloa, Aggie Waiau, Bill Kaliloa, Emmalani Jim and Miki Waiau. Besides hearing them Saturday nights on KTOH, you'd find them entertaining at *luau*, nightspots, fundraisers, political rallies as well as singing from atop flower bedecked floats during Kuhio Day and Kamehameha Day parades.

"It looks funny because the blisters are in straight lines across my arm just as if I had scratched it. Most of these blisters have popped and the skin is beginning to wear away. All of it has healed and there's no need to worry."

Early in 1941, I was happy to learn that one of my four sisters was planning a visit to Kauai. All my seven brothers and sisters had lots of experience in riding streetcars, busses and trains. But none had gone through the bafflement of being a passenger on an ocean liner.

Although I'm the youngest, I behaved as a nice older brother would by sending advice on how to conduct yourself while traveling from California to Hawaii on a Matson ocean liner in a $95 one-way second-class stateroom.

"February 7, 1941 . . . For the past few days I've been pumping all the people I know for information about traveling and staying in Honolulu. The Alexander Young Hotel is about the best hotel for location in town (Honolulu) and for price, too. That's the joint where I stayed when I came over.

"It's in the center of the town and by walking in the four directions from it you can cover the whole village. It doesn't compare at all with the Royal Hawaiian or the Moana, but it is the stopping place for all the travelers from the outside islands when they are in town. I don't exactly know the rates but they range from about two dollars up—and meals may be had either at the hotel or any of the million restaurants in town.

"Maybe I had better start at the beginning and tell you what might happen on your trip, and what you should do.

"When you first get on board the ship, the dining room steward will be at the head of the stairway sitting at a small table taking reservations for meals. In all probability, there'll be two calls for meals, a first and a second. Try the second . . . it's best. It's a good idea to get acquainted with your stateroom companions before you make your table reservations and in that way you'll have a much better time. There is no charge for a table reservation.

"At another small table the deck steward will be making reservations for deck chairs. You'll probably want one to do your knitting or reading. The charge for a chair is about a buck and a half.

"It's then up to you to find something to do while on board {before sailing time). Perhaps it would be best to explore the ship, to find out what kind of a place you're going to live in for the next week.

"During the days on board ship there is always something to do: deck games, horse racing in the lounge, moving pictures, gambling at sea, and sunshine, and, in the evening moonlight, stars and dancing.

"What will you wear? According to the Fountains who are steady travelers, slacks during the day and for breakfast and lunch meals. A sport suit is wonderful for evening wear, starting at dinnertime. But when you are with a gang of girls such as you meet on the liner, you can do what you want to do and wear what you want. The last night out dinner is formal; that is, unless the *wahines* at your table decide to do otherwise. It isn't necessary to go formal, although many do and many don't.

"Now for the tips. The personnel on board ship is paid a very high salary and appreciates a person who remembers their services with a small gift. Don't let it be too large because you'll need the money more than they do, and they know it.

"At the last dinner meal or the last breakfast leave two dollars for the waiter. He gives you the most service. If you use the bath, tip according to the number of times you bathe—from a dollar to two dollars. By the way, the bathing reservations are also made in advance. Try to get yours in the late afternoon. If you require much service from your room steward give him a dollar and a half when you leave your stateroom for the last time, otherwise a dollar is plenty.

"There is also a deck steward who will be paid according to service. If you spend much time on deck you'll become good friends with him and he'll be the nicest of the whole crew. He may not do much for you but because he's such a swell guy you'll leave him two dollars . . . just before you leave the boat.

"Then, if you ever are in need of a bag of peanuts, a candy bar, or seasick pills, the kid in the purser's office will go up to the first class drug counter to get the stuff for you. For this service give him the price of the article before he leaves and a dime when he comes back. He also is paid a high salary. Then altogether your tips will amount to six up to ten dollars.

"About a half hour or so after you have docked (in Honolulu), somewhere on the dock you will find your baggage segregated into groups according to the first letter of the last name. Yours, of course, will be under 'A.' If you have only one or two bags, call for them yourself and take them to the hotel with you. If you have more than you can handle alone, assign the extra bags to a gentleman from the City Transfer who'll contact you just before you leave the boat. Give him your name and where the bags are to be taken and pay him then.

"Will you write me by return mail if you want me to make reservations for you at the Alexander Young Hotel and for the (interisland boat) trip from Honolulu to Kauai. It's not necessary to make reservations in advance. The hotel is four stories high and a block long with millions of rooms. The (interisland) boat is never filled to capacity. If you want to be sure, I'll do it for you, though. I suppose (your friends) Inky and Joe will meet you at the boat so let them tell you what to do while you're spending the days.

"You'll arrive in town (Honolulu) on Wednesday morning about seven o'clock just in time to see the sun rise and listen to the Royal Hawaiian Band playing on the docks. Have a few extra handkerchiefs handy because the scene and music works on your eyes worse than a dozen peeled onions. Maybe you might drop a dime or a quarter to the Hawaiian boys diving around the liner. All day Wednesday and Thursday will be on the island of Oahu.

"The boat sails for Kauai from the Inter-Island Pier at 10:00 P.M., Thursday. Be there about nine-thirty to see the fun of a Hawaiian sailing. As soon as you arrive in Honolulu go to the hotel and then to the office of the Inter-Island at Fort and Merchant Streets for your ticket. After that you're on your own.

"When you arrive in Nawiliwili Bay on Friday morning, I'll be waiting at the pier and from then on you're on my own. You won't need much clothes on Kauai. You'll wear slacks more than anything else. A few blouses and a couple of skirts are enough. Lorraine (Fountain) said two formals are plenty. Why don't you bring that silver formal you have with all the flowers? You may not use both but it's better to be sure.

"I've sorta planned what you might do during the day, and it's up to you if you want to do it. I work during the day, on the air, from six to nine in the morning and from one-thirty to four in the afternoon, but there are some other jobs I must do. We can eat breakfast at the hotel at nine . . ."

And the rest of the letter has been lost.

21

Preparing for a War That Wasn't Supposed to Affect Hawaii

On September 1, 1939, I spent a memorable day at the World's Fair on Treasure Island in San Francisco Bay. It was unforgettable for two reasons. One was the magnificence of the International Exposition. The other was the impact of returning to the city on a ferryboat and seeing a swarm of newsboys at the Ferry Building hawking papers with banner headlines blaring "Nazis Invade Poland." Two days later Great Britain and France declared war on Germany.

From that day forward almost every newspaper front page carried descriptions of the battle in Europe as well as reports that Japan was forging its way through China on its way towards the Malay Peninsula. Radio newscasts anxiously were awaited by mainland Americans, many of whom believed it wouldn't be long before this nation would be drawn into fighting again on foreign soil.

Not so on Kauai. The island's only newspaper, *The Garden Island*, in early September stated its position that the weekly paper "is published on Tuesday but is not distributed on the island until Wednesday morning making the inclusion of war news in its issue only a duplication of the news that had already been released." The local paper suggested that Garden Islanders listen to the two Honolulu radio stations and the high-powered West Coast broadcasters whose reception often was clear at night.

While they weren't considered very newsworthy

on Kauai, the hostilities in Europe and the fighting in the Orient became very serious to mainlanders. I didn't take a survey but it was easy to perceive what was happening.

At that time I was working as a staff announcer for Northern California's only 24-hour broadcast station, KSAN. The term "disk jockey" hadn't been invented yet, but that was my task six nights a week from midnight to 8:00 in the morning. This gave me plenty of time to study for my daytime classes at junior college and read the newswire teletype machines as they printed stories of the growing struggles on the two continents.

Listenership to the all-night broadcast changed dramatically after that September 1939 event in Europe. In those days there wasn't much swing-shift work. Most radio stations shut down at 10:00 P.M. or 11:00 and a few remained on the air until midnight—hardly anyone was awake to listen.

Callers to me, after midnight, usually had been firemen waiting for the alarm bell to ring, police sergeants at their precinct desks, food preparers at the all-night Clinton Cafeterias, hookers waiting for a trick, taxi dispatchers answering calls, some nurses on night duty and garbage men getting ready for their early morning rubbish collection. In the big city just about everybody else slept.

Suddenly there was a dramatic increase in telephone calls from ordinary people who couldn't sleep. Usually they asked for a song that would bring them some pleasure. And in talking with them they often asked for the latest war information on the newswire teletypes. You could tell there was widespread, real concern over the possibility of another world war.

So, I was greatly surprised about six months later when I arrived on Kauai to work at KTOH and discovered the European war and Japan's incursion into China were subjects far from the minds of Garden Islanders. Very little recognition of these ominous events was being given by most folks living here on Kauai. There was no island radio station yet to broadcast the expansion of hostilities and *The Garden Island* weekly newspaper had been choosing not to cover national or international news stories. In many ways, I discovered Kauai to be an extremely isolated community.

By the time Kauai's first radio station, KTOH, went on the air in May of 1940, the wars in Europe and the Far East still had not yet become a common topic of conversation on the Garden Island. Honolulu's two daily newspapers, *The Advertiser* and *Star-Bulletin,* had almost no circulation here and reception from Oahu's two broadcast stations, KGU and KGMB, was limited in its coverage.

The general feeling on Kauai was that America possibly might get involved in some way but Hawaii was too remote ever to be seriously affected. Not many persons, if any, seemed to realize this was the early stage of a great world war that ultimately would directly encompass the lives of everyone on the Garden Island.

Beginning in the summer of 1940, the 33,000 residents of the island of Kauai somewhat half-heartedly joined in practicing the "fire drills" that would make them prepared for the explosive Sunday morning when they suddenly would be face to face with an armed enemy at their doorstep.

It was fourteen months before KTOH's inauguration, that British Prime Minister Neville Chamberlain, on March 10, 1939, had voiced his opinion that "prospects for peace are better than ever." Instead, just a week later, German troops march into Prague, Czechoslovakia, to establish a "protectorate" government for that nation. Within days the British, concerned about Hitler's tactics, take a bold step. Great Britain announces it will support Czechoslovakia's neighbor Poland against "any actions which threaten Polish independence."

At this moment on Kauai, the European battlecry isn't considered as important as the Territory's first income tax plan that places a tax of one-and-one-half percent on all salaries, wages and dividends. Citizens are told the main reason for beginning a direct income tax is that previous methods of taxation aren't raising enough funds for the increasing cost of government.

The world doesn't know that in May of 1939 Germany's Adolph Hitler and Italy's Benito Mussolini join in a "Pact of Steel" that commits them to act "side by side with united forces" for each country's security and maintenance of peace. They make a covenant to come to "the aid of the other should hostilities ever break out."

Germany's mid-March 1939 entry into Czechoslovakia is followed by the September 1 Nazi invasion of Poland. During the previous night, August 31, the Germans carry out a plan code-named "Canned Goods." Nazi storm troopers wearing Polish army uniforms attack a German radio station in Poland and leave behind corpses of German Jews from a concentration camp. These are the "Canned Goods" supposedly slaughtered by the Polish Army. The purpose is to give a basis for Hitler to illustrate Polish "provocative acts."

Two days after the Nazi invasion of Poland, the British Government declares war on Germany in fulfillment of its guarantee to protect Poland's independence. France immediately follows suit.

Almost without recognition on Kauai, another European war begins.

If you're living on the Garden Island, the big topic of discussion isn't President Franklin Roosevelt's declaration of US neutrality but concern over how to halt the increasing number of roller-skating casualties around the island. Roller-skating has become a maddening craze. Nawiliwili's Pier Two, the only large paved surface on the east side, swarms with jocks attempting to learn to stand up on wobbly wheels. Since skating became a fad, two legs have been broken, four arms fractured, and an uncounted number of sprained wrists and skinned knees.

On moonless nights the collisions among skaters on the pier is constant mayhem. In addition to banging into each other, even under a full moon, or just plain falling down and fracturing bones, novice skaters who have learned how to start out on skates but not how to stop, find themselves flying off the edge of the pier and into Nawiliwili Bay. After three beginners find themselves trying to tread water with heavy skates on their feet an emergency is declared. The County is considering a ban on roller-skating on the pier. Commercial rinks quickly go into construction in Waimea, Hanapepe, Nawiliwili and Kapaa. In Hanapepe, alone, there are three rinks; one of them installs an upper level allowing skaters to zip down to the ground floor. Roller-skating is Kauai's big worry—not a war between countries someplace far, far away.

During October and November of 1939, the Soviet Union takes steps to stave off any German attempts to move in Russia's direction by forcing "mutual defense" pacts on neighboring Estonia, Latvia and Lithuania. Then on the last day of November 1939, the Soviet Union, without a declaration of war, invades another neighbor, Finland.

In Asia, Japan is storming through China, fighting its way towards the Burma Road in an effort to stop Britain's shipment of arms to China. With Southeast Asia's French and Dutch colonies now in the hands of Germany, Japan sees the way opening for its possession of these coveted territories. As 1939 winds down, the threat of a Pacific war is drawing near.

There still is little concern on Kauai over these events in Europe and Asia. The major news story of January 1, 1940, is the total destruction by fire of Lindsay Faye's family home on the beach in Waimea. The Kekaha Plantation manager's house and the family's belongings are turned into ashes by the midnight inferno. Except for the clothes the family is wearing and two silver baby cups, the only possession remaining is a very large, brand-new kitchen stove. During the height of the blaze, neighbors join in tearing down a wall and dragging the oversized stove to a safe spot on the lawn. Everything else is gone.

That's the big news story—the fighting in Europe seems so far away. Local concern over the war is summarized in *The Garden Island* newspaper's New Year's editorial reading, "Enemies will never get near our islands but, just in case, we should begin to make some preparations."

And so a few of Kauai's community leaders begin to talk earnestly about the need for preparing for a war that most likely will not affect Hawaii very much. In the months that follow, as Germany, Italy and Japan, carry out bolder and bolder acts of aggression, the mood on Kauai begins to change.

Occasional news reports in the spring of 1940 tell of Germany and Russia making hostile moves against Norway and Denmark. Great Britain retaliates by sending naval forces into Norwegian waters to lay minefields in efforts to block ships trading with the Nazis. Finland's government capitulates to the Soviet Union.

There are no war clouds hovering over the Garden Island. Kauai plantations give all employees a day off to attend the April County Fair. Among the star attractions is "Howdy" Reynolds with "G-Man Joe." "Howdy" sells real estate on Oahu for a living. For fun he joins the circus with his wooden dummy, "G-Man Joe." The two of them make a circuit of Kauai's schools to promote attendance. A record 30,000 admissions are tallied.

To encourage residents to submit items for judging, the County Fair Committee announces, "The richest collection of prizes in fair history." All blue-ribbon winners for exhibits, hobby and skill competitions receive a prize of one dollar each, in cash. High point winners in each category are awarded ten dollars. The overall grand prize is a pair of authentic Chinese vases. This year's fair presents championship matchups for tennis, volleyball, track, girls basketball, amateur boxing, and the biggest crowd pleaser: sugarcane seed cutting.

Folks around Lihue, as well as elsewhere on the island, are preoccupied this spring with engagement parties and preparations being made for the grand wedding of young doctor Sam Wallis to Dora Rice.

No one seems to be paying much attention to news accounts that Germany is amassing two-and-a-half-million troops along its widespread western borders with Holland, Belgium, France and Switzerland.

Then on one single fateful day, May 10, 1940, the course of the lives of everyone on Kauai is altered by three major events. First, Hitler's armies break through the defense of France on one side and conquer neutral Belgium and Holland on the other. Second, Sir Winston Churchill, on that day, becomes Prime Minister of Great Britain in place of Neville Chamberlain, committing the British people to a difficult period of "blood, sweat and tears." And third, Kauai's first radio station, KTOH, on May 10 is inaugurated, opening up a whole new world of information and entertainment for Kauai residents.

Two weeks later on May 23 Garden Islanders are struggling to recover from the heaviest rainstorm ever to strike the island's east side. (As much as 25.43 inches of rain in one daylight period is recorded at one Lihue Plantation Camp.) This doesn't allow many thoughts to be focused on what's happening in Europe where all available boats in Britain are engaged in evacuating 340,000 British troops from Dunkirk. This is the last remaining port of escape for British Expeditionary Forces being routed from Europe by Hitler's tank units. Some 900 ferries, small coasters, fishing boats, tugs, pleasure yachts and naval drifters combine to serve as a lifeline for the withdrawal.

It is on this 23rd of May that Hitler impulsively orders his Panzer forces to stop chasing the enemy. No one knows why such a strange command is given. Postwar strategists believe the Germans lost the war on this day as more than a quarter of a million British troops are allowed to escape and return to the Continent again to fight the Nazis in future battles.

While Hitler is ordering his military leaders not to question his decision to allow the British to escape, Garden Islanders are busy preparing for their own island-wide major event. On that Thursday evening in May 1940 Kauai joins the rest of the Territory in conducting its first practice blackout in preparation for possible enemy air raids.

For weeks prior to the rehearsal, *The Garden Island* newspaper and KTOH carry detailed announcements. Forty-eight hours before the exercise, leaflets written in English, Japanese and Ilocano are dropped from aircraft flying over populated sections of the island.

As people wait that evening to experience frightening total darkness, the moment finally arrives. Sugar mill whistles and pineapple cannery sirens sound eerily for a long minute. All streetlights are blinked on and off before being shut down. In areas with no electricity, sheriff's deputies drive up and down side roads blowing automobile horns to sound the alarm. Cars are halted on roads. Telephone operators take only emergency calls. Boy Scouts and members of the American Legion carry out their duties patrolling roads and neighborhoods to make sure all lights are extinguished. For half an hour folks sit in quiet darkness wondering, "What if?" Ultimately, four aircraft, dropping flares around the perimeter of the island signal the "all clear."

During the next tense month of June 1940, Nazis enter Paris on the 14th and two weeks later France capitulates. Mussolini declares war on Russia and opens up warfare in the Mediterranean with air raids on British air bases on Malta. In the Balkans, the German army presses onward, invading Rumania. The Japanese move deeper into China.

In a rousing radio address Winston Churchill tells the world, "We shall not flag or fail. We shall fight in France. We shall fight on the seas and oceans . . . we shall defend our island, whatever the cost may be. We shall fight on the beaches . . . on the landing grounds . . . in the fields and in the streets . . . in the hills. We shall never surrender."

As Britons muster their strength and resolve, the Kauai Red Cross Chapter expands its activities. Chairman D.E. Baldwin of Makaweli Plantation urges volunteers to join in producing war relief items for use by the Red Cross in Europe.

A *Garden Island* editorial warns that America soon may be confronted by a German, Italian and Russian military block to which the Japanese now have linked themselves. Editor Charlie Fern cautions against "suspicion by hyper patriots tracking spies." There's beginning to be a concern about the loyalty of Kauai residents of Japanese ancestry. The editorial urges "everyone . . . keep his head." A common rhetorical question among many Garden Islanders is, "Suppose you were an American working in Japan and war broke out between Japan and the United States—where would your loyalty lie?"

During July 1940, this apprehension grows as Japanese military leaders place a pro-Axis Japanese government led by Prince Konoye in power. Local Japanese aliens, ages 14 and over, are troubled by an order from the US Government requiring them to appear at any of six Kauai Post Offices starting August 27. They are to be fingerprinted and registered as Japanese aliens. In one month a total of 11,784 comply—virtually all aliens on the island. This is the beginning of a distressing period for Garden Islanders of Japanese ancestry who increasingly are being looked upon with suspicion by some neighbors.

The Fourth of July arrives. Garden Islanders join in observing America's Independence Day with huge celebrations on the east and west sides of the island.

The Waimea Community Association sponsors a three-day celebration including dances, shows and a parade. The July 3rd show titled "The International Blitzkrieg Musicale," is followed by an "International Ball" featuring the Joyland Serenaders. Providing music for the next evening's "Independence Ball" is Al's Troubadours. The final night begins with a lantern parade with participants from all the communities between Pakala and Mana and winds up with the "Popular Ball," with music by Billy's Snappy Pickers.

Eastsiders gather at Wailua Park for a one-day celebration sponsored by the Kauai Post of the American Legion. After a flag raising ceremony and patriotic speeches in the morning, a program of fourteen horse races begins. Fifty cents is the adult admission. Kids pay 10¢. Three Oahu horses are shipped to Kauai including the famed Koa, belonging to Manuel Freitas. Greatest interest for folks betting on the side centers on two races pitting Koa, from Oahu, against Kauai's J.B. Fernandes' horse, Kaneohe. The crowd's favorite competition is the

Kauai Derby for Kauai thoroughbreds only. Biggest spectacle of the day is the exciting Cowboy Relay with teams of *paniolo* and their horses from the island's cattle ranches.

The Japanese merchant marine training ship, Taisei Maru, docks at Port Allen on August 16, 1940, for a weeklong visit. For five days, officers and midshipmen are hosted at lavish celebrations and are taken on tours of the island. On the sixth day the public is invited to inspect the vessel but *haoles* are stopped at the gangway where a ship's officer insists, "No foreigners." Some residents fear the ship's crew is on a sightseeing spy mission and concern over the loyalty of the island's Japanese grows deeper and deeper.

In Europe, during August 1940, Hitler orders stepped-up attacks on any ships engaged in traffic with Great Britain. This is directed towards the United States. He also issues an order to his Luftwaffe to begin bombing Great Britain in order "to destroy the enemy air force as soon as possible." A Nazi invasion of England by sea is planned under "Operation Sea Lion." Massive nightly air attacks are lodged against airfields, radar stations and supply centers in Southeast England.

The initial British defense resists far beyond Hitler's calculations. During one of the early nighttime battles, the Luftwaffe loses 75 bombers while the British loss is 34 fighters. It was this stalwart defense that inspired Churchill's commendation, "Never in the field of human conflict was so much owed by so many to so few."

However, by the end of August Royal Air Force losses are twice as great as for the Luftwaffe. Nazi Field Marshal Hermann Goering advises Hitler that total destruction of Britain's fighter strength and installations in the southeast now is imminent.

Nazi air strikes then turn to daylight hours. The "Blitz" of London goes into full-scale operation. In early September 1940 over 1,000 German aircraft are assigned to hitting the vital docks and central parts of the city. Germany's war records show the British air defense is so tough that Hitler decides to withdraw all

Nazi shipping that had been readied for the invasion and the planned "Operation Sea Lion" attack is postponed until the spring of 1941.

At about the same time, in North Africa, on September 13, 1940, Italy embarks on a new offensive with an invasion of Egypt from Libya, pushing back British forces that have been guarding Egypt and the Suez Canal.

A few days later, in Washington, the Selective Service Act is passed by Congress and Uncle Sam says, "I want you!" to males 21 through 35 years of age who are ordered to register for the Draft. Kauai County Clerk James Burgess' office handles the documentation. On Kauai, a total of 9,196 show up at school registration sites around the island. The Act provides that a committee of members of the community will select draftees for military service for up to twelve months. (The twelve-month limitation is removed in August 1941.) A.H. "Hib" Case, Grove Farm Plantation's financial officer, accepts responsibility for setting up draft boards for the east and west sides of the island.

As usual every year, Kauai's National Guard joins with the Territory's other Guard units for annual training. This year they head for Maui amid rumors that the men will return only to pack up and shove off again— this time for full-time active duty with the Army.

In a major effort to give moral support to British and French troops, Red Cross volunteer knitters busy island-wide all summer send to Honolulu 135 completed items including 60 pairs of sox, 25 mufflers and 50 sweaters.

An ominous development at the end of September 1940 is Japan's formally joining in a "Tripartite Pact" with Germany and Italy. This agreement guarantees Japan will oppose any new country that decides to join the European Allies. This is aimed directly at America.

Most Garden Island residents have no daily paper to follow events in Europe or Asia. The weekly *Garden Island* is covering only local events except for publisher Charlie Fern's editorials. Just a handful of people are relying on costly, late arriving Honolulu papers and national publications such as *Time Magazine*.

As the number of home radios begins to increase, more and more islanders begin listening to the news on the two Honolulu radio stations at those times when their reception is good. The popular KTOH noontime and evening newscasts combine important world events with local stories.

The KTOH five-minute evening world news is received in Morse code by short wave and translated into readable English by Frank Westlake and Herman Loebel at the wireless station on Hanamaulu's Mount Kalepa. It's just a short summary. To this brief report is added news scoops from Lihue's J.C. Plews, an avid short-wave listener, who often calls in to KTOH with breaking news of significant world events. In-depth reports are scarce. Kauaians, never having had a steady flow of off-island information in the past, are just beginning to develop a taste for far away matters.

One of the greatest concerns doesn't seem to be the armed conflict in Europe and Asia or whether Hawaii may become a war zone but, more important, how will first and second generation Japanese on Kauai be treated if Japan and the U.S. become warring enemies.

To help diffuse what he sees as an explosive situation, Charlie Fern in an October 1, 1940, editorial writes, "*The Garden Island* feels that one reason there has been so much loose talk on disloyalty is that the younger generation have been too passive about the matter. We feel that instead of accepting without comment all the various charges made against them, they should take an aggressive stand, and make some of their attackers prove some of their statements."

He continues, "No effort is made to challenge the statements of jingoist Americans who see in every young Japanese a recruit for the Nippon's army. No leading members of the second generation have ever come forward and stated in an outright manner that all the suspicion voiced so loosely can only aggravate the situation.

"On the matter of dual citizenship, no leader

among the second generation has ever pointed out the explanation as to why such a high percentage of his generation were enrolled at the Japanese consulate by their parents.

"The explanation is simple. When the first generation came to the islands, they had no intention of making their home here. They intended to stay only long enough to make some money and return to their homeland. Under the circumstances, they cannot be blamed for the registration of their children with the Japanese consulate. Many an American parent has taken the same step while living abroad.

"While this question is being considered, no second generation parent has ever brought out the fact that exceptionally few, if any, of the third generation are being registered (with the Consulate of Japan). If the second-generation parent thinks so much of his Japanese citizenship, as so many loose-tongued persons have charged, then he would, without doubt, take pains that his child has the same privilege. The absence of any registration of the third generation is one of the best answers to the disloyalty charges."

Then in October, earlier rumors about the National Guard become true as all Kauai officers and enlisted men, active and inactive, are mobilized for full-time active duty. Assembling at hastily constructed campgrounds near the Lihue Armory and County Building, the troops leave on the 22nd for Schofield Barracks on Oahu.

On October 14, a few days after my 19th birthday, a letter is written to my family thanking them for cards and gifts. One portion describes the atmosphere on Kauai as viewed by this naive youth who doesn't understand why there is such a broad mistrust of many of his good friends and neighbors whose mothers and fathers are as American as are his own immigrant parents.

I wrote, "Dear Ma and Pa . . . The National Guard has mobilized and is now parking in the Civic Center in Lihue until it leaves for Honolulu next Tuesday.

"It's just like war around here now. Most of the fellows in town now are in the National Guard and all wear uniforms wherever they go. All during the day and through all the night sentries pace around the town square carrying guns on their shoulders, keeping a lookout for Japanese fifth columnists. Big army trucks drive from the camp to the pier carrying all sorts of supplies for our new army.

"Everybody here expects the (island) Japanese to start some kind of trouble. Very few Japanese people on Kauai are American citizens. The few that are, are all dual citizens . . . a believer in the home government and the American government, but nobody knows what they'll do if a war starts. That's why everybody is getting prepared by looking for good places for concentration camps and other wartime measures . . . Your loving son, Mike"

Note this letter is written fourteen months before the attack on Pearl Harbor.

Meanwhile, in Europe during November the German air offensive continues at a heavy pace, entirely concentrated on night bombing of London and other big cities as well as seaports and industrial centers.

Early in the month, Russia's Foreign Minister Vyacheslav Molotov travels to Berlin to discuss a German suggestion that Russia join the Axis partners. Molotov isn't aware that Hitler has a clandestine blueprint called "Directive #21—the Barbarosa Plan." This scheme lays out strategy for "the Russian Army to be destroyed by daring operations led by deeply penetrating armored spearheads." The Nazis expect to conquer Russia in a series of quick thrusts to take place before the invasion of Britain. Molotov, unaware of Germany's plan to attack Russia, carries Hitler's devious proposal for joining the Axis back to the Kremlin.

On Kauai, the first step is taken in November 1940, to develop an Army air base at Barking Sands. The War Department authorizes construction of housing for 750 men. This is to include barracks, a mess hall and warehouses along with power and water necessary to maintain the new installation. In addition, authorization is given to plan construction of new quarters "as rapidly as possible" for housing an additional 450 men at Burns Field in Hanapepe.

Red Cross knitting volunteers ship another batch of sweaters, sox and mufflers—650 garments to date.

The anxiously awaited Draft lottery begins on November 12, 1940. Kauai's quota for induction in December is 71 young men. On the first day of the lottery when numbers are randomly drawn in Honolulu, eighteen Kauai families learn that a member soon will have to begin being processed for army service.

A large number of Kauai's AJAs, Americans of Japanese Ancestry, are looking for a way to demonstrate their undivided loyalty to America. They join in seeking a quicker way to give up their dual citizenship. Charles Ishii, for east Kauai, and Kazuma Matsumura, for the west side, become co-chairmen for a drive to obtain 3,000 signatures for a petition to the U.S. State Department and Japanese Consulate. Kauai's AJA complain that it seems almost impossible to expatriate from Japanese citizenship. The official procedure, they assert, is too complicated, too cumbersome and too slow, with required paperwork often taking more than a year to complete.

December 1940 arrives. It's now just one year before the attack on Pearl Harbor. On the 10th of December the 71 Kauai recruits leave for army service. Although there are more than 9,000 Kauai registrants to choose from in last November's Draft Lottery list, three Kauai families face the uneven odds of having to say goodbye to two sons each. The sets of brothers are Albert and George Sunada of Hanalei, Walter and Albert Christian of Kapaa, and Koichi and Juichi Takemoto of Lihue.

The year ends with another Red Cross shipment of 205 knitted garments. During 1940 more than 500 volunteers completed 1,040 items of clothing and over 14,000 surgical dressings.

Kauaians greet the New Year of 1941 with increased speculation about the future. Just about everyone is wondering if the war in Europe will directly

In the months prior to the war and during the war years it was in the Kauai Draft Board office that draftees and volunteers were inducted into military service.

involve America and some are beginning to believe United States forces soon will be on their way to Europe. War with Japan becomes a great concern.

A January *Garden Island* editorial reads, "President Roosevelt threw down the gauntlet to the Axis powers in his message to Congress yesterday. There was no question as to what was in his mind when he said that America would not be intimidated by the dictators or influenced by their opinions regarding the aid to nations attacked by aggressors . . . There was plenty for Japan to worry about as the President's message stated significantly that America would aid nations suffering from aggression and this automatically placed China in the category of nations that would be aided."

The militant U.S. position adds fuel to Japan's concern about the security of its position in the Far East. Admiral Isoruku Yamamoto, Commander of Japan's combined fleet, urges military leaders to consider a new strategy for making a surprise military attack on the United States. In the past, aircraft carriers have been used exclusively as a protective force for battleships and other major warships. He proposes a carrier-borne air attack as the opening strike of war. He is ordered to have his staff develop plans for this new and as yet unproven tactic.

On January 10, 1941, Germany and Russia sign a non-aggression treaty. It's the result of Molotov's visit with Hitler in November. Russia doesn't realize the peace agreement is a ploy and soon will be violated by the Nazis.

When Mussolini learns of the pact, he visits Hitler to complain about border difficulties with Russia. The Italian dictator is pacified when he's told of the highly secret "Barbarosa Plan." A week later this clandestine plan is approved by Hitler and by the end of spring, German troops will begin pouring across the Russian border in violation of the treaty.

Kauai's American Legion Post meeting early in January 1941 declares it favors the organization of a Home Guard or Special Police Force to guard utilities, private property, and public property such as waterworks and communications. Three weeks later the proposal is supported by the Kauai Sugar Planters Association and Sheriff William Rice. It's pointed out the force will not be used against any labor disputes. All Japanese and Filipino residents are encouraged to join. They don't have to be citizens. Application blanks for service as Special Police are made available in dozens of locations around the island.

Later in January, a group of Garden Islanders meets to organize a chapter of "The Committee to Defend America by Aiding its Allies." The association's national slogan is, "America can keep out of this war if Great Britain wins." The Committee is engaged in raising funds for humanitarian service in Great Britain—for the relief of the civilian population affected by the war.

In Washington, Congress gives President Franklin Roosevelt authority to lend or lease war materiel to countries believed to be important to America's defense. Called the "Lend-Lease Act," it provides for regular shipments to Britain of ships, arms, tanks, planes and other war goods. The President's intention is to assist Great Britain in winning the war without direct American intervention.

The issue of loyalty comes into focus at the adolescent level as Bernice Hundley, Supervising Principal of Kauai's schools, reports on her visitation to Haena School with a group of off-island Territorial School Commissioners. While chatting with students one commissioner, Dr. Arthur Dean, asks how many are Hawaiian. Most of the children raise their hands. He then asks how many are Chinese, Japanese, Filipino and *haole*. The other students, group by group, lift their hands. He then asks, "How many of you are Americans?" And all raise their hands. When questioned about this, one little boy answers, "Oh, those are our fathers' countries. We are all Americans."

This is followed by another *Garden Island* editorial declaring it's the important duty of civilians to build up trust among all Americans and to stamp out rumors about fellow Americans just because they happen to be of a "certain racial descent."

By February 1941, community leaders are ready to take additional measures in preparation for a possible but unlikely war emergency. While very few residents expect Hawaii to become directly involved, there's concern over any possible interruption of food and other supplies. The Kauai Sugar Planters Association agrees to set aside 1,000 acres for growing basic food crops. Recommended for planting are sweet potatoes, lima beans, pigeon peas, Chinese cabbage, string beans and carrots. Homeowners are urged to make sure their avocado, banana, breadfruit, papaya and citrus trees receive the finest care.

Hitler signs another non-aggression pact in early March 1941. This time it's Rumania. The agreement allows Nazi troops to move through Rumania to establish positions on the border of Greece towards which British troops are advancing.

A crew of Federal Communications Commission engineers arrives on Kauai in March to install a monitoring station in the Lihue Armory. Its mission is to conduct a 24-hour watch to intercept communications from the Orient and to track down any subversive activities by concealed radio transmitters on this island.

In a letter written to my family on March 17, 1941, I describe how uneasy people seem to be as preparations for an unlikely war are stepped up. I wrote, "Dear Ma and Pa . . . From the way the islands are being 'defensed' it really begins to look as if something is expected to happen. I don't remember if I wrote home about the telephone exchange in Lihue being rebuilt to safeguard against sabotage. Thick iron bars have been put in all the windows and an iron gate has been put in front of the door. The Lihue telephone exchange has the only direct communication with other islands (other than the wireless station above Hanamaulu). If it were stopped and if KTOH were put out of order it would be impossible to get word off the island for hours. Boats come to Kauai only twice a week.

"There hasn't been such a hurried improvement in road building in the history of Kauai. A wide, paved road was finished in three months from the airport near Hanapepe to Mana, nearly twenty miles away, where the Army is planning to send seven hundred and fifty men. The road in front of the station going to the port of Ahukini is being widened and paved, too. Ahukini is the closest port to Pearl Harbor on Oahu. Maybe all the improvements are because of a progressive board of supervisors or maybe because they're needed to transport military equipment.

"About two weeks ago we had a city-wide fire drill. All the fire hydrants were turned on at the same time to see how the pressure would be if the city were to catch fire . . . maybe from a bomb attack. Two additional FBI agents have been transferred to Kauai to guard against espionage. Four men from Washington arrived here last Friday to set up a listening station in Lihue to intercept all messages crossing the Pacific to the Orient.

"When the Japanese began to fight in Zamboanga against the Filipinos, the Filipinos on Kauai, the same night, began to start fights with Japanese. Three weeks ago a Japanese field worker bitterly said what he thought his country could do to the Philippine Islands. Two Filipinos jumped from a cane machine and practically butchered him with cane knives. Maybe that's why the Territory is calling for volunteers for a home police force of thousands of men.

"Anyway everything doesn't look good. People

are beginning to say it's just like before the First World War . . . Your loving son, Mike"

When that letter is written, the bombing of Pearl Harbor still is nine months in the future and just about all Garden Islanders continue to believe any expansion of the war in Europe or Asia certainly cannot affect Hawaii directly.

However, Army and Territorial officials continue preparing for the gravest eventuality. An act of the Territorial Legislature requires each government employee to take a loyalty oath. Territory-wide, 200 do not sign the document. Four are on Kauai. Most of these failures are oversights by the individual.

An early March edition of *The Garden Island* publishes the translation of a farewell speech by an unidentified Garden Islander who is returning to Japan to bring his ailing wife back to Hawaii.

He tells his friends who are gathered to bid him aloha, "At first I came to Hawaii with the intention of going back to Japan after staying here for about three years during which time I meant to make a fortune. However, fortunately or unfortunately, no such fortune could be amassed in such short time and in the meantime I built my home here and began a family life. And now Hawaii has become my second native land and I intend to stay here permanently as I am immensely enjoying living here.

"To our deep concern and dismay, the relationship between Japan and the United States has recently been strained. We are putting our sole trust in the efforts of the government officials of the two countries to maintain peace and amicable relationship.

"I firmly believe that it is our duty as parents of the second generation who are American citizens, to encourage them to become good and loyal citizens of America. I also believe that we should be grateful to America for letting us live for thirty or forty years, which is three fourths of one's life, here in blessed Hawaii which is unequalled anywhere else in the world in every respect.

"So, it should be our resolve, first, to help make

our children good and faithful citizens of the United States and, second, to make this our last home and to trust in the protection of the American government.

"Should the worst come to worst, we should resign ourselves to fate and devote ourselves to the welfare of our offspring. At the time of the last great earthquake of Tokio (sp), several thousands of people, who had found their refuge in a certain armory in Tokio, were all burned to death. While searching in the debris, they found a corpse of a woman with her body covering up a child who was still miraculously alive. The mother's love is sacred and sacrificial. We must show the same sort of love toward our children.

"Because of my plan to visit Japan shortly, some have asked me, 'Are you going back to Japan for good?' This is my unhesitating reply to all such questions. 'Why should I go away from this place where I have all my friends? Where else can I find a better place to live?' My real intention of returning to Japan is to bring back my wife who went back to Japan last August on account of her ill health.

"Recently some write from Japan, urging us to return on account of the strained relation between Japan and America. This is to be expected because our relatives are greatly worried about our welfare. But they do not understand our real situation. We have built our homes here and our children are all American citizens and we simply can not and will not move. While in Japan I shall avail myself of all opportunities to make the people in Japan see our point of view.

"The foregoing is a statement of my belief and I wish to make it my parting words. I wish to express my sincere thanks and appreciation to all of you for giving me this splendid farewell party."

Because the speaker in March 1941 was not identified there's no way to learn whether he was able to return to Kauai before December 7.

On Monday, March 10, more than a thousand volunteers pack the Lihue School auditorium to be trained as members of the Kauai Provisional Police. In the first of five Monday night sessions, Lt. Eugene

Kennedy of the Honolulu Police Department describes how legal arrests are made, how much force can be used in making arrests, how and when to use firearms, and how to testify after making an arrest. Under the leadership of Sheriff Rice, the group is told its responsibility is to guard waterworks, power plants, harbors, roads, private property and plantations. The National Guard is a military combat force, not used for police work. "Your job is to protect your own homes and the plantations so that you can continue to earn a livelihood in case of an emergency."

Also in March, at the same time that Nazi General Erwin Rommel pushes his Panzer forces across Africa, Kauai residents join in a community sendoff for the second contingent of 69 draftees from the island.

Because last December's two-hour evening program didn't allow enough time for families to bid their aloha, this parting on March 28 is extended to eight hours, beginning at 1:00 P.M. Groups from all sides of the island, including the Young Buddhist Association and Portuguese Welfare Association, say their good-byes for what is supposed to be a year of military service. Many parents and others wonder whether it'll be just a year for their young men, will it be longer, or will some never return?

The Kauai High School Band is featured along with a Kekaha Young People's Club skit produced by musician, magician and dance bandleader Charlie Kaneyama. "Slim" Holt's Kauai Terminal Polynesians add Hawaiian music to the sendoff. In spite of the attempt to entertain the families, it's not a happy gathering.

A week after the draftees leave, in an early April service, the Buddhist priest of the Kapaia Hongwanji Mission reminds his congregation of the "obligations Japanese parents owe America." He declares their sons now are being sent off to repay a portion of those obligations with military service to America.

The months of April and May 1941 are extremely active both in Europe and Asia as well as on the home front. Japan signs a neutrality pact with Russia. This

From time to time groups of draftees and volunteers assembled in military formation prior to shipping out for processing at Schofield Barracks on Oahu.

frees Japanese forces from its northern border with Russia to march southward to bolster Nippon's expansionist operations in China and Southeast Asia. Germany invades Greece and then Yugoslavia. (KTOH listeners learn this long before others in Hawaii because Jack Plews, Garden Island Motors manager who is dedicated to short-wave radio, calls the station with the latest breaking news stories.) In response to the military moves in Europe, the United States agrees to take Greenland under its protection.

A Kauai Women's Volunteer Motor Corps is organized. Sue Sloggett, wife of Wailua rancher Dick Sloggett, is given the responsibility to see that a team of women becomes qualified for transportation services in the event of an emergency. They're to receive standard Red Cross First Aid training for 20 hours plus an additional ten hours of advanced instruction. Each volunteer must have a car and driver's license, must pass a Red Cross driver's qualification test, must pass a physical exam, be between 18 and 45 years of age and not heavier than 160 pounds. In addition, each one must complete a twelve-hour motor mechanic training course.

In another crucial activity, the Red Cross assigns its surgical dressing instructor, Thelma Akana, to conduct training in all towns on the island. More women volunteers are recruited to roll bandages to meet Kauai's quota of 60,000 surgical dressings. America's total commitment is 40 million.

Construction begins in April 1941 on a new military airfield at Barking Sands. A hundred members of Company I of the National Guard's 299th Infantry commence building an initial five barracks. An increased total of 1,000 men are expected to be housed at Mana for training of bomber pilots and crews. The project is under the command of Kauai's Lt. Francis M.F. Ching, (who later becomes Mayor of Kauai).

Towards the end of the month, 225 members of two additional National Guard companies arrive at Nawiliwili. One, Company M made up of former east Kauai residents, is billeted at Burns Field in Hanapepe. The other, Company C from Paia, Maui, sets up camp at the Wailua Race Track. Another 400 Guardsmen are expected in June—all of this underscoring Kauai's preparations for a war most people still believe is only a remote possibility.

Another marvelous two-day county fair begins on April 18 with ventriloquist "Howdy" Reynolds and his wooden dummy "G-Man Joe" as the star attractions. More Inter-Island Steam Navigation Co. steamers are added and schedules altered to allow neighbor islanders to spend a full weekend at the fair. The plantations declare Saturday to be a holiday.

Each day thousands of fairgoers enjoy band concerts and sporting events including tennis, *sipa,* and the finals for women's softball. Judging takes place for the best *lei, holoku,* vegetables, orchids and other flowers, food specialties, arts and crafts. For the first time, livestock is being judged. Commercial exhibits and food displays attract throngs of onlookers. A contest is held seeking the island's champion sugarcane seed cutter. Churches and community organizations set up food stalls and games of skill for sharpshooters, greased pole climbers and horseshoe players.

A month later, on May 20, Garden Islanders join in another blackout rehearsal with the theme, "Practice makes perfect." A few changes have been made to last year's drill. Among them: headlights on emergency vehicles are covered with blue cellophane. Boy Scouts and American Legionnaires, patrolling plantation camps and rural areas, also dim their flashlights with blue wrapping.

The third Sunday in May 1941 is celebrated nationwide as "I am an American Day." Special services are held on Saturday and Sunday at the Waimea Community Hall, Lihue YBA Hall, and churches around the island. New citizens of Japanese ancestry are honored at Buddhist missions with special programs featuring addresses on the subject of responsibilities of American citizens by Judge Carrick H. Buck and Grove Farm Plantation Manager William P. Alexander, Commander of Kauai's American Legion Post.

Over four hundred people attend a special West Kauai Lions' program in Waimea for sixty-five new American citizens. The principal speaker, Judge Buck, tells those assembled, "The work of keeping America strong and free is at our hands . . . If a greater test comes, America, the land of free men, bound together by American ideals, can meet and conquer anything that may threaten us, our land, or our way of life."

The American Legion, in a move to provide wholesome entertainment for the large number of men in uniform, hosts a dance at Waimea High School's gym. Girls must register in advance for tickets to attend and must agree to rules of conduct, including "formal dress." This causes a big flap. The Legion hastily explains, "formal dresses need not be expensive gowns. Cotton frocks are as good as silk ones. Nice dresses beget good behavior. High standards are needed so mothers of nice girls will allow their daughters to attend."

Only men in uniform are admitted to the gym. GIs are asked to send names of sisters and sweethearts to the Legion for inclusion in the invitation list. The first dance with Charlie Kaneyama's Merrie Melodiers is such a great hit that each of the three companies on Kauai decides to take turns hosting a monthly affair. Money is to be taken from Company funds. The next dance is set for Isenberg Gym in Lihue featuring music by the Rapozo Brothers' Reliance Orchestra.

Hitler's "Barbarosa Plan" is put into effect June 22 as three massive columns of tanks and troops push across the Russian frontier toward Stalingrad, Moscow and Kiev.

At about the same time, Kauai's third contingent of 26 draftees leaves for Schofield Barracks following another stirring community sendoff. A week later another 168 young men who have reached age 21 during the past year register for possible military service.

Food becomes a popular topic. Lihue Store opens its new frozen and chilled meat and produce extension billed with the slogan, "The largest retail market in the Territory—for the first time on Kauai garden fresh mainland frozen vegetables and fruit are available." Across the road, the Tip Top Bakery announces it will begin producing "a new type of bread called vitamin bread" so that "school children now will have nutritious white bread with their school lunches." And, not to be outdone, the Kauai Modern Bakery in Kalaheo reveals it is bringing in a machine that "will actually slice a loaf of bread before it leaves the store."

Along with these innovative food developments, the island's Emergency Food Committee completes its work on plans to feed 35,000 people. Basing its proposal on research by the University of Hawaii and recommendations by the Army and Navy, the committee suggests a daily allowance of 2634 calories. Rations will be based on food crops that can be grown in Hawaii. Every household is asked to plant banana shoots and papaya seeds immediately.

July 1941 begins with several public appearances by Lt. Col. Eugene FitzGerald, commander of troops on Kauai. In speaking with members of the local Japanese-language press and with community groups as well as in a radio address over KTOH, he stresses the fact that the army has no plans to round up enemy aliens in the event war breaks out. "Enemy alien residents will be given the opportunity to live normal lives, as long as they respect that opportunity." All Garden Islanders are urged to "keep life as normal as possible."

As part of the west side's annual three-day

Independence Day celebration, the biggest parade ever seen on the west side takes place. Beginning at Waimea River Park on July 4, marchers pass through Waimea Town to a reviewing stand at the high school. Bands from the Salvation Army and Kekaha Sugar Plantation lead Army units of the 299th Infantry and its mechanized section along with Boy Scouts, Girl Scouts, and members of the Civilian Conservation Corps. For the first time, Garden Islanders witness their own National Guardsmen and Draftees pass in parade in full uniform, pausing to give demonstrations with machine guns, bayonets and hand grenades.

There's also a large turnout for the Fourth of July patriotic and racing programs at the east side's Wailua track sponsored by the island's American Legion Post. Seven events feature horses from Kauai and other islands along with competition between plantations, challenges among rambunctious *luna*, and the daredevil final race: a free-for-all with no holds barred.

On the 7th of July, U.S. Naval transports are dispatched to Iceland with American troops who are to relieve British forces needed in Europe. It brings this country one more step closer to the warfare on the Continent.

On Kauai, as anxiety over questions of loyalty looms greater, Kekaha community leaders initiate a project to seek a means to assure peace in case of a wartime emergency. Committees are formed to educate all ethnic groups regarding their rights and responsibilities as aliens or citizens living in the United States.

A July community meeting of residents of Japanese ancestry is called by T. Takanishi, president of the Kekaha Community Association and Kekaha Plantation Manager Lindsey Faye. The Reverend Tsuruzo Hasegawa, Principal of Kekaha Japanese School, speaking to first generation Japanese, says the prospect of a war with Japan now is facing them and they must prepare for any eventuality.

He points out that military authorities have assured everyone that there will be no concentration camps as long as they are not needed. With the American government offering this protection and privilege, he cautioned, it should be the aim of every Japanese to see that the privilege should never be cancelled. Rev. Hasegawa, outlining the long friendship between Japan and America, said it's to be regretted that this friendship might be ended.

The *Garden Island* reporter covering the occasion continues: "There may be among them (first generation Japanese) persons who felt their national spirit was such that they must do something for Japan, Mr. Hasegawa said. Any person who felt that spirit should consider well before he acted, not what the effect would be on him but what it would be on his friends and neighbors. A man might feel willing to die to strike a blow for his country, but his death would be of little benefit to those who were left behind him to face the consequences.

"The Japanese, he said, will be placed in a difficult position. It would be a simple matter to arouse antagonism among the other residents of Kauai against the Japanese. Therefore, each Japanese should take it upon himself to see that he and his family did everything possible to prevent any causes for the outbreaks of antagonism.

"He asked his audience how many among them would take advantage of an offer of the Japanese government to evacuate Hawaii, if it were offered. Not one person in the audience responded. Mr. Hasegawa used this fact to point out that it was evident that all regarded Hawaii as their home no matter what their ties were with Japan. If they felt that Hawaii was their home, it was only right that they do everything possible to keep it a fitting and proper place to live.

"In closing, Mr. Hasegawa urged his audience to go home with the resolution that if any trouble did come on this island the responsibility for it could never be traced back to any Japanese home in Kekaha."

Week by week the tension over loyalty increases. There's a growing opinion that America may find itself engaged in another world war in which Japan will be an enemy. Yet, there still is wide belief that whatever happens, Hawaii is too remote to be affected other than seeing its young men entering military service and the islands experiencing short-term shipping delays.

Then on the 24th of July 1941 several things happen that, if fully understood, would alert Garden Islanders to recognize all their preparations for war probably no longer are for "just in case." That day, Japan takes over the administration of French-Indo China. A year earlier, when German forces invaded France, Belgium and Holland, Japan made an offer to the new French puppet government to implement a "protective occupation" by Japan of the French-Indo China region. The French Government was in no position to resist.

That "protective action" now is taken as Japan sees its oil supplies dwindling. Virtually all of Japan's oil supplies are imported. It's vitally important for Japan to have oil from Java and Sumatra delivered without delay. By extending her control southward, Japan also will gain access to four-fifths of the world's rubber output and two-thirds of the world's supply of tin.

A bold response is given by President Roosevelt who immediately demands Japan withdraw from Indo China. When Japan refuses, the President freezes all Japanese assets in the United States and places an embargo on oil being shipped to Japan. Then Great Britain and the Dutch Government in Exile also agree to cut off all oil supplies. This places Japan in the position of being trapped in a corner. She either has to give up her grand plans for her Greater East Asia Co-Prosperity Sphere or take a stand to fight for her life.

Another step in the Orient towards confrontation comes early in August. America pledges to defend the Philippine Islands in the event of any attack by a foreign power. General Douglas MacArthur, Chief of Staff under Roosevelt and former military advisor to the Philippine Government, is recalled to active duty. He becomes Commanding General in the Far East.

On Kauai in August 1941, Charlie Fern is appointed Coordinator for Disaster Relief and preparations begin moving at an accelerated pace. He quickly organizes a Major Disaster Council to develop plans for administering divisions relating to law and order, transportation, communications, food, medical, and other vital emergency programs.

Eight Hawaii businessmen, representing commerce and industry of the islands, offer to underwrite three months of start-up costs of the Council. Funds to initiate a civilian defense program are provided by executives of American Factors, C. Brewer & Company, Castle & Cooke, Alexander & Baldwin, Theo. H. Davies, Bishop Bank, Bank of Hawaii, and Hawaiian Sugar Planters Association. Within the next month, committees are formed and urgent action begins in laying plans to meet all possible emergencies.

A Medical Division of the Major Disaster Council develops a training plan under which ten crisis medical units are formed to serve Kilauea, Kealia, Kapaa, Koloa, Port Allen, Makaweli, Waimea, Kekaha and two locations in Lihue. Each medical team of ten volunteers will include two doctors and two nurses along with nurses' aids, litter bearers and clerks.

A decision is made at the Territorial level for the Red Cross to teach first aid at all high schools in Hawaii, to prepare students for assisting in giving urgent care. Kauai High is the first school in the Territory to teach Red Cross First Aid.

The Disaster Council's Transportation Division begins a count of all trucks on the island that could be used in an emergency.

In the fearful atmosphere of their loyalty being questioned, first generation Japanese are warned about a scam being operated by a team of con artists. One member of the conniving group approaches an Issei (first generation) and offers to telegraph a free personal message to his or her family in Japan. The local resident signs a blank paper over which the message is supposed to be written later. Instead, the added text actually declares the individual "would be loyal to Japan and willing to assist Japanese spies." A second team member then calls on the person, pretends to be from "U.S. Intelligence" and asks for $1,000 to "fix" the mistake.

During the summer of 1941, Germany is launch-

In high schools and in all communities around the island Red Cross first aid training went in to high gear—just in case.

ing submarines at the rate of twenty per month. Operating in "Wolf Packs," the submarines seek convoys during daylight hours. When one is located, it is shadowed until the members of the pack converge. At a signal, they all join in a nighttime attack.

It is now September 1941. The United States increases its support of Great Britain by giving fifty over-age destroyers for use primarily in destroying German submarines in the Atlantic. In return, America is granted ninety-nine year leases on sites for naval and air bases in Newfoundland, Bermuda and the Caribbean.

Hitler has reached the point where he is willing to risk war with America by ordering the sinking of all ships carrying cargoes to Great Britain. On September 4, an attack is made on the U.S. Navy destroyer *Greer* off Iceland. President Roosevelt describes the attack as "unprovoked" and "deliberate" and warns, "From now on if German or Italian vessels of war enter these waters, they do so at their own peril."

In the next month, on October 16, another U.S. destroyer, the USS *Kearney*, is torpedoed and heavily damaged.

Then on October 31 the destroyer USS *Rueben James*, escorting a convoy, is torpedoed about 600 miles west of Ireland, sinking within five minutes with the loss of 115 members of the crew.

The next day the American merchant ship *Steel Seafarer* is sunk in the Red Sea. Hitler realizes such attacks could provoke the United States to enter the war. Germany confirms its attack on the *Greer*. The President's command for U.S. naval vessels to "shoot on sight" is widely considered as the establishment of an undeclared war between America and Germany in the North Atlantic.

September sees the beginning of an intense campaign on Kauai to collect aluminum to be shipped to the mainland for use in the defense program. Volunteers from YMCA clubs, Scout troops, Japanese language schools and the Salvation Army pick up the essential material. Kauai's share of the 11 million-pound goal for America is 3,575 pounds.

Two months before the attack on Pearl Harbor, in an October editorial, Charlie Fern echoes the opinion of Territorial and military leaders. He advises Garden Islanders, "the chances of any actual war in the Pacific in reaching these shores is remote. Yet, Hawaii must be prepared for the most remote contingency."

Recognizing the real possibility of war, the Territorial Legislature passes and Governor Joseph Poindexter signs the "M-Day Bill"—Mobilization Day—the day the nation finally mobilizes for actual war. It outlines the many actions to be taken throughout the islands in the event war is declared.

A second group of women's motorcar volunteers begins training. In Kapaa new air raid sirens are installed and tested—their drawn-out, wailing cries causing some anxiety among apprehensive east side residents.

At an island-wide PTA meeting, it's decided to encourage students to buy defense stamps, urge their families to develop home gardens, and practice food conservation. PTA members agree to assist in a survey of all homes that would be available for housing evacuees from Oahu.

Later, in mid-October 1941, an Australian convoy travels across the Pacific and through the Panama Canal on its way to England. While crossing the Atlantic it's attacked by Nazi submarines. U.S. Navy destroyers based in Iceland rushing to the scene suddenly become targets of U-boats. The American destroyer *Kearney* is torpedoed and eleven sailors killed. Germany denies it is responsible for sinking the *Kearney*, saying the act was committed by a U.S. sub to stir up patriotic fervor among Americans.

On that same day, October 16, Japan's Prince Konoye's government is replaced by a group of military leaders under General Hideki Tojo.

Another *Garden Island* newspaper editorial observes, "An active general as head of the Japanese cabinet has brought the possibility of war closer and pushed the possibility of peace much further away."

In another October editorial Charlie Fern writes,

"Japan will strike next when and where it suits the army leaders, and that will be when there is a minimum risk for Japan. However, there is one situation that may qualify that statement. If the Anglo-American-Dutch blockade is having an effect on the Japanese economy and war effort, that many believe, then Japan in desperation may strike in any direction."

It is now just one month before the attack on Pearl Harbor. When November begins, Japan's military leaders gather to discuss a standby plan to attack the United States if America doesn't relax the oil embargo. Japan's oil stocks have declined twenty-five percent in the last six months. One serious consideration by Japan is what will be the Russian reaction in the event Japan attacks the U.S. With Russia hard pressed by Germany in Europe, Japan believes the Russians would be unable to do battle with Japan in the Far East.

Admiral Yamamoto, commander of the Japanese combined fleet, continues to urge a surprise strike to paralyze the U.S. Navy in the Pacific. He describes America as "a dagger pointed at the throat of Japan." On his suggested date of Sunday, December 7, he points out there will be no moon, U.S. Navy ships normally will have returned to port for the weekend, and the warships will not be fully manned.

The precisely laid-out battle plan is reviewed and ultimately approved.

Meanwhile, as General Tojo sends special envoy Saburo Kurusu to Washington on a mission of peace with America, Japan takes the first major step in the attack on Pearl Harbor. On November 19, a submarine force stealthily begins a three-week journey to Pearl Harbor from Japan with five midget submarines in tow. Japanese carriers are standing by in the Kurile Islands awaiting orders to sail for an assault on Hawaii. Admiral Yamamoto is given orders to cancel the Pearl Harbor attack if negotiations are successful in Washington.

Completely unaware of approaching enemy forces, residents of Kauai serenely continue with a "we won't need it, but just in case" scenario. More and more people are beginning to believe war is on the way and are concerned about how it will affect their lives. But there's no feeling of great urgency.

The National Youth Administration begins hospital attendant training on Kauai in November. Twenty-six girls between the ages of 17 and 24 are being taught to take over manual and non-professional medical duties. To be eligible for the course the girls, nicknamed "Canaries," must have completed eighth grade and be unemployed. They'll receive room and board during their nine-months of training.

An island-wide housing survey is conducted in November to determine space available in case Oahu is evacuated. Kauai homeowners and renters are asked to contact friends and relatives in Honolulu to offer emergency shelter. The Council says it will try to assign evacuees according to ages and nationalities to assure a "congenial" relationship.

The Kauai Education Association, meeting at the Lihue School auditorium in mid-November, cites three important measures which must be taken: preparedness among all teachers and students; mutual trust of all races; and, reporting of any subversive activities. Students and parents are praised for their excellent response to the call for buying War Bonds. During the three-month period from August 1 to November 1, $178,663 of War Bonds and $5,959 of War Stamps are purchased from post offices and banks—a grand total reaching nearly $185,000.

Three weeks before the bombing of Pearl Harbor, Kauai's Japanese community, Portuguese Welfare Association and American Legion join in giving a huge send-off to a fourth induction of 33 draftees—unaware of how close they are to the long and perilous march ahead of them.

In another November editorial, Charlie Fern forewarns, "The next few days will determine whether or not there is to be an increase in tension in the Pacific, and possible war with Japan. The Japanese government protests that it desires peace with the United States and in the next breath makes statements that show that the course of Japanese foreign policy is plotted to cross directly with the interests of the United States.

"... There is every possible chance of war with Japan. However, under ordinary circumstances this should cause no more concern on Kauai than it would in San Francisco. There are many who believe that as soon as war is declared, all Hawaii will be placed on a war basis with a war economy functioning and the Territorial M-Day bill going into immediate effect.

"Fortunately for Hawaii this is not true. If war is declared with Japan, it will not cause any immediate change in the normal flow of life on this island. The sugar and pineapple plantations will continue to function as usual, and county government will control the government functions as well.

"Any war with Japan will naturally be a naval war, and if there is any fighting it will be far away from these islands. Kauai cannot expect any form of wartime control, unless Japan finds herself in a position to make an attack or at least a threat of an attack on the islands. As this must mean the destruction of the American fleet and the Hawaiian air force it can be seen that the chances are rather remote.

"Japan could never make any attack on the islands until these two objectives have been accomplished. Even if the American fleet were lost, as it is practically impossible for a carrier based air force to destroy a land-based air force, it can be seen that the chances of the war ever being brought home to Kauai will be a million to one bet.

"This should bring home to the average Kauai resident that if war does come there is no reason to get excited. The people (ethnic groups) of Kauai have succeeded in getting along with each other for a number of years, and they should be able to continue to do so. War will, of course, mean a change in our lives and way of living but war should mean no more to Kauai than to Fresno, California. Both will be very remote from the actual conflict."

These thoughts are expressed just eighteen days before the attack on Pearl Harbor.

This "It can't happen here" sentiment reflects the thinking of most civilian, government and military officials in Hawaii. On November 24, Washington notifies its major commands around the world, "chances of a favorable outcome of negotiations with Japan are very doubtful. A surprise aggressive movement in any direction, including an attack on the Philippines or Guam, is possible."

Three days later the War Department sends another urgent message advising war in the Far East could start at any moment. The November 27 communication warns: "This dispatch is to be considered a war warning. Negotiations with Japan looking for stabilization of conditions in the Pacific have ceased." The nation's intelligence sources predict it probably will be in Burma, Thailand, Philippines or possibly Borneo. The War Department directive concludes with: "Execute appropriate defensive deployment."

All major commands around the world go on full war alert except for Hawaii where no imminent threat is seen. Here the military sees possible sabotage by Japanese living in Hawaii as the greatest threat.

Eleven days before the attack on Pearl Harbor U.S. Secretary of State Cordell Hull, on November 26, tells Japan that the United States desires peace and is willing to give full economic cooperation in return for Japan's withdrawal from China and severing its military alliance with Germany and Italy.

On that same day, weighing anchor in Tankan Bay in the Kurile Islands, the Japanese Navy's main task force begins its journey to conduct its grave mission—a merciless sneak attack on the United States.

While negotiations over the embargo continue in Washington, Japan continues taking each step in its timetable for the attack on Hawaii.

People on Kauai are looking forward eagerly to the first weekend in December. The biggest events are to be two appearances by the Honolulu Interscholastic Champion St. Louis College (high school) football team. The Saturday game at Isenberg Field will pit a local All-Army team against the visiting Oahu Saints with their star, future All-American halfback, Herman Wedemeyer. At halftime, the Women's Volunteer Motor Corps in full uniform is scheduled to exhibit skills in driving army trucks and ambulances, carrying litters and giving first aid. A record crowd also is expected on Sunday when the Honolulu team takes on a squad of Kauai All-Stars in Waimea.

Young people of Kauai eagerly anticipate the arrival of the E.K. Fernandez Circus scheduled to start on Wednesday, the 10th. For more than a month publicity has built up excitement for the arrival of trained animals, carnival rides, side shows, minstrel and girlie shows, along with a broad assortment of booths for food and games of skill sponsored by the island's many community associations and churches. Hundreds of hours of preparation have gone into getting ready for the event to be held in the Lihue Plantation lot near the armory. The circus' advance contingent is on the island to set up tents, booths and rides for the spectacular ten-day event sponsored by the American Legion.

Elsewhere on the island, December 7 junior basketball games are expected to draw good-size turnouts at Kilauea and Hanapepe. Island Christian churches plan early morning worship services celebrating the second Sunday of Advent. The St. Johns Church in Eleele gets ready for its choir and organ concert. Many social events are planned including the wedding of Kauai veterinarian Dr. Bill Parker and Rachel Rankin from the mainland.

Inter-Island Steam Navigation Company announces a revised schedule for the SS *Waialeale*. Beginning on December 6, the steamer will leave Kauai on Saturday nights rather than Friday evenings. This change in schedule will bring the vessel into Honolulu harbor Sunday morning just as Japanese bombers are flying overhead toward nearby Pearl Harbor.

While Kauai continues the week in its normal routine, in Tokyo on December 2 the Japanese Cabinet decides it is being forced into war. Steaming slowly midway across the Pacific, Admiral Yamamoto receives the message, "Climb Mount Nikata"—the coded signal confirming the assault is to be carried out as scheduled.

The attack vessels that have been on a course well north of normal shipping lanes are refueled despite heavy seas. Their speed is doubled from 13 knots to 25 knots. No consideration is being given to a December 6 personal appeal by President Roosevelt to Emperor Hirohito asking that both nations work together to seek peace.

From a rendezvous about 200 miles due north of Kauai on Sunday morning, December 7, 360 Rising Sun aircraft take off and set a course for their targets.

In the meantime, the destroyer USS *Ward* reports it has sunk a midget submarine off Oahu. The Army radar station on north Oahu sees an incoming flight of aircraft approaching Hawaii. Neither report is considered anything to cause alarm. At the Honolulu office of Western Union, an urgent warning message from Washington to the Hawaii military command is waiting for a bicycle messenger to make a delivery. The warning message doesn't arrive at military headquarters until after the attack has begun.

Bombing begins at 7:55 A.M. and continues as scheduled until 8:25. A second wave is launched at 8:40. The initial assault drops torpedoes designed with special fins to guide them accurately in shallow water. Then, an offensive begins with armor piercing shells being dropped as bombs. A total of 3,435 Americans are killed or wounded, including forty-seven civilians killed.

Seven battleships are moored in Pearl Harbor and one is in dry-dock. Four of them are sunk, one beached and the others damaged. Two destroyers are lost and three cruisers damaged. Fortunately, the Navy's three carriers, *Enterprise, Saratoga* and *Lexington,* are at sea.

In a matter of a few hours Japan has gained control of the entire Pacific region.

That cataclysmic moment for which Garden Islanders have been training during the past two years unexpectedly arrives. The direct involvement that "can't happen here because Hawaii is too remote" has surprised the people of Kauai as well as military leaders on

Oahu and all the brilliant sources of intelligence in the nation's capitol.

Charlie Fern is having breakfast at home when he receives the call from Colonel FitzGerald. Immediately, he notifies KTOH to begin making announcements that Pearl Harbor is under an intense enemy attack and everyone should stand by for further reports and instructions. Mike Fern is told by his father to contact every KTOH employee, driving to their homes if necessary, to summon them to the radio station. It's urgent that instructions be translated into Japanese, Ilocano, Visayan and Tagalog.

The news travels like gossip. Families on their way to church debate whether to continue to the Sunday service or go home or drive to the nearest gas station. The lines of cars at Lihue's Garden Island Motors station near the theater and Seki Brothers Service at the town's main intersection stretch out of sight.

The heads of civilian defense divisions, who already have drawn up their wartime instructions for the public, gather to begin printing them for distribution.

At 10:30 Governor Poindexter declares martial law. The M-Day Bill goes into effect. There's no hysteria or panic on Kauai.

Military orders are issued essentially limiting all personal freedoms and activities. The Governor authorizes Charlie Fern, as coordinator of the island's Major Disaster Council, to take control of civilian defense, placing him in authority over all civilian government agencies. Lt. Col. Eugene FitzGerald serves as the military's Commanding Officer and Provost Marshall for Kauai.

KTOH is designated as intelligence center for Kauai. Radio announcements summon all personnel on the island who are enlisted in civilian defense to report to their duty stations. This includes provisional police, air raid wardens, communication center personnel and all other volunteers. K.O. Soong, commander of the American Legion organization, sets up listening posts at strategic locations. All sports activities are cancelled and no public gatherings are being allowed.

No one knows whether Japan's strategy is to take over all of Hawaii. The fear is more air raids, including direct attacks on the island of Kauai, and possibly a barbarous invasion by land.

In a little more than an hour after martial law is declared, Kauai's civilian defense program is completely on the alert. The pieces of a well-rehearsed civilian defense agenda have fallen into place.

The ten island-wide medical stations are manned. An order is issued by Civil Defense Coordinator Charlie Fern to limit the sale of gasoline to no more than five gallons per car and that sales are to be made only to the gas station's regular customers.

The Kauai Motor Corps women, who barely had time to launder their uniforms after yesterday's performance at the football game, rush to the Lihue civilian defense center where the contingent goes on 24-hour duty running errands and servicing emergency calls.

All morning long, Garden Islanders stay close to their radios to see if the Japanese carry out further air raids on other islands or whether an invasion by land is reported. Not knowing what's happening elsewhere in Hawaii is nerve wracking. Many wonder whether Kauai, as the Territory's northernmost sizeable island, will be the target of the next enemy attack—a strategic step for staging an all-out offensive on Oahu.

At eleven o'clock comes the first official word of the air strike: a communiqué from the Army's commander in Hawaii, Lt. Gen. Walter Short:

"Today the Hawaiian Islands were attacked by Japanese airplanes; although a state of war exists, the civilian population has reacted in a calm and satisfactory manner.

"The Army demands the aid and assistance of every person in Hawaii. If you are ordered by the military personnel to carry out a certain order or commission, that order must be obeyed instantly and without question.

"Avoid the appearance of hostility either by word or action.

"Certain enemy agents have been apprehended and detained.

"Civilians who go about their regular duties have nothing to fear; all citizens are warned to watch their actions carefully.

"Any infraction of military rules or regulations will bring swift and harsh reprisals.

"(Enemy) Prisoners when captured will be turned over to the nearest military patrol, the nearest military guardhouse, or the nearest police patrol or police station. Information regarding suspicious persons should be telephoned to the military or police authorities.

"Complete blackout throughout the Territory will go into effect at nightfall. Anyone violating the Blackout by showing a light will be summarily dealt with.

"All civilian traffic except for the direst emergency will cease at dark.

"In this emergency, I assure you that the armed forces are adequately dealing with the situation.

"Each and everyone can best serve his country by giving wholehearted cooperation to the military and civilian government.

"Further instructions regarding civilians will be issued as the need arises. Keep your head and do your part."

Immediately, an order is broadcast on KTOH to clear roads of all unnecessary civilian traffic so that military forces can be deployed in the event of an enemy land attack. All unnecessary phone calls are to cease immediately.

Colonel FitzGerald, now in the position of military commander of Kauai District, issues a list of Martial Law Orders that are broadcast repeatedly by KTOH. They include:

- All civilians who possess firearms are instructed to turn them over with ammunition to their area provisional police coordinator.

- Any information regarding planes or enemy movements, no matter how meager, should be reported to the military district headquarters.

- No games or other meetings are to be held which will attract large assemblies.

- Church services may be held as usual during daylight hours.

- Theaters are to open for matinees only.

- Public schools will function as usual until further notice.

- All Japanese language schools on Kauai are to close until further notice.

- All Shinto temple property will be confiscated and placed in the hands of a custodian.

- No Japanese films are to be shown in theaters.

- Keep your garden hose attached to the nearest faucet; keep buckets handy; have a pile of sand on your lot; clean your attic, garage and closets of papers and other easily burned articles; keep your gasoline and kerosene outside the house in a can painted red.

- The Territorial courts (district courts and circuit courts) will cease to function in all criminal cases until further notice. All offenses will be dealt with by martial law.

- Remove flags, pennants or other markings from buildings, which may attract attention to the building.

- All civilian traffic shall cease at blackout time.

- Keep traffic clear on highways. Any person stopping his car in the middle of the road will be arrested. Draw to the side of the road if you are stopping. Owners of cars parked on the road during the blackout are subject to court martial.

- When driving on highways or roads, draw to the side of the road when a horn is sounded by another passing vehicle.

- No parking of cars in groups. Scatter them or park them under trees.

- It is the duty of every civilian to assist the fire wardens in case of a fire.

• Don't spread rumors about spies. The FBI has the situation well under control. Report your suspicions to the district military commander. Any person caught spreading false rumors will be subject to court martial.

• Obey the laws and you will keep out of trouble and best assist your country win this war.

With repeated warnings to "Keep calm—Keep the peace," KTOH explains the blackout rules, which are to be strictly enforced every day from nightfall to daybreak until further notice. Violations will be dealt with under martial law.

• Get your house ready for the blackout before dark.

• Remain blacked out all night until full daylight. Be particularly careful about lights when you get up in the morning.

• Headlights are to be painted black with a 2½ inch circle of blue slightly below the center.

• Taillights are to be covered with blue. Drivers must have the lights on while passing on the road. The idea of covering is not to provide light for the driver to see by.

• Cover your flashlight with blue if you are to use it out of doors.

• You may use lights inside your house providing you carry out these precautions: cover the light with blue; hang blankets or black paper over all windows, doors, openings or cracks.

• Be careful about opening and shutting an outside door through which the light will show.

• After covering all doors and openings turn on the light, walk around your house and inspect it from all angles to see that no light shows.

• Blackout wardens are on duty in all districts. It is their duty to watch for lights and see that the lights are put out.

With the approach of New Year ceremonies by Chinese and Japanese Garden Islanders, an order is issued prohibiting lighted candles on graves, except during daylight hours. From the FBI list of questionable individuals, 41 Japanese aliens are detained at the Wailua County Jail.

Listeners are asked to write down the name of their nearest blackout and fire wardens who are to be notified if any lights or fires are seen. The district blackout chiefs are Pakala, John Costa; Kekaha, H.V. Rath; Waimea, Alan Faye; Makaweli, P. Baldwin; Port Allen, A.J. Drothzen; Eleele, W.A. McCoy; Kauai Pine Field, Masato Inouye; Kauai Pine Cannery, Thorpe Douglas; Omao, Edward Medeiros; Koloa, J. Kondo; Kipu, Charles Ishii; Puhi, John Klussmann; Lihue, James Langley; Hawaiian Canneries, A. White; Kealia, Neil Moler; Anahola and Moloaa, Les Miller; Kilauea, Antone Perreira & K. Harada; and, Hanalei, Walter Sanborn. (That Sunday evening one resident who allows a light to be seen is arrested and taken to jail.)

To assist automobile drivers during blackout hours, Territorial Highway Engineer Fred Schumacher, is directed to immediately begin painting a white stripe down the center of all main roads. Work gangs, hustling from dawn to dusk paint an endless stripe from Kokee to Hanalei as well as along the Lawai loop through Koloa. Stripes also are laid on the road from Puhi through Nawiliwili and the road to Ahukini. Schumacher's crew finishes the job in one week, striping sixteen miles a day.

For months, instructions on what to do in case of an air raid warning had been published in *The Garden Island,* broadcast over KTOH, and discussed in community gatherings island-wide. But now that the moment of concern has arrived, all listeners attentively, some nervously, concentrate on the repeated advice from Col. FitzGerald:

- The air raid warning signal will be one long and one short blast sounded by your mill whistle or by siren.

- The all clear signal will be two long blasts.

On the day Pearl Harbor was bombed, all residents were instructed: "Trenches for air raid shelters should be dug everywhere. Make them narrow and deep."

- Trenches for air raid shelters should be dug everywhere. Make them narrow and deep.
- When the air raid warning is sounded, get out of the house and lie quietly in trenches or shallow pits either in your back yard or in a ditch in the field.
- If you are driving a car, get off the road immediately, get out of the car and lie flat in the field or clear area.
- Keep away from crowds.
- While walking in groups, in case of air raids, scatter and lie flat in the field or ditches near at hand.
- Keep your children under control. Know where they are at all times.
- The following are Kauai's air raid wardens who can be contacted through the district communication centers:

    Waimea District, Alan Faye;
    Hanapepe, Rev. Masao Yamada;
    Eleele, A.J. Drothzen;
    Koloa District, Herman Brandt;
    Lihue District, Hal McKeever; and,
    Kawaihau District, Manuel Aguiar & Les Miller.

All morning long, one tense moment after another, virtually all residents listen intently to their radios expecting to hear the disturbing report that the enemy has followed up its bombing attack with invasions by land. Who knows what tonight or tomorrow may bring?

Announcements over KTOH urgently are asking for Provisional Police volunteers. "You do not need to fill out a Provisional Police application form. Merely volunteer and accept whatever duty is given to you. If you can volunteer get in touch immediately with one of the following Area Coordinators: Hans Hansen, Kekaha Plantation office; Paul Kahlbaum, Olokele Plantation office; C.C. Christopher, Kauai Terminals office; Ralph Garlinghouse, Lihue County Building; Paul Rice, Kapaa Courthouse; W.K. Mahikoa, Kilauea Gym; and, Fred Conant, Hanalei Courthouse."

Sunday afternoon—1:30 P.M.—Army headquarters on Oahu orders all broadcast stations to immediately shut down. There will be no more news or instructions to the community—just a quiet wait for the frightening unknown.

With the loss of KTOH for communicating with civil defense services, KTOH sends an urgent, last minute appeal for all motorcycle owners to volunteer for messenger service. Civil defense then switches from using KTOH to relying on the telephone and mobile drivers for communications.

After KTOH and the Territory's other three stations are off the air, the only source of news is through international short-wave reports. A rumor circulates that Japan radio has announced "in spite of heavy casualties, the Japanese navy now surrounds Hawaii and the matter of Japanese possession is just a matter of a little time." This creates extreme concern by folks on all sides of the island but still no panic.

During the afternoon, all area Provisional Police Coordinators mobilize their volunteers, assign guards to protect designated buildings, and set up nighttime air raid security forces. An urgent call goes out to pass the word to neighbors that additional volunteers are needed to serve four- and eight-hour shifts with the Provisional Police in patrolling all strategic points on the island.

That evening at midnight the wedding of Rachel

Rankin and Dr. Bill Parker takes place in the bedroom of Sheriff William Rice's home. This is the only large room totally blacked out. Shaded lights are decorated with fragrant white jasmine. The simple ceremony is performed by Venerable Henry Willey of All Saints Church using a dresser as an altar. The bride, escorted by Sheriff Rice, is wearing a dark blue gown—chosen to be appropriate for the blackout. The groom, attended by best man Wayne Ellis, enters from the bathroom, the only other blacked out room. The engaged couple has decided they should get married as soon as possible before any other emergencies upset their plans.

By the evening of December 7, volunteer workers at the Lihue Red Cross Center already had completed enough armbands for civilian defense workers and others so they can be identified by police.

In the days that follow, knitting surges as blackouts limit evening activities. Boys are encouraged to learn to knit items for Red Cross distribution.

Monday morning arrives. America declares war on the Axis Powers of Japan, Germany and Italy. After Garden Islanders survive the suspense-filled night on an air-raid alert, members of the Kauai Major Disaster Council spring into action. Their plans and orders, carefully drafted during the past months, are released to the public.

A.H. Case's Emergency Food Committee places an embargo on foodstuff that had been scheduled to be shipped to Oahu. From now on everything grown on Kauai must be marketed only at local stores. Individual farmers as well as sugar and pineapple plantations are requested to increase their vegetable plantings at once.

The plantations also set in motion their plans that had been laid out earlier in the year. Kauai's Food Production Committee Chairman, J.N.P. Webster, notifies each plantation of its acreage allocation and type of food it's scheduled to plant. It's expected that within two months Kauai's plantations and truck farmers will have had planted enough healthful food to supply the needs of all residents, livestock, poultry and other animals.

In line with the plans prepared months ago by the Disaster Council Emergency Food Committee, the sugar and pineapple plantations with their large areas of dedicated land will grow field crops such as soy beans, peanuts, beans, sweet potatoes, corn, and pigeon peas. They also will plant *koa haole* for animal feed. Truck farmers are assigned cabbage, carrots, green onions, tomatoes and other smaller crops.

During the first week, Food Administrator A.H. Case and his volunteer staff gather all dried beans, soybeans and potatoes from store inventories to use for planting. Crops are assigned according to soil and climate with peanuts going to the west side and Irish potatoes to plantations on the east side of the island.

Sheriff William Rice, who has been in ill health, requests a leave of absence and County Chairman William Ellis appoints the Sheriff's brother, Phillip Rice, as Acting Sheriff. Because Phillip Rice is in Honolulu, Edwin Crowell takes over the duties temporarily.

Instructions to retail food merchants, drafted months earlier, are issued early on December 8 by Food Administrator "Hib" Case.

1. All food sales must be recorded in writing whether for cash or credit.
2. The customer's invoice slip must show name and address of each buyer, along with the quantity and kind of food products sold. These will be kept by all stores for such inspection by officials as may be required.
3. Sell only normal everyday needs. You should know most of your families and should see that they take what they need but not enough to build up a storage. Inform all purchasers that the records will be watched and checked and we will take such measures as deemed necessary against those violating rules. This is an emergency and all persons must cooperate.
4. Merchants may limit their supplies and make distribution of such supplies as they may be

short of so that their customers may be all treated equally.

5.   We suggest that to prevent buying from more than one store, that dealers carefully watch purchasers who are not normally their own regular customers. Do not sell to them if you think they come under this rule. Attempt to get people to use greater varieties of the more available supplies and dispose of the most perishable products first.

6.   Remember that we are attempting to voluntarily accomplish proper distribution of food but if this does not work—rationing and ration cards will follow.

7.   Take an immediate inventory of all food products. Supply this list to the Food Administrator as soon as possible. At the same time answer the following question: How long will this inventory last under normal selling? Full food production has been ordered by all plantations and pineapple companies.

Another martial law regulation orders all stores to keep doors closed until a total inventory is completed and then they are to operate only from 7:00 A.M. to 4:00 P.M. each day. Because gas rationing limits the ability to go shopping, Lihue Store's branches in Lihue, Hanamaulu and Kealia begin home delivery. Orders must be placed early in the day. Delivery trucks begin their rounds at noon.

Keeping the public up-to-date on war news and making sure military orders get as wide a circulation as possible is a serious concern. A *Daily War Bulletin* is produced with the first edition on December 8. To save paper, it's printed bulletin-size on the smallest sheet that can be run through the Garden Island Publishing Company's press. The smallest type size also is used.

Some 5,000 copies are printed daily with distribution at post offices and several civilian defense offices. Residents are urged to share copies and, where possible, post the *Daily War Bulletin* where others can read it. Summaries of important news and military orders also are printed in Ilocano, Visayan, Tagalog and Japanese. The regular, full-size *Garden Island* news continues to be published every Tuesday.

Not everything is going smoothly. There are numerous snafus and glitches as well as questions over misunderstood instructions. It seems everyone is calling either Charlie Fern or Colonel FitzGerald for help.

To alleviate the problem a bulletin is issued advising:

> When you, a civilian defense worker, have a problem arise on which you want authority to act, or, if you have information which should be passed on to either Col. FlitzGerald or Mr. Fern, *do not take it upon yourself to try to reach either Col. FitzGerald or Mr. Fern by telephone or messenger.* Contact the man who is the head of the committee dealing with your problem. This is a democracy and even though we are working under martial law, we are observing the democratic methods.
>
> These are the heads to whom you are to telephone or reach for the settlement of problems.

> > If it concerns
> > **Food:** contact A.H. Case
> > **Transportation:** G.N. Hitchcock
> > **Police:** Acting Sheriff Edwin Crowell
> > **Communications:** W.L. Ralston
> > **Purchasing of Supplies:** B.D. Pratt
> > **Fire Wardens:** Robert Morton
> > **Air Raid Wardens:** Leslie Miller
> > **Air Raid Stations:** K.O.Soong
> > **Medical Operations:** Dr. Sam Wallis
> > **Medical:** Dr. V.A. Harl
> > **Red Cross:** Andrew Gross
> > **Provisional Police:** Philip Rice
> > **Blackout:** E.F. Shackleton
> > **Morale:** Father Maurice Coopman, whose headquarters are at Station KTOH
> > Paul H. Townsley will be **in command as first lieutenant** to Mr. Fern every night from 6:00 P.M. to 6:00 A.M., at the Lihue County Building.

According to plan, Red Cross workrooms are opened immediately after Martial Law is declared. Beauty shops, dressmaking shops and other small busi-

Entire communities—men, women and children joined in tasks to further the war effort. Evacuation camps were established in valleys and mountainsides. Clearings had to be created for shelter in the event of an enemy invasion by land. For this, foot and horse trails had to be widened to accommodate trucks that would transport residents from coastal and plains areas. Tent sites were leveled. Latrines dug. Food storage and kitchen facilities had to be prepared.

Other civilian defense projects cleared away *kiawe* and other thick scrub growth along shorelines that might conceal enemy landing parties. This shrub removal also made it easier for soldiers to string fences of sharp-pointed barbed wire along island beaches. Hundreds of "Kiawe Korps" volunteers showed up in large community groups. Each member carried a *kaukau* tin, a bottle of water and a working tool: shovel, hoe, axe, pick, saw, or whatever other implement might be used to help protect Kauai from the danger of covert enemy landings.

nesses operated by women and temporarily out of business are turned into sewing rooms.

To prepare for the possibility of casualties from an air raid or land invasion on Kauai, the Red Cross' first big task is equipping the island's hospitals and medical units set up for disaster work. The Red Cross issues 35,000 surgical dressings and bandages plus surgery gowns, caps, scrub aprons, towels, swabs, sheets, and other hospital supplies. Placed into hospital inventories are 400 blankets and other pieces of bed clothing. Assistance in heavy lifting and loading of crates is given by athletes from Oahu's St. Louis College who were stranded after their Saturday football game.

The lifestyle of Garden Islanders suddenly becomes topsy-turvy.

Schools temporarily are closed. Many students work on agricultural projects. High school boys are sent to help farmers. Little children collect seeds for food plants.

No more nightly movies. Theaters are open only for one matinee at three o'clock on Saturdays and Sundays.

Those plantations (and any other businesses or individuals) with clocks that are set to times other than standard time must now follow the time as broadcast over KTOH.

Currency (all coins and paper money) is limited to

no more than $200 per individual, with a man and wife being considered as one individual. Any amount of cash over $200 must be deposited in a bank or savings and loan company. This includes any currency in a safe deposit box. Checks in any amount are okay. Businesses are limited to $500. In addition, no one may withdraw more than $200 cash per month from his or her bank account. The penalty for violating currency regulations is a $5,000 fine or five years imprisonment or both. This is being done to make sure that if Japanese forces do take over Kauai, the enemy will not have a supply of U.S. money to use in world markets. (Later all paper money was recalled and replaced with special bills on which was printed "U.S.Currency. Hawaiian Series.")

The penalty for violating gas-rationing rules also is stiff. As the month progresses the Gas Adjusters Force is quadrupled from its original size and begins to conduct regular sweeps of gas stations to search for duplicate applications or cards. Motorists are reminded that breaking the rule is a violation of a military order. "There will be no second chance."

Anyone wanting to place a radiotelephone call to the mainland or to other islands now faces a restrictive list of conditions. The instructions require that you give the operator your telephone number, name, address, occupation and the subject of your conversation and whether it is personal, business or other class. Then you must give the name, address and occupation of the person being called. If you want to talk to several others at that number, you must give the name, address and occupation of each of these persons. The same information must be provided for anyone else at your end wishing to talk.

No calls can be placed from public telephones or any other phone that can't be traced. The conversation must be in the English language and cannot include military subjects of any kind; arrivals and departures of ships; the movement of officials, troops, war materials; "location of mine fields, internment camps; conditions of social, political or economic unrest; weather conditions, blackouts, air raids or any other matter which might give aid or comfort to the enemy or prejudice the foreign relations of the United States and its allies."

Sons and daughters living with parents who are Japanese aliens are told they have an important responsibility in maintaining peace with their neighbors. Alien owners of short-wave radios may keep them without having the short-wave bands disconnected as long as the aliens are living with a citizen over eighteen years of age. Families are advised there is no law against citizens listening to Radio Tokyo but common sense should prevail. They are told that because of the possibility of more Japanese attacks, "Many of your neighbors have the jitters. You can avoid being talked about and you can avoid arousing the suspicion of your neighbors by explaining to your parents that you are not going to tune in on the Japanese language programs from Tokyo until after the public has recovered from the jitters."

After KTOH returns to the air, a new system for dispatching County police officers is put into effect. Garden Islanders needing immediate police assistance are told to telephone KTOH where either Jack Wada or Katashi Nose, both communication engineers, will clear the calls. In each district, officers in several police cars are given a radio tuned to KTOH. Regular radio programs are interrupted to dispatch police as needed. Everyone listening to the radio hears all the police calls being made. Anyone alarmed by a rumor is instructed not to call the FBI but to check the rumor with William Moragne at KTOH.

Merchants are given further directives that prohibit the sale of meat on Tuesdays and Fridays. They agree to sell no meat—fresh, canned or frozen—and suggest substituting fish and cheese. Customers are reminded, "Using leftover meat on Tuesdays and Fridays defeats the purpose of meatless days."

Farmers and ranchers fear that limited shipping will be concentrated on delivering food for human consumption while cutting back on animal feed. Menus are published for feeding cows, horses and mules. They include suggestions for specific amounts of panicum grass, cane molasses, soy beans and soybean meal,

Kauai's "Last Ditch Fighters"

When the plan for a Provincial Police Force was first outlined, adult males of all nationalities were urged to enlist for volunteer duty. U.S. citizenship was not a requirement. But after the bombing of Pearl Harbor, service by "those of Oriental blood" was brought to a halt "for their own protection." According to

Civil Defense officials, "It is understood that the Army feels that soldiers, or volunteers, of Oriental ancestry would run the risk of being shot down by our own armed forces in case of an invasion."

Young men of Japanese, Chinese and Korean ancestry then became the bulwark of Kauai's air raid defense program, serving as volunteer fire fighters, participating in blood donor programs and in the planning and administration of the island's evacuation program.

It wasn't long after the war began, that a call went out for "every able-bodied man from the age of 18 up except those of Oriental blood" to enlist in the Kauai Volunteers Regiment. A total of more than 3,000 Garden Islanders, mainly Filipinos, lined up at the twelve recruiting centers on Kauai to join ranks as "Last Ditch Fighters." Three full battalions quickly were organized under the leadership of Col. Paul H. Townsley, office manager of Lihue Plantation. One battalion was established for the west side of Kauai, another for Kalaheo, Koloa and Lihue, and the third to include volunteers from Kapaa to the north shore.

Each man was required to furnish his own khaki uniform. The Army provided arms, ammunition and intensive combat training on Sundays and after *pau hana* on weekdays. The bolo (a large cane knife with its edge honed razor-sharp) became authorized equipment. On special occasions regimental parades took place, including a marching band and the appearance of the mounted volunteers whose civilian defense duties were to ride *mauka* trails and to search through the undergrowth for possible enemy infiltrators.

coconut meal, pineapple bran and *koa haole*. Dairy farmers are told at least 12 pounds of soybean meal is necessary to produce 30 pounds of milk and that urea also can be used, with one pound of urea providing the nutrition of seven pounds of soybean meal.

Dairymen do not expect a milk shortage but because there will be no replacement of glass milk bottles in the foreseeable future, all empty milk bottles must be returned to the store—no empty bottle, no milk. That's an order.

The *Garden Island's* big attention-grabbing story of the December 7 attack comes from Niihau, the privately owned island 17 miles northwest of Kauai.

Late in the morning following the attack on Pearl Harbor a single-seater Japanese Zero fighter plane crash-lands on the island while returning to its carrier. This is a sudden, shocking revelation for the people of Niihau who finally get a close-up look at the contraption that sometimes has been seen soaring over the Kauai coastline.

Not many Niihauans have ever heard a radio broadcast. The occasional newspaper that reaches the island is printed in English—a foreign language. The Robinson family, owner of Niihau, has been vigilant in helping the island community maintain its traditional native culture. People who leave seldom return. The news from elsewhere doesn't reach Niihau.

So, on that Sunday morning, without realizing Pearl Harbor is under attack, the people of Niihau greet a slightly injured, dazed visitor from Japan as a controversial, armed guest. According to witnesses, he's taken first to the Robinson home where he's made comfortable. There's some suspicion among residents but it's decided to act calmly until the next morning when Aylmer Robinson, Niihau's manager, is due to arrive on his motor sampan for his weekly visit.

Robinson doesn't show up as scheduled. Military orders prohibit him from leaving port. For several days the Japanese pilot meanders around the tiny village, making friends with the only two Japanese residents: Yoshio Harada, the island's beekeeper, and ranch-hand

Ishimatsu Shintani. During this time, the pilot secretly is searching for the person who took his pistol and war papers from the downed plane's cockpit.

With Harada's help, the pilot recovers the pistol but not the highly secret war documents. They are being held by Hawila Kaleohanu, a Niihau Hawaiian. Learning this, the pilot sends Shintani to bribe Hawila with all of the pilots' money—about 200 yen. When Shintani fails, he runs into a wooded section of the island to hide rather than face the wrath of an edgy Harada and the agitated pilot.

On Friday, six days after the bombing of Pearl Harbor, Hawila asks five other cowboys to join him in rowing a whaleboat across the choppy channel to Waimea, the closest town on Kauai's west side.

On that same day, the pilot and Harada remove the machine gun from the plane and attach it to the Robinson's horse-drawn carriage. First they burn the plane and then set fire to Hawila's house, demanding the papers be returned. At the end of the day, when the papers have not been recovered, the duo enters the village wildly firing the machine gun. Everyone scatters for the woods and nearby caves.

Saturday morning, Harada and the pilot go down to the shoreline caves and ask another Niihauan, Benehakaka Kanahele, to help search for Hawila. Benny knows Hawila has gone for help but agrees to lead the pair into the nearby woods where the group spends the morning shouting for Hawila. Benny's wife is with them. Eventually the pilot becomes more enraged and, waving a shotgun over his head, threatens to shoot everyone on the island if he isn't told where Hawila is hiding. Benny sees the pistol stuck into one of the pilot's boots and begins looking for an opportunity to overcome the irrational enemy airman.

As the pilot is passing the shotgun to Harada and reaching for his pistol, Benny jumps the pilot. His wife grabs the pilot's arm and twists it to his back. Harada grabs the struggling woman, pulling her away from the pilot.

As translated to a *Garden Island* newspaper

reporter, Benny Kanahele says, "Then the flyer started to shoot at me. His first bullet went into my ribs on the left side. I jumped him again and he shot me again. This bullet got me in the hip. Then he shot at me once more and that bullet hit me in the groin. Then I got mad.

"I picked up that flyer and I threw him against the stone wall. I knocked him cold. Then I turned to go after Harada because he had the shotgun. But Harada was using the shotgun on himself. He put the muzzle into his *opu* (abdomen) but he was in such a big hurry that he missed himself.

"The shotgun kicked itself out of his hand. He picked it up and he aimed at his *opu* again. This time his aim was a little better. The gun went off and did its work all right.

"While Harada was shooting himself, my wife was going into action. She was plenty *huhu* (angry), that woman. She picked up a big rock and she started right in to beat that flyer's brains out. She did a pretty good job.

"By that time, I wasn't feeling too good, with all those bullets, but I was all right. My wife ran away. She ran to the village for help. But while the help was coming out to me on horseback, I walked to the village."

News of the struggle on Niihau causes great anxiety among Japanese living on Kauai. They hear the anti-alien remarks of those people who always had questioned their loyalty. "I told you so" is heard from time to time. However the overwhelming majority of Garden Islanders see the combat on Niihau as an isolated incident.

Shintani is picked up by military authorities, imprisoned, and returned to his Niihau family after the war is over. In 1960 he attained U.S. citizenship.

Many honors were bestowed on both Kanahele and Kaleohano. In April of 1942, American Legion Heroism Medals were awarded both men. And both were presented letters of commendation from the President of the United States for their "demonstration of exceptional courage." In 1945 Benehakaka Kanahele, in ceremonies at Oahu's Fort Shafter, was awarded the

Purple Heart for his wounds and the Medal of Merit for his bravery. A year later Hawila Kaleohano received the United States Medal of Freedom.

Meanwhile, in mid-December of 1941, pieces of wreckage and cargo from a ship are beginning to appear on beaches along the east side of the island. First a life ring and a drum of high-grade alcohol are recovered. Then more drums and countless bags of onions are washed up in the area from Ahukini to Kapaa.

KTOH broadcasts a warning that all salvage is the property of military authorities. When found, the items are to be hauled above the high water line and the police notified. The source of the debris is a Norwegian freighter torpedoed on December 7 while approaching Hawaii. Its 35 crewmembers were rescued by another vessel and brought to Honolulu where they were released as "distressed seamen."

Kauai's warfare doesn't end with the Battle of Niihau. In the early morning hours of December 30, residents in Nawiliwili and Lihue are awakened as brilliant flares light the sky and distant explosions are heard. Many families take shelter while others turn over and go back to sleep thinking it's a Civilian Defense exercise or that someone has begun shooting off New Year's fireworks one day early.

For the Pat Shannon family living in Nawiliwili it's very real. They hear a series of explosions and suddenly shrapnel begins to pierce their living quarters above Shannon's boatworks. Every room is hit. As Pat with his wife and mother huddle in the ground-level office, one large piece of shrapnel slices through one side of the second story and smashes its way out of the other side.

It's an attack by a Japanese submarine firing about fifteen shells into what the Japanese mistakenly believe is a military installation.

One shell cuts its way through the upper section of a Shell Oil gasoline storage tank and sinks to the bottom of the fuel. Fortunately it doesn't go off.

As a cane fire starts in a field above Nawiliwili, the well-trained Civilian Defense Corps springs into action.

Can you imagine the shock when a member of the William Alexander household opened the front door on New Year's Eve morning, 1941, and found an unexploded bomb on the doormat? Grove Farm Plantation field workers had found the shell in a canefield above Nawiliwili during the day after a Japanese submarine had shelled the harbor. Not knowing what to do with a live bomb, they placed it on the plantation manager's doorstep knowing the big boss had all the answers.

Fire units successfully battle the blaze with help by neighbors. The Lihue medical station quickly is manned. Home Guard members report to their stations and all Civil Defense standby officers report for duty.

In the morning an unexploded shell is found by a Grove Farm work gang in a field above Niumalu. The crew sets it aside for the rest of the day. At *pau hana* it's thrown onto a labor truck heading back home over bumpy roads, and then the explosive is dropped off on the front steps of the Grove Farm manager's home for safekeeping.

No one is injured in this second surprise attack in Hawaii. Most of the shells are duds. A Tokyo short-wave broadcast is reported as claiming, "Our warcraft shelled and completely demolished important military objectives at Nawiliwili, Kauai."

This frightening incident and the immediate Civil Defense response bring Garden Islanders a sense of assurance that the island seems to have prepared itself well for whatever emergency the war may bring.

After the initial burst of activity following the declaration of war and establishment of Martial Law,

Charlie Fern in an editorial "Can you take it?" writes, "For the present at least the storm is over.

"The war has passed on to other areas and there is every likelihood that Kauai will now enter upon a long period of extreme boredom which won't be relieved by even a nuisance raid.

"Headquarters reports that the response of Kauai's entire population, when every one was called on for self-control, vigilance and unusual effort, was magnificent. Every one who was asked to do emergency work acquitted himself handsomely.

"Now that the first excitement is over, the civilian population is being asked to pitch in and do an even harder job. You are being asked to obey the rules with cheerfulness, to do without complaint the unexciting work that lies ahead, and, while being bored by the blackout and other necessary precautions, to remain courageous and alert."

Continuing the editorial Charlie Fern writes that Colonel FitzGerald has said for quotation in the newspaper: "This is a war of nerves. People must compose themselves. This monotonous stage is one that will last for a long time. The blackout may also continue for a long time. People must get accustomed to it. And people should now try to get accustomed to different food. They will not be able to get the foods to which they are accustomed in the same quantities as heretofore. There will be plenty of food on this island to keep everybody in good health. But you must learn to enjoy new and different foods."

And so, the people of Kauai now settle in for close to three-and-a-half years of wartime personal restrictions and material shortages.

Ultimately, on May 8, 1945, the German High Command signs the Instrument of Unconditional Surrender, closing the last chapter of the fighting in Europe. Then four months later, on September 2, 1945, Japanese military representatives place their signatures on a surrender document aboard the battleship USS *Missouri* anchored in Tokyo Bay. A week later an American flag, that had flown over the Capitol in

Washington when Pearl Harbor was bombed, is raised over Tokyo.

Soon the GIs from Hawaii begin returning from the battlefields of Europe with highest honors for their bravery, dedication and skill. Kauai had sent more than 1,300 young men and women to war. Never to come home again are 63 sons—51 are Americans of Japanese Ancestry.

Altogether 18,134 individual decorations for valor were awarded to members of the 100th Infantry Battalion and 442nd Regimental Combat Team. These units were formed in September 1942 and February 1943 when the United States allowed Americans of Japanese Ancestry to enlist. When the call went out for AJAs to volunteer, over ten thousand throughout the United States offered themselves. Twenty-five hundred were from Hawaii.

The 100th Infantry Battalion was the unit that, in October 1944, rescued the U.S. Army's Lost Battalion that had been surrounded and trapped by the German army. The number of members of the 442nd killed and wounded was four times the number of soldiers rescued. Known as the "Purple Heart Battalion" its members were awarded more than one thousand purple hearts.

Only eight army units have ever received a Presidential Unit Citation for courage under fire. One of these is the 442nd Regimental Combat Team, which fought on some of the bloodiest battlefields in Italy and Germany from 1943 to 1945. Some 650 of its men were killed in action. It is America's most decorated unit.

Any question of loyalty has been emphatically answered.

Glossary

All listed words are Hawaiian except for:

    Chi = Chinese
    Fil = Filipino
    Jpn = Japanese
    Kor = Korean
    Pid = Pidjin
    Por = Portuguese
    Tah = Tahitian

A

akamai		smart
alaloa		long road, belt road
alii		chief
aole pilikia		"no trouble"
auwai		irrigation ditch
auwe		"Oh!" "Too bad!"

B

bagoong	Fil	fermented fish
bakatare bobura	Jpn	crazy pumpkin head
bandorya	Fil	stringed instrument
benjo	Jpn	toilet
bento	Jpn	lunch box
bonodori	Jpn	rhythmic, repetitive, religious dance
botoboto	Pid	an unprintable word
bufo	Pid	bullfrog
bulaia	Pid	"Bull! Liar!"
bunelos	Fil	filled pastry, dessert

C

| calabash cousin | Pid | very close friend, extended family member |

chamarita	Por	folk dance
cone sushi	Jpn	cooked rice in tofu wrap

D

daikon	Jpn	pickled vegetable similar to radish/turnip
da kine	Pid	"that thing"

F

fado	Por	folk song
furo	Jpn	community bathtub

H

hala		Pandanus tree
Hale Aina		house of food
hale ko		sugar mill
ham sup	Chi	aggressive lover
hanabata	Pid	dripping nose, "honey butter"
hana ebi	Jpn	dried shredded shrimp
hanahana		work
hana hou		repeat
hanai		adopted
hana make		kill, destroy
haole		foreigner, usually Caucasian
hapa Filipino		part (half) Filipino
hapa keiki		child of mixed nationalities
hauna		smelly
haupia		coconut pudding
hee nalu		surfing
hekka	Jpn	Japanese stir fry
hemo		loosen, free
hikie		large couch
hilahila		bashful
hoito	Jpn	glutton
holoholo		go for a ride
holoku		long dress with a train
holomu		long dress without a train
honohono		fragrant hanging orchid
hoomalimali		flatter
hoomanawanui		"take it easy"
Howzit?	Pid	greeting: "How is it?"
huhu		angry
hui		partnership

huki		pull
hukilau		surround-net fishing
hula		Polynesian dance
hula halau		hula instruction, hula group
hulihuli		turn over, rotisserie

I

ichiban	Jpn	number one
imu		underground oven
Issei	Jpn	first generation Japanese immigrants

J

jan ken po	Pid	scissors-paper-stone hand game

K

kahili		royal standard made of feathers
kai		sea
kalua		bake in underground oven
kamaaina		native-born, long-time resident
kanaka maoli		native person
kane lua		men's restroom
kanikapila		play music
kapakahi		crooked
kapu		taboo
kaukau	Pid	food, to eat
keiki		child
kiawe		Algaroba tree
kim chee	Kor	spicy pickled vegetables
kini popo		ball
koa		Acacia tree
koa haole		Common shrub noted for its brown seeds
kokua		help
kolohe		naughty
komo mai		"Come in."
kona		leeward wind
kukae		excrement
kuleana		responsibility
kulikuli		"Be quiet!"

L

lanai		veranda, porch
laulau		pork/fish/taro tops, cooked in ti leaves
lava lava	Tah	wraparound garment
lei		garland
lele		to fly
lilikoi		passion fruit
lolo		goofy
lomi lomi salmon		salted salmon with onions and tomatoes
luau		feast
luhi		weary
lumpia	Fil	similar to Chinese egg roll
luna		overseer

M

mahalo		thank
mahape		tomorrow, afterwards
maile		fragrant vine used for important occasions
mai tai		rum drink
maka ainana		commoner
make-die-dead	Pid	to die
makule		aged
malasada	Por	ball-shaped doughnut
malihini		newcomer
Mama-san	Jpn	older woman
manini		stingy
manuahi		free of charge
manukina		injured
mauka		towards the mountains
mea		thing
miso	Jpn	soybean-based broth
moemoe		sleep
mokihana		Anise-scented green leaf/berry
momona		to be fat

N

namasu	Jpn	vegetables marinated in rice vinegar
niele		inquisitive

Nissei	Jpn	children of first generation Japanese immigrants
niu		coconut

O

obake	Jpn	ghost
Obon	Jpn	festival of the dead
ohana		family
ohia		tree with red blossoms
okole		bottom side
okole maluna		bottom up
oluolu		comfortable
ono		delicious
opihi		small Limpet shellfish
opu		abdomen

P

paakiki		stubborn
pahee		slide
Pai Gow	Chi	card game
Pake wahine		Chinese female
palaka		blue-white checked cloth
palekoki		petticoat
pali		steep hill, cliff
pancit	Fil	stir-fry vegetables with noodles
paniolo		cowboy
pao duce	Por	sweet bread
papale		hat
Papa-san	Jpn	older man
pareu	Tah	wraparound garment
pau hana		end of work
pehea oe		"How are you?"
piko		belly button
pilau		stink
pio		pass out
pipikaula		beef jerky
poho		out of luck
poi		edible paste made from cooked taro
poke		raw fish pieces with seaweed and flavored paste

pololei		all right
pua		flower
puka		hole
punee		movable couch
pupule		crazy

S

sabidong	Fil	agricultural spray
sake	Jpn	Japanese alcoholic beverage
salalabit	Pid	S.O.B.
shaka	Pid	friendly hand wave
shibai	Jpn	make believe
shoyu	Jpn	wheat and soybean sauce (soy sauce)
sipa-sipa	Fil	soccer-like game with ball of palm leaves
s'kebei	Jpn	aggressive lover
sushi nori	Jpn	cooked rice wrapped in seaweed

T

tamaraa	Tah	Tahitian feast
taro		tuber from which poi is made
teriyaki	Jpn	shoyu/ginger marinade

ti		broad-leaf plant in lily family
tiki	Tah	torch on pole
tuberose		small fragrant lily-like flower

U
uka		upland
uku		flea, lice
ulu		breadfruit tree

V
vahine	Tah	woman

W
waha		mouth, talk too much
wahine		woman
weliweli		fearful
wiliwili		native tree

Y
yukata	Jpn	summer kimono

Z
zoris	Jpn	thong slippers

K A U A ʻ I
HISTORICAL
S O C I E T Y
ESTABLISHED 1914

MISSION

To collect, preserve and disseminate the oral, written and pictorial history of Kauaʻi County; to protect and preserve historic sites; and to educate ourselves and the public about the history and cultures of Kauaʻi and Niʻihau.

The Kauaʻi Historical Society was founded in 1914 by people dedicated to the preservation of Kauaʻi County's history. Today, the Society remains the only general historical archive for Kauaʻi County and is open to the public on a regular basis for education and research purposes.

COLLECTIONS

The archives of the Society contain these collections and more:

A library of approximately 4,000 volumes.

A collection of over 4,000 photographs and audio-visual materials.

A wide assortment of maps, technical drawings and blue prints.

Subject files of short pieces and news clippings.

Materials from the Kekaha, Kilauea and Lihuʻe sugar plantations.

Manuscripts, such as personal papers from the Sanborn and Arruda families; organizational records from the Mokihana Club, YWCA, Kauaʻi Polo Club, Department of Health, and more.

The Garden Island newspapers from 1913.

Grace Guslander's Hawaiiana Collection from the Coco Palms Resort Museum.

OTHER KAUA'I HISTORICAL SOCIETY PUBLICATIONS

Kaua'i History & Culture Map

Cook 'Em Up Kaua'i
The Kaua'i Historical Society Cookbook, 1994

Koloa Plantation, 1835–1935
Arthur C. Alexander, Reprint 1985

Queen Emma and Lawai
David Forbes, 1970

Wailua-Nui-A-Ho'ano
Wichman & Faye, annotated map

Touring Waimea
Christine Faye

Touring the Legends of Koke'e
Frederick B. Wichman

Coming Soon:

Lihu'e: The Heart of Kaua'i
Pat Griffin

Touring the Legends of the Northshore
Frederick B. Wichman

A Walking Tour of Historic Downtown Kapa'a
Marie Fifield

Stories of Wailua, Kaua'i
Read by Lyle A. Dickey 1915, Reprint 2004

For information about these publications and how to become a Kaua'i Historical Society member contact us at:

> Kaua'i Historical Society
> P.O. Box 1778
> Lihu'e, HI 96766

Or visit our website at www.kauaihistoricalsociety.org

KAUA'I
HISTORICAL
SOCIETY
ESTABLISHED 1914

Production Notes for
  Ashman • KAUAI AS IT WAS IN THE 1940s
  AND '50s

Cover, Jacket and Interior designed by
  Santos Barbasa, Jr., in Galliard, with display type
  in Quirinus Bold.

Layout and Composition by Santos Barbasa, Jr.

Printing and Binding by
  The Maple-Vail Book Manufacturing Group

Printed on 55 lb. MV Bright White Tradebook, 360 ppi.